For Graham Fairbairn

DEWI HUGHES

FOREWORD BY CHRISTOPHER WRIGHT

POWER AND POVERTY

DIVINE AND HUMAN RULE IN A WORLD OF NEED

IVP Academic
An imprint of InterVarsity Press
Downers Grove, Illinois

InterVarsity Press
P.O. Box 1400, Downers Grove, IL 60515-1426
Internet: www.ivpress.com
E-mail: email@ivpress.com

Published in the United States of America by InterVarsity Press, Downers Grove, Illinois, with permission from Inter-Varsity Press, England.

InterVarsity Press® is the book-publishing division of InterVarsity Christian Fellowship/USA®, a student movement active on campus at hundreds of universities, colleges and schools of nursing in the United States of America, and a member movement of the International Fellowship of Evangelical Students. For information about local and regional activities, write Public Relations Dept., InterVarsity Christian Fellowship/USA, 6400 Schroeder Rd., P.O. Box 7895, Madison, WI 53707-7895, or visit the IVCF website at <www.intervarsity.org>.

ISBN 978-0-8308-2809-8

Printed in the United States of America ∞

InterVarsity Press is committed to protecting the environment and to the responsible use of natural resources. As a member of Green Press Initiative we use recycled paper whenever possible. To learn more about the Green Press Initiative, visit <www.greenpressinitiative.org>.

Library of Congress Cataloging-in-Publication Data

A catalog record for this book is available from the Library of Congress.

P	19	18	17	16	15	14	13	12	11	10	9	8	7	6	5	4	3	2	1
Y	25	24	23	22	21	20	19	18	17	16	15	14	13	12	11	10	09		

CONTENTS

FOREWORD

It is a joy to commend this book, and not merely for the friendship that Dewi Hughes and I share. In addition to being from the Celtic margins of the United Kingdom (Dewi from Wales, and I from Northern Ireland), we share many hours of stimulating theological reflection in meetings of the Tearfund's Theological Panel and the Lausanne Theology Working Group. Above all, we share the immeasurable support and joy of the two fine ladies whom we are privileged to have as our wives, as we once agreed over a long cold drink on a pavement café in Budapest.

A friend once told me that before he became a Christian he used to go to All Souls Church, Langham Place, London, to listen to John Stott preaching. He found it infuriating; although he constantly wanted to disagree or argue with what Stott was saying, he could not do so without finding himself in conflict with the author of whatever passage of the Bible Stott was preaching from. Stott was doing nothing more than making clear what the original writer meant to say and how it applied to us today, and it was difficult to disagree with him without disagreeing with the Bible. I was reminded of this when reading *Power and Poverty*.

It is so constantly biblical—again and again letting the simple text of the Bible speak for itself before drawing some implications for how we ought to respond to it today. I hope readers will not find this infuriating, like my friend (unless, of course, they are minded to disagree robustly with Dewi and the Bible at the same time), but rather exhilarating and illuminating. It is, frankly, refreshing in an age when even many who claim the name *evangelical* seem to sit very loose to the Bible in their preaching and writing, preferring more popular confections of social analysis, prophetic speculation or anecdotal fascination. If you want to let your mind be filled again and again with the simple but powerful impact of the Word of God on the issue before us, then this book is a feast in store.

More than *constantly* biblical, this book is also *comprehensively* biblical—as a glance at the index of scripture references will show. Dewi sets the issue of poverty in the light of the whole Bible, from the roots of the problem in Genesis to its ultimate solution in Revelation. In doing this he avoids several regrettable tendencies that tend to vitiate evangelical efforts in this field. Some draw only on the teaching of Jesus and the New Testament, and do so in a heavily individualistic way in relation to personal Christian discipleship. While this may produce a powerful ethical challenge, it overlooks the substructure of scriptural narrative and teaching on which

Jesus and the apostles built. Others sense the value of many Old Testament passages to the battle against poverty but content themselves with quotations of the most powerful texts without perceiving the importance of the whole paradigm of a redeemed community under the governance of God's law that confronts us—in its achievements and its failures, both equally instructive—in the Old Testament.

Dewi Hughes avoids both extremes. He shows how the Old Testament's analysis of the causes of poverty, and its systemic response to it, still speak eloquently today. He draws on my own work on Old Testament ethics as he does so, but both of us share these concerns and perspectives with many others, including agencies such as the Jubilee Centre in Cambridge and Dewi's own beloved Tearfund.

Dewi also shows how Jesus and the New Testament must be central to any evangelical approach to this issue. And he refuses to separate the teaching and example of Jesus in relation to poverty, from the significance of his atoning death. The cross is central to our social ethics at this point, for if poverty is one major result of sin, then God's answer to sin must be connected to his answer to poverty.

What, then, does it mean to live as Christians, and as the church, in a world of appalling poverty? Dewi speaks of the church as a transformed and transforming community, of people who live in the world but by the standards of the reign of God as taught in the whole Bible. Among other things, this is a prophetic stance, and Dewi does not hesitate to put his finger on examples of rank wickedness and injustice in our world today—some of them uncomfortably linked to our own national and even religious identities. But again and again I find that his use of telling examples, facts and figures, illustrative anecdotes and the like serves the purpose of amplifying and applying the voice of Scripture itself.

The conclusion of the book still haunts me, as it challenges us to decide which story we live in—or rather, whose empire/kingdom we belong to. Picking up for the last time the theme of the crying of the poor (which is first heard by God in the company of Abraham as an outcry against Sodom and Gomorrah as early as Genesis 18:20-21), Dewi writes,

> It is better to listen to the crying now and respond in prophetic speech, prayer and acts of love, because we belong to a kingdom where there will one day be no more crying, than shut our ears and say and do nothing, because we belong to a kingdom in which crying will never cease.

May we indeed be among those who hear—like the God of Old Testament Israel, like Jesus of Nazareth—and on hearing, choose to act.

Christopher J. H. Wright

PREFACE

It is now a few years ago that Graham Fairbairn, Tearfund's Deputy Director and my manager, reminded me that Tearfund would be 40 years old in 2008 and that it would be good if I could produce 'a substantial theological work' (Graham's phrase) to mark the occasion. I am certain that producing a really 'substantial' work of theology is way beyond my ability, but I did agree to write something.

I have been a Tearfund employee for more than half of its 40 years and have served under all four of its Chief Executive Officers. The gestation of this book happened while our newly appointed current CEO, Matthew Frost, was leading us through another round of strategic review that embedded 'integral mission' deeper than ever as a description of what we aspire to do. The term 'integral mission' (*mision integral*) hails from Latin America and reflects the debate among evangelicals during the last half century or so about the respective roles of evangelism and social service/action in Christian mission. Integral mission implies that it is impossible to separate words and actions in describing the Christian mission. 'Holistic' is another word used to express the same idea, although it is arguable that 'holistic' does not convey the idea of inseparability as clearly as 'integral'. For me it is a cause of deep frustration that this is still a bone of contention among evangelical Christians. I hope this book, which rarely uses the term 'integral' will reassure those who are afraid of 'integral mission' that what we say, are and do under God are inseparable.

Another result of the most recent strategic review in Tearfund was a very strong reaffirmation of the role of the church in integral mission. We now describe ourselves as Christians who are 'passionate about the local church bringing justice and transforming lives – overcoming global poverty'. Straplines like this are not precise theological statements but evocations of hope tied to a specific commitment. I believe it is consistent with what we learn from the Bible and from Christian tradition about the significance of church in God's economy. In an older Tearfund document I had the privilege of working on with others, the church was described as 'a caring, inclusive and distinctive community of reconciliation reaching out in love to the world'. I hope that I have done justice to this vision of church and its potential in this volume.

Concern for theological training has been an important component of my work as theological advisor for Tearfund. I believe that if we are going to see more and more churches fulfilling the vision described in the previous paragraph we will need more and more church leaders committed to integral mission. An obvious way to make sure this happens is to make sure that church leadership training programmes are integral in their approach. By this I do not mean the introduction of optional courses that will help pastors in ministering to the poor – although it is a good idea to have such courses in many colleges. What I long to see is the whole curriculum of leadership training courses infused with the spirit of integral mission. Bible, history, dogmatics and practical aspects of the curriculum should all be taught integrally, which means that the whole course should be grounded in the life of God and of the people whom the trainee has been called to serve. My hope for this book is that theological educators in particular, as well as church leaders and educated Christians, will be encouraged by it to teach more integrally.

Ever since becoming acquainted with Abraham Kuyper and his followers many years ago I have been convinced of the importance of the whole Bible in formulating Christian doctrine and the principles of Christian practice. They also convinced me that if Jesus is Lord, then he must be Lord over *all* of life. But the person who has helped me more than any other to see how this approach is worked out in detailed exegesis and exposition of the biblical text is Christopher J. H. Wright. His *Living as the People of God* (1983) was seminal for me when I joined Tearfund and I have benefited greatly from the more substantial works he has published since. Through common involvement on various bodies in the last few years I have also got to know the man behind the books as someone who is serious about practising what he preaches. He was certainly gracious in agreeing to read the manuscript of this book and in commending it. Stephen Nantlais Williams was another faithful friend who agreed to read (although a colleague in an e-mail that should not have reached me considered him crazy to do so!). I am sure it was a holy madness, because his many searching comments have made this book a lot better than it would have been without them. I would also like to thank Dr Phil Duce of IVP for being an understanding and supportive editor.

As stated above it was my manager, Graham Fairbairn, who pushed me to write this book. As boss and friend he has encouraged me throughout the process of writing in his own gentle, but persuasive, way. This would have been enough of a reason to dedicate the book to him, but his passion for the Bible and the church has led him to train for non-stipendiary ministry in the Church of England so that it has now become even more appropriate that I should do so.

Dewi Hughes
Theological Advisor, Tearfund

INTRODUCTION

One striking fact that needs to be kept in focus as we start this book is that throughout history poverty has been largely unnecessary. Generally the earth and human ingenuity have always ensured enough provision for everyone. Poverty is fundamentally a matter of distribution of the adequate provision that has always been there. Throughout history a proportion of the earth's population has always enjoyed an abundance of the goods available at any one time while a proportion suffered want of the most basic goods needed to sustain life at all.

Evolutionary theory argues that there is a physical reason for this. It is a priority for every organism to pass on its genetic imprint to another generation at all costs. If this means capturing a disproportionate control of the goods available to secure the flourishing of the next generation and in the process eliminating fellow organisms, then so be it. It is a matter of the survival of the fittest. But most scientists and philosophers committed to the evolution paradigm have argued that this 'physical' law, which is supposed to explain the appearance of all creatures on earth including human beings, cannot provide the ethical principles needed to condition the way in which human beings ought to relate to each other and the rest of the natural world. Curiously evolutionists on the whole have argued that the principles of morality should take us in the opposite direction to the principles of physical evolution. Morally, they say, we should make every effort to fit as many as possible of our fellow organisms for survival, although our 'selfish' genes are pushing hard in the opposite direction. It seems to me that there can be only one result when two trains travel on the same line in opposite directions!

There is clearly a need for a deeper, spiritual understanding of the origin of human beings and the type of human behaviour that leads to poverty and away from it. The conviction underlying this book is that the Bible provides such an understanding. The approach taken to the Bible is canonical, which means attempting 'an appraisal of the [biblical] material . . . according to the interrelationships of its parts in the form in which it has been received'.[1] The work done by scholars in the historical reconstruction or deconstruction of the text is not dismissed as irrelevant, but is not considered as essential for grasping its meaning. The message explored is the narrative presented in the canon of Scripture as it stands. Finally the whole study is based on the conviction that what the Bible says speaks at a profound level to our contemporary circumstances.

The underlying theme of this book is that poverty has to do with the way in which human beings use the power God gave us when he created us. The core meaning of 'power' is the ability to do something. So this book begins with an examination in the biblical 'Book of Origins' (Gen. 1 – 11) of the source of the immense power vested in human beings and the reason why some often use that power to the detriment of others. The Book of Origins ends with the two defining stories of human history. On the one hand, we have the story of the Tower of Babel, which epitomizes the pride of human beings in their rebellion against God as they seek to concentrate power and build an empire (which inevitably involves violence and oppression). On the other hand, we have the genealogy of Noah's son Shem down to Abram, who was destined to be the source of God's alternative way of giving power away. In chapter 2 below, what the covenant with Abraham tells us about God's answer to the endemic evil use of power is explored. Then three chapters follow on the Mosaic covenant. Chapter 3 looks at what God revealed about those who were to exercise power among his redeemed people. The power that causes or prevents poverty is human power. The vast number of human beings in our day who suffer because of poverty is overwhelmingly the result of the ungodly use of power by other human beings. Among those who use power to the detriment of others, rulers are the most culpable. It is amazing to see that the

---

1. J. G. McConville, *God and Earthly Power: An Old Testament Political Theology* (London: T. & T. Clark, 2006), p. 169. See pp. 1–11, 169–174, of this book for a scholarly description of my approach to the Bible.

types of rulers required for just government are clearly described in the Mosaic covenant. Just rulers exist to administer just law, so chapters 4 and 5 look at the pro-poor elements of the Mosaic law. Chapter 5 concludes by focusing on what we learn about what it means to be poor from the pro-poor laws. Chapter 6 deals with the nature and development of governance after Israel had settled in Canaan and on their failure to keep the Mosaic covenant, which culminated in loss of the land, exile and the prophets' prediction of the establishment of a new covenant focused on a divinely anointed Ruler, who would exercise his power through suffering.

The concept that justice will be established by suffering rather than by inflicting violence comes through clearly in the last Suffering Servant song in Isaiah 53. It is the most intense expression of another fundamental theme that runs through the book – that a living faith in God is needed to enable us to live in a way likely to reduce rather than increase poverty. Insecurity, leading to exclusion and risk aversion, is a key spiritual force that ensures the persistence of poverty. The source of this insecurity is our universal alienation from God. So the restoration of our relationship with God is a key factor in overcoming poverty. Risky faith in God is a prerequisite to doing what is right and just. This fundamental principle has far-reaching implications for the ongoing debate among Christians as to how to overcome poverty. If nothing else, it reminds the advocates of the free market, on the one hand, and the advocates of state intervention, on the other, that the problem of poverty is essentially a spiritual as well as an economic problem. My hope is that the focus of this book will help to move the Christian debate away from the arid polarization between the so-called right and left wings that has prevailed since the 1980s.

The revelation of the power of God, which brings justice and the elimination of poverty in its wake, reaches its fulfilment in Jesus the Messiah. 'Messiah' in Hebrew means 'anointed ruler' (and its Greek translation is 'Christ'), so the coming of Jesus is, therefore, the ultimate revelation of the rule of God. It is at the profoundest level a political revelation because it has to do with how God is going to order human society in such a way as to bring glory to his name and blessing to human beings and the rest of the earth and its creatures.

Because the Bible clearly sees Jesus as the ultimate revelation of the rule or kingdom of God, the largest section of the book focuses on Jesus. Chapter 7 begins by examining his superiority as compared with the major Old Testament (OT) revealers of God's rule and then goes on to look at how Jesus has or will fulfil the various types of ruler as well. The focus in this chapter is on the superiority of the person of Jesus as supreme ruler. Chapter 8 focuses on what Jesus did. He touched the untouchable, drove out unclean spirits and forgave sins, but his supreme act was to offer himself as an atonement for sin and to rise from the dead in proof of this. I argue that the traditional evangelical understanding of the atonement is vital for understanding the nature of God's rule, and that the 'evangelical' social activists who reject this understanding undermine the very foundation of significant contemporary social change for good.

Chapters 9 and 10 deal with the teaching of Jesus by means of a reflection on the Sermon on the Mount, where the sermon is seen as providing an ethic for contemporary living. Chapter 11 looks at what Jesus has done and continues to do since his ascension. The focus in this chapter is on the work of the Holy Spirit in individual believers, seen as the fountainhead of the ability to change human circumstances for good – including overcoming poverty. God rules by his Spirit through King Jesus. Then chapter 12 examines what Jesus is yet to do, which deals with the significance of the final judgment, when God 'will judge the world with justice by the man he has appointed' (Acts 17:31).

The third and final section of the book focuses on the church, which is seen as the ordered society established by Jesus through the power of the Holy Spirit in the midst of societies ordered to reflect the general human rebellion against God. It is through the churches that the power of God is now manifested. They are bridgeheads of divine order in our disordered world. In this sense, they are 'political' societies, even if they are not political in the sense in which the term is usually understood in the world. They are societies that have a Ruler whose 'law' governs every aspect of their lives. The structure of the section on church is based on Oliver O'Donovan's contention that the church is shaped by the Christ-event, summarized in the four moments of *advent*, *passion*, *restoration* and *exaltation*. So chapter 13 looks at the fact that, reflecting the advent, the church is a gathering people. Here it is argued that the divisions among evangelicals over evangelism and social action have never been over the crucial importance of proclaiming the good news (evangel) of Jesus but over the content of the good news. The advocates of social action insist that the gospel includes the invitation to become incorporated into the church, the body of Christ, and that a new way of life is implied in belonging to the ordered society ruled by Jesus. Chapter 13 also considers the church as a suffering people, which reflects the *passion* of Jesus. Here the inevitable conflict between the kingdom of God and the kingdoms of this world is examined. The insecurity and riskiness of kingdom living is to the fore here. Jesus leaves us with a real hope of transformation, and there are plenty of historical examples where the witness of the church has led to changes for good in the behaviour of earthly governments for the blessing of the poor. But such examples are exceptions rather than the rule. The sporting adage that there is no gain without pain is true more often than not in this context – and it is resolute faith in God that can see the gain beyond the pain.

The third moment in the Christ-event is *restoration*, and this is recapitulated in the joy of the church as it experiences the resurrection power of Jesus. This is the theme of chapter 14. The power of the resurrection makes the church a joyful people. Here the focus is on the delight that more than counter-balances the pain considered in the previous chapter. Because Jesus is raised from the dead and endowed with indestructible life, things can change, people can be rescued from sin, demonic oppression and sickness, poverty can be overcome. Finally (chapter 15) the church reflects the *exaltation* of Jesus in being a people who speak the living words of God. The words of God are powerful and these are the only offensive 'weapons' given to the church to transform the world. They come in the form of prophecy and prayer. These are the ultimate weapons given to the churches as they gather from the world to pray and then scatter into the world to prophesy. This is how a foretaste of the just government (without sorrow or poverty) to be manifested when Jesus returns in glory can be enjoyed even today in our broken world.

This is not a book, then, about the practical details of overcoming poverty from a biblical perspective. What has been attempted is a discussion of the twin themes of power and poverty against the background of some of the fundamental theological themes of the Bible as a whole. This has been done with a deep conviction that to experience the truth of these themes is the most effective antidote to poverty.

PART ONE: OLD TESTAMENT

The revelation of God that has been preserved for us in the OT is a wonderful mixture of different types of literature that in metaphorical terms makes it look much more like a wild natural forest than a formal arboretum favoured by the neoclassical minds of the Renaissance period. Yet a story with various themes can be clearly detected. One key theme is that the earth and all its creatures, including human beings, have been created by a good God and are sustained by him. This explains the staggering beauty of the forest. Another key theme is the disorder that has been introduced into life on earth as a result of humankind's rejection of the Creator's authority. This explains those elements that introduce decay and death into the forest. A third theme describes the initiatives taken by God to restore his forest to its pristine glory. This explains what God does to deal with the forces of death and decay so that the beauty and majesty of his forest can be seen again.

Humankind as the crown of God's creation plays a pivotal role in the story. Our abilities are so great that we are clearly the dominant species on earth. Climate-change scientists now say that the way we are using the earth's resources could lead to catastrophic destruction of the environment on which our life depends. Even if the apocalyptic vision of some scientists is not fulfilled, it is already clear that many people are going to suffer as a result of the way some of us live. There has probably never been a time when it is more important for us to understand our origin and nature as human beings. Why are we so powerful? Why do we use our amazing abilities in a way that makes some very wealthy but leaves others in abject poverty? Why are we able to be so destructive and yet also so creative? Is there any hope for us? These are the questions presupposed in the whole of this book, and the foundations of the biblical answers are found in the book of Genesis.

1. FINDING THE ROOTS OF POVERTY IN GENESIS 1 – 11

The story of humankind begins with God's assurance of provision for their needs linked to the command to multiply and rule. Human beings were made with the ability to have dominion over the rest of creation (Gen. 1:28–29). The context and key characteristics of human rule were a garden and caring cultivation. The man was placed in the Garden of Eden 'to work it and take care of it' (2:15). The verb translated 'to work it' is commonly used for cultivating the soil, but is also often used in the religious sense of 'serving' God. The core meaning of the Hebrew translated 'take care' is 'guard'. Interestingly these two verbs are often used together when describing the duty of the Levites in the tabernacle (Num. 3:7–8; 4:23–24, 26). In the garden as well as the tabernacle, the calling is to serve and guard God's holy things.

God, humanity and the soil

In the UK, town councils are obliged to make plots of land called 'allotments' available for rent so that they can be used as gardens by town dwellers who have little or no land attached to their homes. I became a tenant of one of these allotments some years ago. The previous occupant had not worked the soil as a servant, so I found it exhausted and infertile. To bring back the soil to fertility means giving back as much as taking from it. And this is not something that concerns a middle-class Western academic like me who has a passion for growing some of his own food. The whole future of humanity on earth actually depends on the 30 centimetres or so thick crust of our globe that we call 'soil'. We neglect, abuse or just cover more and more of it with asphalt at our peril. It came to us from the Creator so that we might serve him by working it in a way that proves we care for it.

That we have the power to use the soil is clearly one aspect of the dominion God gave us as human beings at our creation (Gen. 1:28). So it is unsurprising that one of the key consequences of the rejection of God's authority by the first humans has an impact on their relationship to the soil. This is the sentence God passes on Adam:

> Cursed is the ground because of you:
> through painful toil you will eat of it
> all the days of your life.
> It will produce thorns and thistles for you,
> and you will eat the plants of the field.
> By the sweat of your brow
> you will eat your food
> until you return to the ground,
> since from it you were taken;
> for dust you are
> and to dust you will return.
> (Gen. 3:17b–19)

God has placed Adam and Eve in a garden he formed for them. The hard work has been done. When the soil is prepared and the fruit-bearing trees and bushes planted, where there is an ample supply of water, as in Eden, working to preserve the fecundity of the soil is not a hard task. Having rejected God's authority, though, Adam is banished from Eden 'to work the ground from which he had been taken' (Gen. 3:23). The ground (*'ădāmâ*) from which Adam has been made is not the richly prepared earth of the garden but the uncultivated granules of soil – the mere dust (*'āpār*) of the earth (Gen. 2:7). This ground, this soil, to which he is banished to provide for his subsistence, is now cursed so that the process of food production becomes a difficult and risky business, as many things threaten success. And as humans struggle with this soil they are also continually faced with the reality that this is what they themselves will one day become.

As a result of the fall God's original command to Adam and Eve to 'be fruitful and increase in number' and to 'fill the earth and subdue it' (Gen. 1:28) is fulfilled in the context of curse. The woman and the man are not cursed in themselves but the processes by which they can fulfil God's mandate to increase and subdue the earth come under a curse. Childbearing becomes a very painful business for the woman and producing food from the soil is the result of 'painful toil' for the man (Gen. 3:16–17). Although at the beginning the woman bore only the pain of childbirth and the man the painful toil of cultivating the soil, historically, because of his physical and cultural dominance, in many societies the man has forced the woman into the *double pain* of childbearing and soil cultivation.

Adam and Eve's firstborn, Cain, worked the soil and probably followed his father in doing so (Gen. 4:2). Abel, Cain's younger brother, became a shepherd and did not work the soil but depended on the soil's spontaneous growth to feed his flocks. Both felt the need to offer something of the fruit of their labour to God. In the light of the covenant God made with Israel after the exodus, the cereal and animal offerings Cain and Abel brought to God were legitimate offerings. We can but conjecture as to why Abel's offering found favour with God while Cain's did not. It is possible that Abel brought the best part (the fat) from the firstborn of his flock, which meant that he thought of giving to God before taking for himself. Cain on the other hand did not bring the first fruits but simply 'some of the fruits of the soil', which suggests that he did not think of God before he saw to his own needs.[1]

The legacy of Cain

Cain's reaction to the rejection of his offering is to become very angry. Guilt easily transmutes into anger where there is an unwillingness to accept responsibility. Cain cannot accept that the rejection of his offering is his fault. To complicate matters he has to contend with the fact that his younger brother's offering has been accepted. So he blames his brother for the rejection of his offering, and his anger towards the unseen God transfers to his tangible brother. God in his goodness warns him that he has embarked on a path leading to disaster. The option to take the right path is still open. Rather than being angry with God and his brother, he can revisit his own motives in bringing his offering and do what is right. But anger has blinded his mind, so the crouching demon of sin takes its spoil and Cain murders his brother.

---

1. See the comment on Gen. 4:4 in Gordon J. Wenham, *Genesis 1–15*, Word Biblical Commentary on CD-ROM, vol. 1 (Dallas, Tex.: Word, 1998).

As with Adam, Cain's rejection of God is punished. But to emphasize the seriousness of his sin, Cain himself is put under a curse. In Adam's case, the ground was cursed because of him, while Cain is cursed from the ground/soil:

> The LORD said, 'What have you done? Listen! Your brother's blood cries out to me from the ground. Now you are under a curse and driven from the ground, which opened its mouth to receive your brother's blood from your hand. When you work the ground, it will no longer yield its crops for you. You will be a restless wanderer on the earth.' (Gen. 4:10–12)

A new and persistent reality is introduced into the story of humankind at this point. The earth/ground that had been created to yield blessing and bounty under human management is polluted when innocent blood is shed on to or into it. Cain's act is typical of all self-centred acts that result in the suffering and death of the innocent, including the oppression of the poor by the powerful. Gordon Wenham comments:

> 'Your brother's blood is crying to me.' The four Hebrew words used hardly require comment. Compressed into them is a whole theology whose principles inform much of the criminal and cultic law of Israel. Life is in the blood (Lev 17:11), so shed blood is the most polluting of all substances . . . Here Abel's blood is pictured 'crying' to God for vengeance. *ṣ'q* 'cry' is the desperate cry of men without food (Gen 41:55), expecting to die (Exod 14:10), or oppressed by their enemies (Judg 4:3). It is the scream for help of a woman being raped (Deut 22:24, 27). It is the plea to God of the victims of injustice (Exod 22:22[23], 26[27]). The law, the prophets (Isa 19:20; cf. 5:7), and the psalms (34:18[17]; 107:6, 28) unite with narratives like this (cf. 2 Sam 23; 1 Kgs 21) to assert that God does hear his people's desperate cries for help.[2]

Cain was a farmer who drew his sustenance from the soil. Now that he has polluted the soil with his brother's blood the very soil itself rejects him. Violence and injustice make life even more insecure and riskier than it had been as a result of Adam's banishment from Eden.[3] Cain's heinous act, born

---

2. Comment on Gen. 4:10 in Wenham, *Genesis 1–15*.
3. Later in the OT it is made clear that murder deserves the death sentence (Gen. 9:5–6). Cities of refuge were designated where those charged with murder could flee for sanctuary from the avenger of blood (Num. 35:12), who would normally be the closest male relative of the murdered person. Alleged murderers would be safe in these cities until their case was brought to trial and their guilt or otherwise was

out of guilt and jealousy, not only leads to the death of his brother but to the destruction of his family. The resulting curse not only puts a greater distance between him and the ground God originally blessed, but also between him and his family. Without the protection of his family Cain's insecurity is doubled, even though God promises protection despite his terrible act (Gen. 4:15). Having taken a second massive step away from Eden, Cain finds himself a wanderer in the land of Nod. Since Nod means 'wandering', the very land in which he finds himself reminds him of his fate.

The narrative continues with a brief account of Cain's genealogy that speaks loudly of the tragedy and glory of fallen humankind. Throughout the brief passage where Cain is the main character, he is portrayed as someone who feels that he does not deserve the treatment he gets. He is someone who believes very deeply that there is nothing wrong with him and that the source of any problems he encounters are not in him. For Cain it is inconceivable that he is to blame for God's rejection of his offering or even for the sentence passed on him for murdering his brother. He cannot accept that he has not done what is right. Even when he finds himself alienated from God, from his closest relations and from the earth/ground that provided his sustenance, he is incapable of facing up to his responsibility for what has happened to him.

There is a profound insecurity at the root of his being as a result of this triple alienation, which helps to explain various aspects of his genealogy. In the first place, Cain and his family become the first city builders. Early cities were unquestionably places where a number of human beings came together for mutual protection from external threats. They were expressions of the attempt of alienated people to find security and cease to be a vulnerable 'restless wanderer' (Gen. 4:14).[4]

Cain's family was also significant in the development of culture. This happened in the family of the polygamist Lamech in the seventh generation from Cain. One son became the pioneer of a nomadic life dedicated to animal husbandry.[5] Another son pioneered the use of musical instruments, while a third pioneered the forging of tools from metals. Although there is no suggestion

---

safely established. Where violence leading to murder happened within a family, loyalties would be divided. It seems that in this case banishment became an alternative punishment to the death sentence (2 Sam. 13 – 24).

4. We shall return to this theme when we come to consider the significance of the Tower of Babel narrative at the end of the Book of Origins (Gen. 11:1–8).

5. This is interesting because the nomadic life is a combination of Abel's profession and the wandering life to which Cain was sentenced.

of this in the text, forging metals has often been associated with developing better weapons. The boasting of Lamech in his song that concludes the story of Cain's line confirms that senseless violence had become endemic in the family. God had reassured Cain a sevenfold vengeance in the event of his murder, which should have told him of his continuing value to God, but he preferred to trust in his own resources to right any wrong against him. It is unsurprising that his descendant Lamech became the archetypal dominant male bully who boasts to his two wives that he has killed a young man who dared to injure him, but unlike Cain he will be avenged not seven but seventy-seven times (Gen. 4:23–24)!

The flood and its aftermath

The very bleak picture we have of the development of humankind in the line of Cain in Genesis 4 is affirmed when we come to the story of Noah and the flood in Genesis 6. Between these two chapters we have the genealogy of Adam and Eve through Seth. It was the line of Seth that 'began to call on the name of the LORD', and to which the Enoch who walked with God belonged (Gen. 4:26; 5:24). But something happened even among the descendants of Seth that led to the corruption of the godly line, so that Noah became the only just man left in his generation.[6] In stark contrast to seeing what he made at creation as very good, God now saw 'how great man's wickedness on the earth had become, and that every inclination of the thoughts of his heart was only evil all the time' (Gen. 6:5). The crown of God's creation had become comprehensively corrupted. Rotten to the core, humankind spewed out rottenness on each other. The word used to describe this manifest rottenness is 'violence' (Gen. 6:11, 13). Wenham comments:

> Animals and men had been intended to fill the earth (1:22, 28); instead, 'violence' (*ḥms*) fills it. This important term . . . is most often paired with *šd* 'oppression.' 'Violence' denotes any antisocial, un-neighborly activity. Very often it involves the

6. The key to what happened is probably the mysterious narrative in Gen. 6:1–8 of the sons of God being attracted by the daughters of men. The heavy emphasis in the OT on the corrupting influence of unbelieving women who do not belong to the covenant supports the traditional interpretation of this passage. It is also possible that a Middle Eastern myth of divine beings consorting with women could have been used to make the point.

> use of brute force, but it may just be the exploitation of the weak by the powerful or the poor by the rich (e.g., Amos 6:1–3), or the naive by the clever (Prov 16:29). '*Chamas* is cold-blooded and unscrupulous infringement of the personal rights of others, motivated by greed and hate and often making use of physical violence and brutality' (*Theological Dictionary of the Old Testament*, ed. G. J. Botterweck and H. Ringgren 4:482). In this context, Genesis 4 well illustrates the meaning of 'violence,' although the word itself is not used there.[7]

Because of this violence the earth itself had been corrupted and ruined to the point that God was left with but one alternative – the destruction of all human beings and animals except for Noah, his family and the animals he would take with him into the ark.

The first thing righteous Noah does on coming out of the ark is to build an altar on which he offers burnt offerings. In the future, burnt offerings were the way Israel could make atonement for their sin and appease God's wrath. Commentators disagree as to whether Noah's sacrifice was meant to be propitiatory or simply an expression of thanksgiving, but God's response suggests the former. Accepting the sacrifice as atonement for sin, God vows never again to curse the ground (*'ădāmâ*)[8] and all living creatures in a flood (Gen. 8:21). From now on, and as long as the earth lasts, God promises that days and seasons will follow each other in orderly progression so that the ground will always yield its fruits for the blessing of all his creatures. This is confirmed in the covenant of the rainbow in Genesis 9:8–17. That this is a covenant between God and the whole of his creation is emphasized again and again in the passage (vv. 12, 13, 15, 16, 17). The strong evidence of the reality of human-induced climate change calls for a theological re-evaluation of this promise, but is beyond the scope of this book. The cursing of the ground indicates the persistent conflict between God's endowment and the way we use it, but we now face the possibility that we may be able to damage the earth to such an extent that it will impoverish a very large proportion of the world's population. There has never been a time when our power in relation to the earth itself has been greater, and there has never been a greater need to face up to the spiritual and moral implications of the way in which we use our power.

---

7. Comment on Gen. 6:11 in Wenham, *Genesis 1–15*.
8. When God says in Gen. 8:21, 'Never again will I curse the ground because of man,' he does not rescind the curse of Gen. 3:17. The curse referred to here is the curse of a comprehensive flood.

This affirmation of God's care for all creatures is conditioned by the reaffirmation and modification of God's original command to humankind in Genesis 9:1–8. God blesses Noah and his sons and commands them to multiply and increase (Gen. 9:1, 7; 8:17; cf. 1:28). All other creatures are given into the hands of Noah and his descendants, with their dread of humankind being evidence that this is indeed the case (Gen. 9:2; cf. 1:28).[9] Finally the creation of humankind in the image of God is reaffirmed and seen as the basis for a very high view of the value of human life, so that murder opens an account that can be paid only by the blood of the murderer. Cain was indeed Abel's keeper (Gen. 4:9b). Many Christians believe that this text means that capital punishment is the just response to homicide. To discuss this is beyond the scope of this book, but if poverty is primarily the result of oppression, then those who cause the death of the poor through oppression are guilty of murder. The way we live in luxury in the minority world while millions die in poverty could well make us liable for the blood of the poor before God. Ignorance and a lack of intent can reduce culpability, but there could still be blood on our hands. And as the 'cities of refuge' law reminds us, those who kill unintentionally need a refuge (see Num. 35)![10]

The development of nations

In Genesis 10, we get the account of the descendants of Noah's sons that is really the fulfilment of the renewed command to humankind to increase in number and fill the earth. As people increase in number they disperse over the face of the earth, and as they become more remote from each other they develop different languages and cultures. When people who share a common language and culture come to think of themselves as sharing a common origin, history and place, an ethnic identity with its strong sense of solidarity is born. This is underlined in the refrain at the end of the genealogy of each of Noah's sons that speaks of their clans, nations, languages and territories (Gen. 10:5, 20, 31). All this is seen as a perfectly natural outcome of God's command to multiply and fill the earth.

The sections on Nimrod and the Tower of Babel (Gen. 10:8–12; 11:1–9) teach us that the process of nation formation that happens when human

---

9. One important difference between the original command and the situation after the flood is that humankind is given permission to eat meat as well as plants.

10. I believe that in view of the teaching of Jesus, it is right to abolish capital punishment.

beings obey God's command to scatter over the face of the earth happens in the context of the continuing sinfulness of humankind. Nimrod is a great warrior, someone addicted to violence. He builds a kingdom with blood, and Babylon is one of the first centres of his empire. Babel is also Babylon. Having found the good broad valley of the Euphrates and developed building materials that would enable them to construct large buildings, these descendants of Ham decided to build a city with a tower reaching up to the heavens. Their motivation was to make a name for themselves and 'not be scattered over the face of the whole earth' (Gen. 11:4).

The fundamental insecurity we found in Cain is still present in the builders of Babel. They are continuing to look for a safe place without God, and believe that the only way to create such a place is to build a city where they can defend themselves against the threat of others. They build on the assumption that complete security will only be gained when they have divine status. The tower they set out to build has to be so high that it will awe everyone and make the citizens of Babel invincible. To achieve this, both human and material resources have to be drawn into the city rather than dispersed from it. Godless power is a centripetal force. The city sucks into its vortex people with military, administrative and all sorts of creative gifts, but also a majority of oppressed people who are needed in order to carry out its grandiose schemes. The security of the few has to be bought with the oppressive sweat of the many. Then the bigger the pretensions the larger the sum of resources needed in order to achieve them. Since large human resources are required to build the invincible city, they can be deployed most effectively in a monolingual context. Therefore, God's command to scatter and diversify linguistically has to be resisted at all costs.

Babel was the first of many attempts by rebellious humankind to make themselves secure by grasping at divinity.[11] In Babel's case, the language was confused and the people found themselves unable to communicate; and without communication the ambitious project was doomed to failure. So the people scattered as God had intended they should. God's power is a centrifugal force. But the fact that human beings were forced to do what God had intended does not mean a change of heart. Human nature remains polluted at its source. Alienated humankind will always have problems with its God-given abilities as long as those abilities are not submitted to the Creator.

---

11. Shi Huang Di, the first emperor of China, who commissioned the making of the terracotta warriors, spent thirty years of his life trying to assure his own immortality!

Conclusion

What, then, are the roots of poverty that have been exposed in the Book of Origins? Alienation from God the Creator is fundamental. Much has been written about the precise nature of the 'original sin', but even from the surface of the story of the fall one obvious consequence is that human beings become focused on themselves rather than on God. Whereas before the fall decisions were taken with and before God, now decisions are taken in independence of God. With Cain this leads to a rejection of the Creator's right to judge our actions. God warns Cain about the danger of not doing what is right, but even when Cain has perpetrated the most heinous crime of fratricide there is no suggestion he felt any guilt. To be able to murder with impunity is the limit of this narcissism and absolute proof that fallen humanity is endemically preoccupied with self.

Insecurity is a fundamental consequence of this preoccupation. Since our true identity is found only in our unity with God, away from God we exist in a constant crisis of identity. Unable to be content to be made in God's image, we feel the need to assert our superiority over others. The last thing we can do is admit that we are insecure in ourselves away from God. From the perspective of fallen humanity, to walk with God is to walk away from this pathological human longing for self-centred security.

That we have become self-centred creatures does not mean we have lost our social or relational nature. We still value marriage, family, clan, tribal and ethnic identities. But we struggle to be truly social beings and our relationships too often become means either to satisfy our own ego or to protect us from our fears. This explains our readiness to dominate and to be dominated. For example, the original creation story in Genesis 1 implies a total equality between man and woman in terms of their creation in God's image and the mandate to rule and have dominion. The elaboration in Genesis 2 emphasizes the difference between the sexes and focuses on complementarity rather than equality. There is nothing in these two chapters that would lead us to expect the total preoccupation with boys and the male line in the genealogies that follow the account of the fall. The domination of the female by the male seems to be the first place where human beings looked to assert their identity and meaning at the expense of others once they had been alienated from God.

The insecurity of humankind is further increased after the fall as a result of God cursing the ground. The contrast between the Edenic and post-Edenic state is not between leisure and labour but between secure and insecure labour. Work in Eden was unfailingly productive, with no possibility of a nutritional deficit. Outside Eden there is no such certainty. Producing food from the ground is now fraught with difficulty. Given this insecurity, it was inevitable, as humankind increased in number, that food production would become an issue of power and control as well as a struggle against the curse.

The desire to be significant, coupled with the desire to have a secure supply of things taken from the ground, which includes food as the most basic good, has been a driver of the desire for power and domination throughout history. God made us powerful creatures as human beings. Exercising dominion is in our nature, and many ecologists have charged Christians with interpreting Genesis 1 in a way that justifies human domination and exploitation of the earth's resources. We may need to plead guilty to this charge in some cases, but it is undeniable that humankind is the dominant species on earth, whether Christians have encouraged that domination or not. 'That' humankind dominates is not the issue, but 'how' we dominate. What Genesis shows is that the exercise of power by human beings alienated from God leads to the domination and exploitation of human beings and the rest of the earth and its creatures by those able to assert their power over others for the sake of a name and security. This happens at every level of social organization, from marriage and the family through to government and business to large multiterritorial empires. The Book of Origins ends with God bringing to nothing the first attempt at establishing an empire. However, this is not the end but merely the beginning of empire building. Its cargoes of all manner of goods including the 'bodies and souls of men' have arrived in its ports throughout the ages and will continue to do so until the announcement of the wedding feast of the Lamb (Rev. 18:13; 19:7). In a world alienated from God, poverty and oppression of the excluded is inevitable. But this is not the whole story of human history. The more significant story of God's redemption shines a glorious light into the dark history of the empires of this world. And that story begins in earnest with Abraham.

2. GOD'S COVENANT WITH ABRAHAM AND ITS SIGNIFICANCE IN THE HISTORY OF REDEMPTION

Genesis 3 – 11:8 tells the story of the deep darkness that descended on earth as a result of humankind's rebellion against God. It takes the rest of the Bible to tell God's story of redemption. This story of redemption begins with an unlikely childless couple, Abram and Sarai, who were both descendants of Seth and Noah through Shem.[1] Their family lived in one of the most advanced cities in the world, Ur of the Chaldeans, in the second millennium BC. The ruins of its famous tower reaching up to heaven are still visible in Iraq today. Abram and most of his father's house or extended

1. Christopher J. H. Wright captures the wonder of this divine intervention beautifully: 'What can God do next? Something that only God could have thought of. He sees an elderly, childless couple in the land of Babel and decides to make them the fountainhead, the launch pad of his whole mission of cosmic redemption. We can almost hear the sharp intake of breath among the heavenly hosts when the astonishing plan was revealed. They knew . . . the sheer scale of devastation that serpentine evil and human recalcitrance have wrought in God's creation. What sort of an answer can be provided through Abram and Sarai? Yet that is precisely the scale of what now follows. The call of Abram is the beginning of God's answer to the evil of human hearts, the strife of nations and the groaning brokenness of the whole creation' (*The Mission of God* [Nottingham: IVP, 2006], p. 199).

family leave this centre of civilization and worldly empire for the land of Canaan, but settle in Haran in northern Mesopotamia (Gen. 11:31). In obedience to God's command, Abram then leaves his newly adopted country of Haran, his people, his father and most of his extended family and proceeds on to Canaan, which was the intended destination when the family originally left Ur (Gen. 12:1).

As Abram leaves Haran, God makes him a promise that becomes a central theme in the story of redemption:

> I will make you into a great nation
> and I will bless you;
> I will make your name great,
> and you will be a blessing.
> I will bless those who bless you,
> and whoever curses you I will curse;
> and all peoples on earth
> will be blessed through you.
> (Gen. 12: 2–3)

It is striking that the blessing God promises Abram was what the builders of Babel aspired after – a numerous people and a great name. God was clearly setting out to establish an 'empire' that would be an alternative to the Babels of this world. The major difference between the Babel type of empire and the sphere of divine rule was that not only under God's rule would all nations be blessed but even all 'peoples', in the sense of 'kinship groups', would be blessed. While this world's empires destroy the diversity of nations and peoples to create a magnificent uniformity, God's 'empire' is a blessing to all, which must mean the flourishing of all nations and peoples.

The story of Abraham and Sarah

Before looking briefly at the way this pivotal promise was worked out in the story of Israel and finally in Jesus the Messiah, it is worth focusing on the story of Abram and Sarai. The promise is a sovereign declaration of how divine government is going to be re-established over the earth and its peoples, but Abram and Sarai are not dispensable cogs in the machinery that is going to make the promise a reality. What they were and how they responded to God was indispensable for fulfilling the promise. As crucial links in the purpose of God in history, their obedience of faith also tells us a great deal about the nature of divine government that is going to deal with the violence and crying caused by humankind's rebellion against God.

Leaving Ur and Haran

The story of Abram begins with an account of departure from the two cities of Ur and Haran. It seems he left Ur under the authority of his father, Terah, although later references suggest this departure was also the result of a divine command (Gen. 15:7; Neh. 9:7). His departure from Haran was in response to a direct command from God to leave his country, his people and his father's household (Gen. 12:1). This suggests the family had been in Haran long enough for them to think of the city and its environs as *their* country. That he was commanded to leave his 'people' or clan, a kinship group larger than the father's house but smaller than a tribe, suggests that Terah's move from Ur with his family might not have been an isolated one. God's hand was probably on Terah's move from Ur, but such a move was also typical of how human beings have behaved throughout history. People have always been attracted to cities as centres of power and prosperity, and those adventurous enough to leave one place to settle in another often become pioneers for other members of their family, clan and nation to follow. This is why cities often become cosmopolitan with people from many nations seeking security within their boundaries. In obedience to the voice of God, Abram leaves the security of the city of Haran, his clan and his extended family and sets out, trusting God's promise to show him where he should go.

As Joshua reminds Abram's descendants many centuries later, his departure also marked a religious conversion. He rejected the gods his family had worshipped in Ur and Haran and began to worship the God who had called him to leave his father's house (Josh. 24:2, 15). He thus left his people's idolatrous worship when he obeyed the voice of God.

Abram's departure from the city does not mean that Abram's God was endorsing the nomadic or pastoral life as the superior way to live. As we shall see, God's promise to Abram was that his descendants would become a great nation, and as the fulfilment of this promise progressed it became clear that this great nation would have a great city at its heart. It was not a matter of rural culture being superior to urban culture, but that human life, which had been so terribly marred by the rejection of the Creator's authority, could be restored only on the basis of trust in God. This trust in God that Abram was asked to show meant taking big psychological, social and economic risks. It meant a departure from all the things that make us feel safe and a stepping out into the unknown, because he knew that a future with God was far more secure than everything Haran could ever offer.

The dispute with Lot and its resolution

Leaving Haran was only the first major step of faith taken by Abram. The next major test came in Canaan as a result of a dispute with his nephew Lot. Lot was the son of Abram's brother Haran, who had died before the family left Ur. He had probably been adopted by Terah and was considered to be Abram's brother. When Abram and Sarai chose to leave Haran with all their servants, animals and portable possessions, Lot decided to join them with his family and possessions. When they eventually came to Canaan, the God who had *spoken* to Abram in Haran now *appeared* to him and told him that Canaan was the land that was to be given to his descendants, the place where they would become a great nation (Gen. 12:7).

Because of famine, Abram left Canaan for Egypt and, although his behaviour there showed a lack of trust in God and exposed flaws in his character, he and Lot returned to Canaan, having become 'very wealthy in livestock and in silver and gold' (Gen. 13:2). As their flocks increased, tensions emerged between Abram and Lot's herdsmen that eventually led to a decision to separate. Generously Abram allowed Lot to choose how they were going to separate, knowing full well that Lot would choose the best land. Abram was left in the more challenging mountainous area of Canaan, while Lot made his way to the plain of Jordan, where he eventually settled down again as a city dweller in Sodom. Wealthy Lot was lured by the prospect of even greater wealth, and moved away from the company and divine protection of his godly uncle until he eventually made his home in a city that became a byword for wickedness. Abram, because of his trust in God, was resolute in clinging to the path of peace and generosity, even if that proved costly to him in psychological, social and material terms. God's sovereign promise made to Abram when he left Haran, that his descendant would become a great nation, was reaffirmed as soon as Lot left. God told Abram to leave Haran and go to the land he would *show* him; he now tells Abram that Canaan is the land he is *giving* him (Gen. 12:1; cf. 13:17).[2]

---

2. Cf. Gordon J. Wenham's comment 'the generosity and peaceableness displayed by Abram on this occasion is applauded from one end of Scripture to the other (e.g., Lev 19:17–18; Pss 122; 133; Prov 3:17, 29–34; Heb 12:14; Jas 3:17–18). Indeed, peacemaking and reconciliation are so central to God's character revealed in Christ (cf. Matt 5:22–26; 43–48) that Paul often calls God "the God of peace" (e.g., Rom 15:33; 2 Cor 13:11; Phil 4:9; 1 Thess 5:23; cf. Eph 2:14–17). It may be that, as elsewhere in the patriarchal story, this reaffirmation of the promises (cf. 22:16–18) is viewed as a blessing given to Abram in virtue of his prior faith and

Rescuing Lot

But Abram's life was not entirely peaceable. When a coalition of eastern rulers came to subdue a rebellion of Canaanite city states, including Sodom, resulting in the capture and abduction of many people and possessions, including Lot and his family, Abram jointly with a couple of other Canaanite rulers went in pursuit of the invaders. In an expedition that reminds us of Gideon's later exploits, Abram and his allies were totally successful despite the heavy odds against them. They returned to Canaan with all the people who had been abducted and a great deal of loot. The first to welcome back the victors was Melchizedek, the priest-king of Salem. He came out with bread and wine and as a priest of God Most High blessed Abram and blessed God Most High for granting him success in his campaign. In response, Abram gave Melchizedek a tenth of all the spoils. The welcome of the king of Sodom was in stark contrast to that of Melchizedek. He brought no food or drink and we can feel his resentment in his curt greeting: 'Give me the people and keep the goods' (Gen. 14:21). Abram knew that the king of Sodom presided over a wicked regime and had vowed to God that he would take none of the loot, in the event of success, so that the king of Sodom would not be able to claim that he had made Abram rich. So Abram responded, 'I will accept nothing belonging to you, not even a thread or the thong of a sandal, so that you will never be able to say, "I made Abram rich"' (14:23).

This fascinating incident in Abram's story tells us a lot about his values. He was prepared to take an enormous risk to right an injustice. Whatever could be said about the relationship between a group of wicked kings from the east and a group of wicked Canaanite kingdoms, the abduction of Lot and his family was unjust in Abram's eyes. He may have regretted that Lot had been attracted to the wicked city of Sodom and that he had eventually settled there, but he was still a relative and fellow pilgrim. Without hesitation he set off in pursuit of a massively superior force, trusting only in God to give him success. This sets the tone for the whole history of God's people as a clan, tribe or nation among the clans, tribes and nations of their world. What success they were to have would never be because of superior military might. Military power would never be the means by which they would establish a just society.

Footnote 2 (*continued*)

good works, illustrating the principle summed up in our Lord's well-known words "Blessed are the peacemakers, for they shall be called sons of God" (Matt 5:9)' (final paragraph of 'Explanation' of Gen. 13:1–18, in *Genesis 1–15*, Word Biblical Commentary on CD-ROM, vol. 1 [Dallas, Tex.: Word, 1998]).

The account of the meeting between Abram and the mysterious figure of Melchizedek the priest-king of Salem, because of Psalm 110, contributed significantly to the Jewish and Christian conception of the Messiah.[3] From the human perspective, as a ruler of a city state in the area where the nomadic Abram lived, it made sense for him to make peace with someone who had just proved himself to be the leader of a successful military force. In this context, his coming with food to share with Abram was also an invitation to enter into a peace treaty. But there is clearly more to the story than this. Melchizedek also came to affirm God's promise to Abram. God had declared Abram blessed; now Melchizedek declares him blessed by his Canaanite God, El-Elyon, God Most High. He also blesses El-Elyon for delivering Abram's enemies into his hands. Abram accepts this affirmation and sees no problem identifying Yahweh with El-Elyon.[4] Then Abram gives Melchizedek a tenth of the spoils, which indicated his subordination and recognition of a superior authority. It is easy to speculate about the significance of the fact that Melchizedek was the priest-king of Salem. Ancient tradition has it that this Salem was the place that would later become Jeru-salem. 'Salem' means 'safe' or 'at peace', so it is easy to see how inspired imagination in due course came to identify this Melchizedek with a type of priestly rule associated with the safety, security and peace only God can provide. By bowing to Melchizedek, Abram was recognizing that security can ultimately be found only in the Lord (Yahweh), who is God Most High (El-Elyon), creator of heaven and earth.

The way the king of Sodom approached Abram contrasted sharply with Melchizedek's, as did Abram's response. The wicked hate to admit that the godly have done well. Making peace with the godly is never on the agenda. A grudging offer of the spoils is made to minimize contact, so the Sodomites can return to their wicked ways as soon as possible. The darkness does not want to be in the presence of light for a moment longer than necessary. What Abram did with the minimum contact was shine the light with even greater intensity. He refused to be indebted to a wicked king and, in the process, was very generous towards someone who was clearly hostile towards him. In view of the teaching of Jesus and Paul on how to treat enemies, there is a strong suggestion of the ethical profile of God's redemptive purpose here right at the beginning of its outworking (see Matt. 5:43–48; Rom. 12:18–21).

---

3. The New Testament (NT) references to Melchizedek are in Heb. 5 – 7.

4. See Gen. 14:22: 'But Abram said to the king of Sodom, "I have raised my hand to the LORD, God Most High, Creator of heaven and earth, and have taken an oath."'

Interceding for Sodom and Gomorrah

That the promise has become intertwined with the quality of Abram's life is further underlined in the amazing account in Genesis 18 of his intercession for Sodom and Gomorrah. This happened after God had changed Abram's name to Abraham, 'a father of many nations' (Gen. 17:5). Amazingly God was very insistent that his promise would be fulfilled through Abram's wife, Sarai, whom we have known to be childless since the genealogy of Terah at the end of Genesis 11. As the time approached for this unlikely promise to be fulfilled, God also gave Sarai the name Sarah, saying that 'she will be the mother of nations; kings of peoples will come from her' (17:16). This happened when the Lord appeared to institute the covenant of circumcision with Abraham. Shortly afterwards the Lord appeared as one of three men and again declared that Sarah would soon bear a son. The other two men were angels on their way to destroy Sodom and Gomorrah, and, as Abraham accompanied the three on their way, after they had enjoyed his hospitality, the Lord decided to share with him what was about to happen. Speaking to Abraham or, maybe, to the two angels God gives the reasons why he is taking Abraham into his confidence. Electing grace, Abraham's response of faith and his appropriation of the Lord's character into the way he lived were intertwined as reasons for taking Abraham into the divine confidence:

> Abraham will surely become a great and powerful nation, and all nations on earth will be blessed through him. For I have chosen him, so that he will direct his children and his household after him to keep the way of the LORD by doing what is right and just, so that the LORD will bring about for Abraham what he has promised him. (18:18–19)

The way Abraham had acted in the dispute with Lot as well as his behaviour towards Melchizedek and the king of Sodom witness to the fact that his experience of the Lord God was being reflected in keeping his way. This was not the first time God had spoken or appeared to him. Whatever else he had learnt from his encounters with God, it was clear to him that the way of the Lord was very different from the way of Ur, Haran and Sodom. So his encounters became the source of his generosity and peaceableness that made the Lord confident he would teach his children and his substantial household what it means to do 'righteousness' and 'justice'. These two terms, which occur hundreds of times in the OT, are at the heart of its ethical teaching. When used together, Chris Wright suggests that possibly the nearest English expression to the double word phrase would be 'social justice', although he goes on to point out that this phrase may be 'too abstract for the dynamic nature of this pair of Hebrew words . . . That is, righteousness and justice are actual things that you do, not concepts you reflect on.'[5] So the NIV translation, quoted above, is a good translation of the meaning of the text in this instance: 'by doing what is right and just'.

Wright goes on to explain that the account of Abram's intercession that follows God's decision to share with him his intention to destroy Sodom and Gomorrah illustrates what it means to do what is right and just. God tells Abram that 'the outcry against Sodom and Gomorrah is so great' (Gen. 18:20). What is referred to here is the cry for justice of the victims of those wicked cities. It is right that these cities have been held up as supreme examples of moral putrefaction, but it is the cry of those poor people who were being oppressed and exploited so that others could indulge their lusts that was God's priority. We are reminded here of the blood of Abel crying out to God from the ground and God hearing his enslaved people in Egypt crying out because of their slave drivers. Such cries do not go unheard by God (Gen. 4:10; Exod. 3:7). They touch his heart and invite his judgment.[6] It is probably the oppression of people in order to enrich Sodom's occupants that is the sin in focus here. But when Ezekiel came to compare the Israel of his day with Sodom, it was the neglect of the city to use its wealth to care for the poor that was in view: 'Now this was the sin of your sister Sodom: She and her daughters were arrogant, overfed and unconcerned; they did not help the poor and needy' (Ezek. 16:49; cf. Prov. 21:13). Causing and ignoring the cry of the poor invite God's judgment.

When he learns that God is about to destroy Sodom and Gomorrah, Abraham pleads for mercy on the basis of a conviction that God's judgment cannot be undiscriminating. Although Abraham never mentions Lot, he is bound to be at the forefront of his mind as he intercedes for the cities. Surely, he argues, God is not going to destroy even a small minority of righteous people along with the unrighteous? He says boldly, 'Far be it from you! Will not the Judge of all the earth do right?' (Gen. 18:25b). After finally assuring Abraham that he will not destroy the two cities if there are but ten righteous in them, the Lord ends the conversation. Abraham returns home convinced

---

5. Christopher J. H. Wright, *The Mission of God* (Nottingham: IVP, 2006), p. 367.
6. 'At verse 20 God speaks again to Abraham, and the first word in what he says is *zĕʿāqâ* – "cry for help". The trigger for God's investigation and subsequent action is not only the appalling sin of Sodom but the protests and cries of its victims. This is an exact anticipation of what motivated God in the early chapters of Exodus . . . The way of the Lord, which Abraham is about to witness and then to teach is to do righteousness and justice for the oppressed and against the oppressor' (ibid.).

that God's judgment is just and with some hope that Lot will be spared. In the process, he has set the tone for the relationship of the redeemed to their ungodly, and at times intensely wicked, cities. Their task is to pray for the well-being of their cities, to offer mercy and to work for transformation and leave judgment to the God who will always do what is right (Jer. 29:7–8; Jonah).

Sacrificing Isaac

The climax of Abraham's story is his obedience to God's request to sacrifice his son Isaac, through whom God promised to make him a 'father of many nations'. Abraham many times acted in a way that seemed to fly in the face of reason because of his faith in God – good examples being his leaving Haran, choosing the less prosperous part of Canaan and rescuing Lot, which have been considered in this chapter. When God asks Abraham to sacrifice Isaac, 'flying in the face of reason' is taken to another plane. God now asks him to destroy the means by which God himself said he would fulfil his promise. But despite the fact that God seems to be contradicting himself, Abraham still obeys. We must resist the temptation to read this strange story through Western 'psychologized' lenses. The proper backdrop is the terrible consequences of rejecting God's authority since the fall of Adam and Eve and most recently seen in the horrible wickedness of Sodom and Gomorrah. In stark contrast, Abraham proves his total submission to God, because his beloved son Isaac is on the altar and his arm is raised and about to slay him when the angel of the Lord intervenes. A ram is provided to take Isaac's place on the altar, and for the last time in the story the Lord confirms the promise first made when Abraham left Haran. Abraham's obedience of faith is so significant that the Lord God now swears by himself that it will be fulfilled:

> The angel of the LORD called to Abraham from heaven . . . and said, 'I swear by myself, declares the LORD, that because you have done this and have not withheld your son, your only son, I will surely bless you and make your descendants as numerous as the stars in the sky and as the sand on the seashore. Your descendants will take possession of the cities of their enemies, and through your offspring all nations on earth will be blessed, *because you have obeyed me.*' (Gen. 22:15–18; my italics)

This final affirmation shows clearly that the spiritual and ethical life of those to whom God reveals himself is a part of his redemptive purpose for the earth. We now know this purpose was eventually worked out through a Son, who, unlike Isaac, voluntarily offered himself as a sacrifice for sin, but it also includes the obedience of faith of those who are being transformed into the Son's likeness.

The content of the covenant with Abraham

A great nation

We can now turn to the content of the promise made to Abraham and a brief outline of its fulfilment in Israel and Jesus. First there is the promise that God will make his descendants into a 'great nation'. 'Nation' is a political concept referring to a people sharing a language, territory and government. A great nation will have a large population and extensive territory. This promise is also made to Abraham's son Ishmael (Gen. 17:20; 21:18), but the focus in the OT is on its fulfilment through Isaac, the long-awaited son from Abraham's barren wife, Sarah. This promise is fulfilled literally in the reigns of David and Solomon, but from the beginning the promise is conditioned by faithfulness to God. The fact that Abraham's descendants are to be a blessing to all peoples rules out an empire built on oppression and injustice.

The whole promise to Abraham is saturated with blessing. There is a strong echo here of the story of creation when God blessed the water creatures, birds, land creatures, human beings and the seventh day (Gen. 1:22, 28; 2:3). In the case of the creatures, including human beings, success in breeding is an important aspect of the blessing. To be blessed is to multiply. A great nation is a nation with many citizens. God confirms this to Abraham (as he proves his love for God in the way he lives) by saying that his descendants will be as numerous as the dust of the earth and the stars in the sky (Gen. 13:16; 22:17). In a world that has now been anxious about population growth for half a century or more, we are losing the ability to rejoice in this blessing of God. This is not the place to write at any length on this issue but we probably need to be reminded that all children are a blessing because they represent not only the potential for despoiling the earth by their consumption but for blessing the earth and its people by their creative production. We may need to limit population growth for various reasons but children are always a blessing.[7] But to be blessed in the OT is not just to increase in number but includes prosperity in every sense – not only children but plenty of food and drink, property, security from enemies, wealth enough to lend to others, long

---

7. In many countries, the elderly still depend directly on their children for their sustenance. In wealthier countries with a national-insurance system, elderly people seem to be able to cope without depending on their children. But with older people living longer and with too few insurance-paying people in the next generation, any national-insurance system is likely to become unsustainable and collapse.

life and, central to it all, the presence of God (Lev. 26:4–13; Deut. 28:3–15; Isa. 65:20–25). To be blessed is to enjoy the security lost with banishment from Eden.[8]

The descendants of Abraham became very numerous in Egypt where they were enslaved in the interest of ungodly and idolatrous imperial pretensions. Like every other empire, the Egyptian was built with the unjust exploitation of labour.[9] Seeing the injustice and suffering of Abraham's descendants and hearing their cry for help God comes to their rescue and calls Moses from exile in Midian to lead them to freedom (Exod. 3:7). After their escape they are led to Mount Sinai, where God establishes his covenant with them declaring that they are to be 'a kingdom of priests and a holy nation' dedicated to him. But almost as soon as the Israelites have solemnly agreed to the covenant, they turn their backs on God to worship a golden calf! Seeing the nation's incorrigibility, God says to Moses that he will make him into a great nation (Exod. 32:10), but Moses intercedes on the nation's behalf and the project to make them great proceeds. Moses' intercession is the first in a long series of cases where a faithful individual, often with or on behalf of a faithful remnant, represents God's intention for the nation as a whole. This pattern reaches its climax in the Suffering Servant of Yahweh in Isaiah. At this point the great nation melts into the background and is replaced by the Servant as the focus of God's blessing to the nations. The New Testament is insistent that Jesus was the Servant described by Isaiah and the seed of Abraham that would bring blessing to all nations.

A great name

The second promise is of a great name. In Babel, they set out to make a name for themselves, but it is God who promises to make a name for Abraham and his descendants. Here again this process is conditional on obedience to God's standard of justice. The nation that comes from Abraham will be great only to the extent that it lives in a way consistent with God's character or name. The tragedy of Israel is that it rejected God and his ways and adopted the ways of

---

8. I'm reminded here of the first two lines of a hymn by William Williams: 'Yn Eden, cofiaf hynny byth, / Bendithion gollais rif y gwlith . . .' (tr.: 'In Eden, I will ever remember this, / I lost blessings as numerous as the dewdrops . . .').

9. Ironically Gen. 47:21 seems to imply that Abraham's great-grandson Joseph may have contributed to this development by the 'servitude' to which he reduced the Egyptians. But the Egyptian servitude was very different from the servitude to which the Israelites were subjected.

the nations around it. God had warned Solomon at the dedication of his magnificent temple that disobedience would lead to disaster:

> But if you or your sons turn away from me and do not observe the commands and decrees I have given you and go off to serve other gods and worship them, then I will cut off Israel from the land I have given them and will reject this temple I have consecrated for my Name. Israel will then become a byword and an object of ridicule among all peoples. (1 Kgs 9:6–7)

The greatness of Israel's name was dependent on their respect for God's name. Solomon had built the temple but it was God who adopted it and consecrated it to his name. While he was worshipped there and his character was reflected in the lives of the rulers and people of Israel, Israel's name would be great simply because God is great. Sadly Solomon conformed increasingly to the world's image of empire, in such acts as building alliances on the basis of foreign wives who introduced idolatry into Israel, or using forced labour, so that Israel's golden age was really only a prelude to disaster. Again foreseeing the final collapse of Jerusalem and its famous temple Isaiah prophesies a new name for the city that will be a witness to the nations:

> For Zion's sake I will not keep silent,
> for Jerusalem's sake I will not remain quiet,
> till her righteousness shines out like the dawn,
> her salvation like a blazing torch.
> The nations will see your righteousness,
> and all kings your glory;
> you will be called by a new name
> that the mouth of the LORD will bestow.
> You will be a crown of splendour in the LORD 's hand,
> a royal diadem in the hand of your God.
> No longer will they call you Deserted,
> or name your land Desolate.
> But you will be called Hephzibah,
> and your land Beulah;[10]
> for the LORD will take delight in you
> and your land will be married.
> (Isa. 62:1–4)

---

10. 'Hephzibah' means 'my delight is in her', and 'Beulah' means 'married'. The idea is that Jerusalem will be joined to God as a wife to her husband.

According to Revelation, this prophecy is fulfilled in the marriage union of the church with Jesus Christ who is 'great Abraham's greater son' (as the hymn writer says). Just as ultimately the greatness of the nation that descended from Abraham was focused on Jesus Christ, so is the greatness of its name (Rev. 21:1–3, 9–11, 22–26). Because Jesus died, rose again and ascended to heaven, the centre of the divine empire promised to Abraham is not on earth but in the very presence of God. It is the ascended Jesus who has been given a name above every other name (Phil. 2:9). So the final fulfilment of the promise of a great name for Abraham will be seen in the final revelation of Jesus and his redeemed from every nation.

A blessing to all peoples/nations

The third promise is that Abraham would be made a blessing to 'all peoples on earth' (Gen. 12:1). As in the case of the great nation and great name, the great blessing is dependent on obedience to God. How, then, were the descendants of Abraham to be a blessing to all nations (18:18)? By showing that true 'prosperity' is not the result of the pursuit of power but the pursuit of God's justice. Worldly empire is always built with military or commercial power or, more often than not, a combination of both. Its prosperity is always bought with the blood and sweat of many. Its 'peace' and 'freedom' mean war and bondage to those perceived as threats to its stability. This being the case, it is impossible for the empires of this world to be a blessing to all peoples.

The God who owns the whole earth decided to give a part of it, the land of Canaan, to the enslaved nation of Israel. But Israel still had to occupy the land of Canaan, and it is fair to ask how this invasion differs from other invasions in the interest of worldly empire.

First the Israelites did not arrive at the borders of Canaan as a result of bloody rebellion. The one act of bloody rebellion recorded in Exodus cost Moses forty years of exile in Midian (Exod. 2:11–15). When he returned as God's emissary to lead the people to freedom, he did not become the leader of a violent slave rebellion as he had once hoped he would be, but became an announcer of the mighty acts of God. It was the power of God and not the power of the sword that gave birth to Israel as a nation.

Secondly it is true that the land was already occupied, but the people who occupied it had long lost their title to it because of the wickedness and injustice of their ways. No nation has a right to continue to own land they have polluted with blood, especially the blood of children offered as sacrifices to their idols (see Gen. 15:16; Lev. 18:24–25; 20:22–24; Deut. 9:5; 12:29–31). Israel was eventually removed from its land for precisely the same reasons as the Canaanites.

Thirdly Israel travelled to Canaan via Sinai. There God laid down the conditions on which he was giving Israel the land. If Israel would obey the law of the God who had saved them from slavery, then they would establish a society where equity and economic justice was the norm. If Israel had been able to establish a nation embodying the principles of the law revealed at Sinai, that would have been one way in which the nation could have been a blessing to all the nations. They would have shown how the power of God leads to blessing for all. Sadly the law was unable to penetrate and change Israelite hearts, which are, like all human hearts, deeply infected by evil, and for much of its history the nation was not a blessing to any other nation. A new covenant that could penetrate the heart was required. However, the heart of the law still provides principles that, if put into practice, will lead to the establishing of nations in which all the citizens will experience life as a blessing.[11]

In his foundational covenant with Abraham, God laid down the tracks on which the progressive revelation of his redemptive purpose would run. The events cumulatively known as the exodus put a powerful new engine on the tracks. This 'engine' is the focus of the next three chapters.

---

11. For a more comprehensive discussion of this topic, see Christopher J. H. Wright, *Old Testament Ethics for the People of God* (Leicester: IVP, 2004), pp. 472–480.

3. DIVINELY ORDAINED GOVERNMENT IN THE OLD TESTAMENT

God told Abraham to leave Haran and go to live in the land he would show him and promised he would make Abraham a great nation. God also made it clear that the promise would be fulfilled through his childless wife, Sarah. By the end of his life Abraham had been further tested by his daughter-in-law Rebekah's initial childlessness, but the non-identical twins Esau and Jacob were born fifteen years before the old man died. So he died having seen his child's children but having to exercise considerable faith still to believe that his descendants through Isaac would become a great nation that would be a blessing to all nations. God had also revealed to Abraham after Lot had separated from him that Canaan was the land in which his numerous descendants would become a great nation, although when Abraham died he owned nothing in Canaan except a grave.

It took centuries for Abraham's descendant through his grandson Jacob/Israel to multiply into what would now be regarded as a small nation or ethnic group; and when significant multiplication happened, they were enslaved by the Egyptians. Their escape from Egypt under the inspired leadership of Moses, the revelation of God's law to them as an emerging nation at Sinai and their eventual possession of Canaan under Joshua's leadership are seen as a crucial new phase in the fulfilment of God's promise to Abraham.[1]

---

1. Moses would have been the leader of the escape and settlement had it not been for the recalcitrance of the Israelites.

As such these events are also a crucial phase in the revelation of the nature of divine government.

Israel was a nation founded in fulfilment of God's promise on the twin pillars of *divine rescue* and *divine law*, and Moses, as the divinely appointed leader, played a vital role in both the rescue and the giving of the law. He became the paradigm of the divinely instituted governor or ruler. In order to understand government in the context of the exodus and settlement of Canaan, we need to look at what God expected of his divinely instituted governors and the law by which they were expected to govern. Moses himself is the obvious place to begin.

Moses as a ruler

The context for the divinely instituted rule of Moses over Israel is the imperial rule of the Egyptian Pharaohs, which is typical of the empires of this world. The Pharaohs were perfect examples of what Galbraith calls condign power vested in a person.[2] Claiming divine status, the Pharaohs unified the power of the dominant cult and their control of the military to coerce their people into submission. This same power was used to enslave the Israelites.

The Pharaoh used a strategy that has been used often in the history of empire. To enslave the Israelites he needed popular support, so the first step was propaganda to create fear and suspicion. It was put abroad that this immigrant population, these Israelites who did not really belong in Egypt, had become very numerous. The purpose of this was to make people fearful and suspicious of them. This fear was then intensified by the suggestion that they could potentially join with an enemy and threaten the security of Egypt. Interestingly what the official propaganda indicates the government feared most was not that the Israelites could take over the government if they joined with an enemy, but that they might take the opportunity provided by joining with Egypt's enemies to leave the country (Exod. 1:8–10). Having whipped up fear and suspicion while emphasizing the importance of the Israelites for the Egyptian economy, enslaving them would have been the obvious and pertinent thing to do, and the suffering and misery caused by the brutal way in which they

2. Galbraith argues that there are three instruments for wielding power (the *condign* [coercive], *compensatory* and *conditioned*), and that there are three sources of these instruments: personality, property or wealth and organization. For an outline of this thesis, see J. K. Galbraith, *The Anatomy of Power* (Boston: Houghton Mifflin, 1983), pp. 4–6.

were treated would have been considered justifiable in the circumstances. That it was fear of losing their economic value to Egypt that led to their enslavement also explains why it was so terribly difficult for the Pharaoh to allow them to leave. What is so chilling about this typical example of the way empire works is that the decisions to treat people with intense brutality comes to appear so reasonable to those who take them. History is littered with examples: the Nazi decision to adopt what they called the 'final solution', which led to a concerted attempt to exterminate all European Jews,[3] or the decision to use the atom bomb on Japan, or the decision to stamp on Tutsi 'cockroaches' in Rwanda, seemed perfectly reasonable decisions to those who perpetrated the atrocities!

In the event, even brutal treatment did not restrain the numerical growth of the Israelites – so the brutality intensified. It reached its climax in the command to all Egyptians to kill, by throwing into the Nile, every Israelite boy they came across. At this point the main plot of Exodus begins to be revealed. The time had come for God to lead his people out of Egypt, so his promise to Abraham that his descendants would one day occupy Canaan could be fulfilled. A leader needed to be prepared for this great task.

Moses should have been drowned, but as the adopted son of a princess he was raised to rule. However significant or insignificant his mother may have been in the pecking order of Pharaoh's court, he would have become very familiar with the way power was exercised in the greatest empire of his day. He would also have been indoctrinated into the political philosophy of Egypt in which the Pharaoh figured as a god with absolute power over the lives of his subjects. But Moses never forgot the knowledge of his origins that had been instilled into him by his mother, despite the fact that he would probably have been a very young child when he left her to be raised as an Egyptian. However, it is unsurprising that it was to the Egyptian way that he resorted as a mature adult when trying to right the wrong suffered by one of his fellow Israelites. Making sure there was no Egyptian witness, he killed an Egyptian who was ill-treating an Israelite. There is no indication in the biblical text as to how premeditated an action this was, but the response of an Israelite the next day when he tried to stop him ill-treating a fellow Israelite suggests that Moses may have been thinking about leading an Israelite rebellion. The Israelite whom Moses

---

3. The film *Conspiracy*, starring Kenneth Branagh, is a powerful recreation of the two-hour meeting of Nazi intellectuals and SS officers, where the decision was taken to exterminate European Jews. Cf. Dietrich Bonhoeffer's statement 'One is distressed by the failure of reasonable people to perceive either the depth of evil or the depth of the holy' (*Ethics* [London: Macmillan, 1965], p. 65).

tried to restrain made it clear that Moses' authority was not accepted when he said, 'Who made you ruler and judge over us?' (Exod. 2:14). Without support for his violent strategy of liberation, Moses was left exposed and had no alternative but to flee from Egyptian jurisdiction.

Forty years later God considered Moses ready to become a leader and judge over Israel. Moses was very reluctant to obey, but little by little realized that all he had to do was proclaim God's word and that God would do the rest. This led to the amazing chain of events that eventually left the Israelites free by a sea shore with the remains of the military might of Egypt floating in the sea before them. The Israelites had been freed without one of them having to strike an Egyptian in anger!

Once Israel was free, Moses faced forty years of ruling and judging Israel in very difficult circumstances in the desert. The secret of his success was his almost total submission to God – a lesson he had learnt well in the conflict with Pharaoh. He is described as 'a very humble man, more humble than anyone else on the face of the earth' (Num. 12:3). 'Humble' here translates *'anaw*, which has the primary meaning of 'poor' – and poor in the sense of disinherited victims of exploitation by others, people without rights. The term is clearly used in a metaphorical way in this description of Moses. He never experienced literal poverty, but felt his poverty before God very deeply. He had no confidence in his own ability as a ruler and it took him quite a while before he began to have confidence in God. God almost had to drag him to Egypt under protest. The result of his lack of faith in his own abilities was a growing trust in the power of God and a willingness to be led by God. He had to face a lot of complaining, insubordination and what came close to rebellion in the desert, yet not once did he take dealing with problems into his own hands but looked only to God to vindicate him.

In humility, he led the freed slaves to Sinai and there received the law that was to condition the way in which the Israelites were to live on taking possession of the Promised Land. Again, listening to God, he built the tabernacle and instituted its priesthood and sacrificial system to ensure God's continuing presence with his people. When the tabernacle was built, the camp of Israel was organized around it and provision was made for an orderly decamp when the time came for the people to move. Interestingly his father-in-law, Jethro, gave him sound advice when he saw Moses exhausting himself trying to act as a judge for the whole of Israel. As a result he organized the judicial process into clan, tribal and national levels.

Moses became so committed to God that when God offered to make him personally a great nation because of Israel's idolatry with the golden calf, he rejected the offer and pleaded for forgiveness for Israel, because their destruction in the desert would reflect unfavourably on the name of God. Although life in the desert would make it difficult for any leader to profit from his people, there is no evidence that Moses was tempted in this way. He took valuables from the people to build the tabernacle, but there is no evidence that he asked for anything for himself, and he certainly did not enrich himself by accepting bribes to pervert justice. His family joined him in the desert and probably died with the whole generation that passed away in the forty years of wandering, because no issue of his is mentioned in the genealogy of the tribe of Levi (Exod. 18:5; 1 Chr. 6). So neither he nor his family profited from his role as ruler. Finally his greatness as a ruler is seen in the fact that he took great care in training his successor. Joshua became Moses' close companion soon after the escape from Egypt, and Moses made it clear that Joshua would succeed him as leader, so that there would be no doubt about the leadership after his death. To the end, the glory of God and the well-being of Israel were his primary concerns. It is unsurprising that Deuteronomy, commenting on his life after his death, says that 'no prophet has risen in Israel like Moses, whom the LORD knew face to face' (Deut. 34:10).

Israel's four categories of ruler

A *prophet* is one of four types of leader/ruler whose ideal qualities Moses describes in Deuteronomy 16:18 – 18:22. The other three are *judge*, *king* and *priest*. Together these four encompass the method of God's government of his rescued people. It is interesting that Deuteronomy, looking back on Moses' life and work, uses 'prophet' as the best term to describe his leadership role. But he was clearly more than a prophet, because he acted as a judge and, as God's spokesman, gave Israel their judicial system. He also had a priestly function as a mediator between God and the people and as the one who instituted the cult and its priesthood to carry on his priestly role. Although he displayed some of the qualities of the ideal king, Moses foresaw that monarchy as a form of government would become an option for Israel once they were settled in Canaan. Monarchy becomes a possible form of government only when there is a national security to defend. What Moses says about these four types of ruler tells us much about what a government that would be a blessing to people looks like even in a fallen world. We shall examine briefly what is said about each role in Deuteronomy.

Judge (Deut. 16:18–20; 17:8–13)

Interestingly the judge was the first type of leader described by Moses. This reflects the fact that Israel's life as a redeemed people was conditioned by the revelation of their Redeemer's law. That a judge might be needed testifies to human fallibility, while the existence of a just law to apply testifies to the existence of a way back for society to the right path. The judges were to have a number of characteristics.

First they were to be accessible by being based in every town (16:18). Judges are of little use unless they are accessible. The system envisaged was really an extension of the structure of authority that already existed in a society organized into father's households, clans/kinship groups and tribes. The father's households would provide the pool from which the clan elders would emerge, and the clan elders would be the pool from which the tribal leaders would emerge. Judges would be clan or tribal elders gifted with the ability to ensure that the law was observed especially on behalf of the most vulnerable in society. The book of Job presents a vivid picture of such a judge, as Job described his public life before disaster overtook him. The picture is not of a judge meticulously applying statute law to particular circumstances but of a person involved in making sure that the weak and vulnerable in society are protected:

> When I went to the gate of the city
>   and took my seat in the public square,
> the young men saw me and stepped aside
>   and the old men rose to their feet . . .
> Whoever heard me spoke well of me,
>   and those who saw me commended me,
> because I rescued the poor who cried for help,
>   and the fatherless who had none to assist him.
> The man who was dying blessed me;
>   I made the widow's heart sing.
> I put on righteousness as my clothing;
>   justice was my robe and my turban.
> I was eyes to the blind
>   and feet to the lame.
> I was a father to the needy;
>   I took up the case of the stranger.
> I broke the fangs of the wicked
>   and snatched the victims from their teeth.
> (Job 29:7–17)

Secondly they were to 'judge the people fairly' (Deut. 16:18; literally 'judge a righteous judgment'). What this meant is shown by the three commands that follow (v. 19):

1. 'Do not pervert justice', which means that where law was embodied in a statute it should be applied to the letter, that no attempt should be made to 'bend' the law away from its original intention.
2. 'Do not show partiality', which means that the social status of the accused or accuser should be immaterial.
3. 'Do not accept a bribe', which means that a judgment cannot be bought. A judge should not be influenced by the reward offered by accused or accuser.

Thirdly a commitment to 'justice and justice alone' (v. 20) has a direct bearing on the continuing prosperity of the people: 'so that you may live and possess the land the LORD your God is giving you'. Possessing and using the land to generate wealth was dependent on judges administering the law justly. The people had been told in Deuteronomy 15 that there would be no poor people among them if they fully obeyed all the Lord's commands (vv. 4–5). Judges were – and are – needed because God recognizes the difficulty of achieving complete obedience to his commandments. They may not operate on the level of the moral law, with its emphasis on love of God and neighbour, but by just application of God's just penal law they are able to restrain evil and make a significant contribution to creating a society where the poor can hope for a better future. Where laws are unjust and judges crooked the poor have no hope. That is as true today as it has ever been.

The Israel who settled in Canaan under the leadership of Joshua was a loose federation of tribes, and where national security was concerned it survived without a permanent central military authority for around three-and-a-half centuries. During this time the nation's focus of unity was to be the tabernacle and its worship and a high court that was to be closely linked with it (17:8–13).[4] Cases involving serious physical and civil conflict, where it could be difficult for a local elder/judge to be impartial, were to be referred to this higher court. Linked to the sanctuary would be Levites, whose calling was making sure that God's law was preserved and taught. Some would become experts in the law. Presiding over them would be a chief justice, who would probably be chosen from among the tribal elder/judges. The decisions of this court were final, and contempt was to be a capital crime. But no judicial system can remain just without upright judges, and in the history of Israel even this court at times became corrupt and its judges subjects of prophetic

4. It was a system that reflected what Moses had established during the wilderness wandering (see Deut. 1:15–18; and cf. Exod. 18:17–26).

condemnation. It was a descendant of this court that condemned Jesus the Messiah to death!

King (Deut. 17:14–20)

Israel as a nation was conceived as a type of pluralism under divine guidance and not a monarchy. That is why judges are the first community leaders to be mentioned. Since the nation was to be established on God's law, the judges who administered the law were indispensable. This is probably why the charismatic military leaders who arose to rescue Israel from oppression after the land of Canaan had been settled under Joshua's leadership were called 'judges'. Some, like Samuel, may have literally acted as judges and heard individual cases, but their main function was to call the people back to God as their ruler and saviour.

The book of Judges ends with five chapters showing a nation prone to idolatry, immorality and division as the context for the repeated refrain 'In those days Israel had no king; everyone did as he saw fit' (Judg. 17:6; 18:1; 19:1; 21:25). These chapters must have been written in the time of David or Solomon when things were a lot better, but history testifies that monarchical government also failed to keep Israel from the sins that often prevailed in the time of the judges. In fact, when the people insisted on adopting monarchy as their form of government, Samuel retorted that their motivation for doing so was a rejection of God's rule over them and that their kings would inevitably disobey the law for kings revealed in Deuteronomy (1 Sam. 8:10–17). What, then, were the key principles of that law?

1. *The king was to be a person chosen by God (v. 15a).* This is what happened when the monarchy was established in the time of Samuel. The corollary that an unfaithful king could be rejected by God and another chosen in his place was also the case in the beginnings of Israelite monarchy. Even when God made a covenant with David that would lead to the establishment of a dynastic monarchy, he did not give up his position as the one who ultimately chose the ruler of Israel. David's ancestors could be chosen or rejected by God. Even the Servant Messiah who was to bring justice to the nations was Yahweh's chosen one in whom he delighted (Isa. 42:1b).

2. *The king was to be an Israelite (v. 15b).* He needed a good understanding of the basis of Israel's existence in God's saving acts as a hindrance to leading the people into idolatry.

3. *He was not to put his trust in military power (v. 16).* The chariot was considered the state-of-the-art weapon in the time of Moses. So the more horses a king had, the more chariots he could muster and the more powerful he would be. What is more, Egypt would have been the obvious place for an Israelite king to buy horses to build his arsenal of chariots. The thought of Israel depending

on the military might of Egypt for its defence was utterly abhorrent to God (Ps. 20:7; 2 Kgs 18:24; Isa. 31:1). This is one area where Israel was to differ radically from other nations. Its security was not to be dependent on military might. There was no need to spend a high proportion of its resources on weapons. The nation was to trust God to defend it against its enemies, which would have been a ridiculously risky policy from a non-Israelite perspective – and which was, sadly, considered too risky by Israelite kings for much of the nation's history.

4. *He was not to acquire a large harem (v. 17a).* Having many wives was an important status symbol in the ancient world. The king would be expected to have the largest harem. Kings would also acquire wives in the process of making alliances with surrounding nations. By welcoming this convention Israelite kings would import women with idolatrous beliefs into the very heart of their nation. Marrying foreign wives was strictly forbidden to an Israelite, and kings were not above God's law. Ignoring God's directive in this area was a key factor in Solomon's undoing (1 Kgs 11:1–4). The clear teaching of God's law should have given Israelite kings the courage to reject this diplomatic convention of their age, while the theological account of human origins in Genesis 1 – 2 should have caused them to reject the use of women as pawns in a diplomatic game.

5. *His position was not an opportunity to accumulate great wealth (v. 17b).* It is at this point, maybe, that the clash between the ungodly concept of power as a means to self-aggrandizement and the godly concept of power as an opportunity for service is most acute. The temptation to use power to accumulate wealth is intense, because power provides ample opportunity to do so. In God's eyes, power and wealth are not synonymous. The world where the rich and powerful still exploit and oppress the poor for their own benefit desperately needs such teaching.

6. *The king was a servant of God and his law (vv. 18–20).* In this respect, a king was to see himself as on the same level as any other citizen or brother in his nation (v. 20). Like everyone else he was subject to God's law and should do everything in his power to keep it. An essential prerequisite to keeping the law would be knowing it, and this could be ensured by having a copy at hand to refer to as well as experts who could bring relevant laws to his attention in different circumstances.

The positive and negative prescriptions of this law of the kings would yield a political leadership that would be as radical and counter-cultural now as it would have been in the ancient Near East. It is a servant-kingship model in which the rulers would see themselves as servants of God and the people. Fundamentally that meant they were guardians of a law that, if obeyed, would ensure there would be no poor persons in the nation. Plenty of countries today could do with this type of ruler administering this type of law.

Priest (Deut. 17:9; 18:1–8)

God commanded Israel to set aside one of its twelve tribes to be devoted entirely to the spiritual needs of the nation, because they had been chosen 'to stand and minister in the Lord's name always' (Deut. 18:5). They were not given a block of tribal land but dispersed in cities among all the other tribes. Their support was to come from the tithes and sacrifices of their fellow Israelites. Unlike priestly classes in other nations, the ban on owning land made it more difficult for them to build a power base in Israel. They were consigned to perpetual dependence – like the poor. In return for this support, they were given two key functions in the life of the nation.

1. *They were to preserve and teach God's law.* We have seen that a legal case too difficult for a local judge to deal with was to be taken to the central sanctuary, where the Levitical priests as well as the judges based there would be consulted. This was because the priests at the central sanctuary were to be devoted to knowing and teaching God's law (Deut. 17:9; Lev. 10:11; 2 Chr. 17:7–10; Neh. 8:7–9). But the tribe of priests were also scattered in the cities that had been given to them in the midst of all the other tribes. They, like the judges, were accessible. While the judges applied the law to particular cases, the priests and Levites preserved and taught the story of God's dealing with humankind and particularly with Israel. They bolstered the teaching that went on in Israelite homes that provided the motivation for keeping the law (Deut. 6:7).

2. *They were responsible for the upkeep of the central sanctuary and presenting sacrifices to God on behalf of the people (18:1b).* They kept the need for reconciliation with God before the minds of the whole nation. They also instructed the people in the ways of holiness that included teaching the rules of ritual purity (e.g. Lev. 11 – 13).

Because of their calling to make sure that Israel knew the story of God's dealing with humankind as a whole, and especially with Israel, and to preserve Israel's relationship with God through sacrifice, they had a key role in fulfilling God's purpose of blessing the nations through Israel. They were crucial to God's intention that the whole nation of Israel should be a 'kingdom of priests and a holy nation' (Exod. 19:6). Their task of being priests for Israel was to make the whole of Israel priests for the nations. They had a key place in God's government of his people by keeping them obedient and humble. By preserving and teaching God's law they reminded the people what God required of them; by maintaining the cult of the central sanctuary they reminded the people of their sinfulness and need for reconciliation with God. Divine government always needs priests in this sense.

Prophet (Deut. 18:14–22)

The list of 'detestable practices', such as divination, sorcery and omens in Deuteronomy 18:9–13, witness to the deeply felt need of human beings for supernatural guidance and approval, particularly when crucial life decisions need to be taken. The law taught by the priests would be adequate to guide life in general, but there would be many points in the history of individuals, families and the whole nation when a direct word from God may be required. God promised to provide prophets for such times and that his prophets would be like Moses:

1. They would be called to their task by God. No true prophet is self-appointed (v. 18a).
2. They would speak God's message, not their own (v. 18b).
3. One test that they were genuine was that their predictive prophecies would come to pass, although this was not an infallible test (vv. 21–22; cf. 13:1–2).

By being told by God what was going to happen beforehand, the true prophets were really witnessing to the fact that history is meaningful. God took Moses into his confidence when he called him to lead the Israelites out of their captivity. He told him what he was about to do, so that Moses was a witness to the outworking of God's purposes in history.

The prophets called by God, who predicted many future events that happened as they had said they would, had two central messages for their contemporaries: they condemned idolatry and the social injustice that accompanied it.

Elijah, whose appearance on the mount of transfiguration marks him out as the greatest of the prophets after Moses, set the tone in his message to Ahab as he took unjust possession of Naboth's vineyard (1 Kgs 21). The story of the way Naboth was dispossessed is a classic case of idolatry leading to injustice. Because she had no respect for the God of Israel, Ahab's wife, Jezebel, had no hesitation in paying people to give false testimony against Naboth, which led to his death by stoning. In doing so, she trampled all over everything sacred in God's covenant with Israel. In condemning Jezebel's heinous deed (done with Ahab's connivance), Elijah acted as the spiritual and social conscience of the nation.

Prophets are divinely inspired counter-cultural revolutionaries. They come to proclaim divine judgment and hope. They declare what God is going to do, and when it comes to pass, faith in God is strengthened. Having been taken into God's confidence, they are able to stand against the stream and challenge the powers of this world. They are often rejected and persecuted, but are always in evidence when God is moving to establish his rule.

Judges, kings and priests are the institutional expression of what the prophets do. Moses was such a great prophet because through him God rescued his people Israel and gave them the law that would shape their life as a nation in the Promised Land. They needed judges, kings and priests to maintain their integrity as God's people. But with the inevitable decline in the effectiveness of the maintainers, the extraordinary contribution of the prophets was always an option for the renewal and progress of divine government. As a result of the redemptive work of Jesus Messiah, prophecy moves into centre stage as the central means for the expression of divine government in the NT age.

Conclusion

This chapter on Moses as a ruler and the various types of rulers Deuteronomy envisaged for Israel adds substantially to what we have come to understand of the method of divine government from the life of Abraham. The contrast between divine government and the government of this world is also deepening. In the life of Moses, the cruel oppression of the Egyptian model is added to the example of Cain, the situation before the flood and Babylon. In the story of divinely instituted rule, we now have Noah, Abraham and Moses. As with Noah and Abraham, divine election and righteousness/justice are at the heart of the events in which Moses is the chief actor. But Moses was called to lead a people to a life of freedom in their own land where they would share 'a memory of deliverance from slavery, the provisions for the worship of the God who delivered them, and the pervasive presence of *torah* throughout [their] corporate life'.[5]

A memory of redemption, a pervasive need to worship and the law were to be the foundation of what looks like a pluralistic and somewhat democratic form of government. It was pluralistic in the sense that there were different types of rulers responsible for different aspects of the lives of Israelites, and

---

5. J. G. McConville, *God and Earthly Power: An Old Testament Political Theology* (London: T. & T. Clark, 2006), p. 98.

all, including the rulers, were expected to be subject to the law (Torah). Since all were expected to have at least a working knowledge of the law, all were to be treated as responsible citizens. This is a world away from the Egyptian model of a divine king, whose task was to use his people to enhance the glory of his name through oppression and conquest.

4. THE LAWS TO PREVENT POVERTY

Having looked at the different types of leaders who were given authority over the lives of God's people in the OT, we now turn to the law that was meant to condition all their actions. There is a temptation at this point to rush to those parts of the law that have to do with hindering or alleviating poverty, but there is a need first to emphasize the unity of the law. The legislation that gives opportunities for all to provide for themselves, or welfare for the needy, cannot be divorced from commands prohibiting idolatry or that provide a way (through sacrifice) to deal with sin. In the law, the physical is tightly linked to the spiritual. True respect for God and for neighbour are inseparable.

The integral character of the law becomes very apparent in the work of the prophets. They continually remind the people and their rulers that the religious, social and economic life of the nation has become something very different from what God intended for them. The prophets use graphic pictures to illustrate this. Isaiah compares Israel/Judah to a vineyard stocked with the best vines and for which everything has been done to ensure a good crop. Tragically the vineyard produces nothing but bad fruit. Isaiah explains the meaning of the illustration:

> The vineyard of the LORD Almighty
>   is the house of Israel,

> and the men of Judah
> are the garden of his delight.
> And he looked for justice, but saw bloodshed;
> for righteousness, but heard cries of distress.
> (Isa. 5:7; cf. 1:15–17; 3:13–15)

Despite everything God has done for his people in rescuing them from slavery and giving them his law, they still end up behaving in the way that led God to destroy most of humanity in the flood. What God saw in Judah was a society in which the rich and powerful used their position to exploit the weak and needy. God had come to rescue his people from Egypt because he had seen their misery and 'heard them crying out because of their slave drivers' (Exod. 3:7). Now he was hearing the cries of distress coming from his people again, but this time the oppressors were their own judges and rulers.

The consistent condemnation of the economic inequality that had become endemic in Israel during the period of the monarchy is clear proof that God's intention for his people (and by implication for all societies: Deut. 4:6–8; Isa. 49:6) is a high level of economic equality. Immediately after the 'Song of the Vineyard' referred to above, for example, Isaiah goes on to proclaim judgment on those

> who add house to house
> and join field to field
> till no space is left
> and you live alone in the land.
> (Isa. 5:8)

As Samuel had warned, monarchy had led to the establishment of an aristocracy in which a small number of individuals and families were enriching themselves at the expense of the majority of the population. Ahab and Jezebel's oppressive method of acquiring land was not subtle, but in various ways an aristocratic rich and powerful class was able to manipulate the legal and economic framework in which Israelites/Jews lived, so that they were able to build smart mansions where they enjoyed a very high standard of living while the majority of the people, who were paying for the pleasure of the elite, lived in abject poverty. Unsurprisingly the prophets proclaimed judgment on the mansions (Isa. 5:9; Jer. 5:26–29; 22:15–16; Amos 3:15; 5:11).

Another picture used by the prophets is that of the unfaithful wife. God is portrayed by Jeremiah as a bridegroom who lavishes gifts of jewellery on his bride. But despite such generosity, the wife has become adulterous and prefers other lovers. Consequently:

On your clothes men find
the lifeblood of the innocent poor . . .
(Jer. 2:34)

Ezekiel develops this theme into an extended allegory of a man finding a baby girl abandoned to death, caring for and finally marrying her and lavishing all manner of precious gifts on her. She repays her husband's love by becoming a prostitute who paid for men to visit her! This unfaithfulness was a picture of the nation's idolatry, which reached its zenith with the adoption of child sacrifice, military alliances with idolatrous nations and injustice towards the poor. Where oppression of the poor was concerned Israel/Judah had become worse even than Sodom, which, as we have seen, was 'arrogant, overfed and unconcerned' and 'did not help the poor and the needy' (Ezek. 16:49).

What, then, were the laws that if kept would have made it impossible for Israel to become the unjust and exploitative society condemned by the prophets?

The significance of the land for Israel

Before mentioning any specific laws, something needs to be said about the significance of the land Israel occupied. In a pre-industrial context, land is the crucial economic resource.[1] But for Israel it also had a profound theological significance. The land was a gift God had promised to Abraham's descendants many centuries before the Israelites found themselves camped on the eastern side of the Jordan ready to invade. Possessing the land was going to take effort and sacrifice, but with faith in God the outcome of the invasion was certain. Because of lack of faith and zeal, they made much heavier weather of possessing the land than they should have – but they did possess it. When enough progress had been made with the invasion, the land was divided among the tribes, clans and families so that everyone was provided for. Humanly speaking, the Israelites would have been unable to possess the land without God's help. The truth of this would have been seared into the mind of the people through the forty years of wandering in the wilderness as they realized the consequences of a lack of faith.

It was God who enabled the Israelites to take possession of the land. But having brought them into possession, he also claimed ultimate ownership that

1. Even in an industrialized society, land continues to have significance at least as an indicator of wealth.

gave him the right to determine the terms on which Israel could continue to possess it. In the jubilee legislation, God declares, 'The land must not be sold permanently, because the land is mine and you are but aliens and my tenants' (Lev. 25:23). Land, which is the most fundamental source of sustenance for humankind, could not be traded freely in the open market in Israel. It was lent as a sacred trust to the tribes, clans and families of the nation, with conditions attached. This principle has profound implications for biblical economics. The most basic resource needed in order to produce wealth in an agrarian economy was not the private property of the owners to be disposed of as they saw fit. This means that any concept of private property in Israel cannot be divorced from a whole raft of social obligations.[2]

When the time came for Joshua to organize the division of the land (see Josh. 13 – 19), the portion of each tribe was described as 'the inheritance of the tribe of . . . , clan by clan' (Josh. 13:15). It is clear from this that the tribes, which traced their ancestry back to one of Jacob/Israel's sons, were divided into numerous smaller subgroups translated 'clans' by the NIV and other translations. This subgroup was not a clan in the way the term is normally used by anthropologists and sociologists, because the Israelite clans did not practise exogamy (marriage outside the clan), their land was not held communally and power was not strongly centralized in the clan leader. However, these Israelite 'clans' were highly significant because it was to them that specific parcels of land were allocated, and it was their responsibility to ensure that the families or fathers' households of the clan retained their inheritance within the clan lands. The clan did not own the land, but it had the responsibility of preserving the land and clan members for its fathers' households. There was no ownership of land in the absolute sense in Israel, but there was ownership of the right to use the land and this right was given only to families.[3]

A father's house was made up of all the living descendants of one living male ancestor. This could include the wife/wives, their sons and their wives, the sons' sons and their wives and all unmarried girls. It could be quite a large establishment in a polygamous society. How new fathers' houses would come into existence when a family grew numerically and the relationship of new houses to the resulting diminishing land resource are unclear in the biblical material, but the ideal was that land should belong inalienably to fathers'

---

2. This is also the case for the concept of private property in the NT.
3. It is clear from passages such as Judg. 6:11 that the land belonged to the father's house, so this was the level at which there was communal ownership. The levirate law in Deut. 25 also reflects such a situation.

houses.[4] Naboth's response to Ahab's offer to buy his vineyard, or to give him a better one somewhere else, illustrates how deeply ingrained this principle had become in the hearts of the people: 'The LORD forbid that I should give you the inheritance of my fathers' (1 Kgs 21:3). Christopher J. H. Wright comments:

> The Lord did forbid it. This piece of land was not really Naboth's to give, sell or exchange. He held it in trust from the Lord for the benefit of his family. It was not just a question of 'human rights' or 'natural justice'. It was a staunch upholding of the right of a member of the Lord's people to maintain that part of the national inheritance which the Lord had assigned to his personal household.[5]

God's laws that condition Israel's occupancy of the land

The two principles that God was the ultimate owner and that the families of Israel were to have a share of it in perpetuity are fundamental to the laws that conditioned Israel's occupancy of the land. It is time to look at some of the specific tenancy laws and their implications for overcoming poverty in the OT economy.

The seventh year release of the land (Exod. 23:10–11; Lev. 25:2–7; Deut. 15:1–11)

The law in Exodus states that the land was to be released from cultivation in the seventh year. Whatever grew of itself was available to the poor and the wild animals. In a sense, ownership of the land reverted to God, who then made it equally available to all the people and to the wild animals. The Leviticus passage underlines that reaping was forbidden (Lev. 25:5). The family who normally cultivated the land were allowed, with the poor and wild animals, to use what grew of itself for their immediate needs, but they had no greater rights to such produce than the poor or the animals. Like the poor, for this special year, even the owner's enjoyment of the fruit of the land was for subsistence and not profit. Patrick Fairbairn's observation on this law is still valid:

---

4. Christopher J. H. Wright, *God's People in God's Land: Family, Land, and Property in the Old Testament* (Carlisle: Paternoster 1990), pp. 44–58.
5. Christopher J. H. Wright, *Old Testament Ethics for the People of God* (Leicester: IVP, 2004), p. 90.

> Such an institution was utterly opposed to the niggardly and selfish spirit which would mind only its own things, and would grind the faces of the poor with hard exactions or oppressive toil, in order to gratify some worldly desires. No one could imbibe the spirit of the institution without being as distinguished for his humanity and justice toward his fellow-men, as for his piety toward God.[6]

Whereas in Exodus and Leviticus the land was to be released from cultivation and made available for common use, in Deuteronomy the focus was on 'release' from debt (Deut. 15:1). The Hebrew root *šmṭ*, meaning 'to release', is used in both Exodus and Deuteronomy.[7] This suggests that there was a direct link between releasing the land from cultivation and releasing debtors. The probable scenario in view here is a farmer having to borrow from a neighbour in order to survive the hungry months, as many subsistence farmers still do today. The only way the debtor could repay was by pledging a proportion of future crops, which practically meant giving a parcel of land to the creditor as security against the loan. Such loans could be paid over a number of years. What the law of release from debt did was to put a limit on the number of years this type of debt could be carried. This would mean that the type of loan in view here would always be negotiated with the seventh year release in view. For example, if a loan had to be taken out the year after the sabbath year, repayment could be agreed over six years. However, the beauty of the law for the debtor was that if the debt had not been paid in full by the seventh year then it was to be cancelled. The seventh year was clearly an ideal year to do this because no creditor could expect to receive any payment from a debtor in the year when the land was not to be cultivated for profit. Some scholars have argued that the debt cancellation was only for the sabbath year and that the debtor would be expected to continue to pay the debt once the sabbath year was over. Free market interpreters are particularly fond of this interpretation![8] However, it seems difficult to understand Deuteronomy 15:9a if this were the case: 'Be careful not to harbour this wicked thought: "The seventh year, the year for cancelling debts, is near," so that you do not show ill will towards your needy brother and give him nothing.' It is clear from this verse that the closer the seventh year was when the loan was made, the greater the risk. When there

6. Patrick Fairbairn, *The Typology of Scripture*, 6th ed., vol. 2 (Edinburgh: T. & T. Clark, 1882), p. 464.
7. See Christopher J. H. Wright, New International Biblical Commentary, *Deuteronomy* (Peabody: Hendrickson, 1996), pp. 187–188.
8. See E. Calvin Beisner, *Prosperity and Poverty* (Westchester: Crossway, 1988), pp. 58ff.

were five years left to repay a loan, the creditor could expect the debtor to be able to pay a good proportion of the loan before the sabbath year. It would be unlikely that the debtor would have a whole series of bad harvests. If there was only one harvest between taking out the loan and the sabbath year, the risk for the creditor was much greater. Verse 9a makes sense only if there was a risk. If a debtor was expected to resume paying the debt after the sabbath year, there would be no risk. It is unsurprising, therefore, that Jewish interpreters have understood the debt cancellation of the sabbath year as absolute.

This interpretation is also consistent with the relational view of justice found in the law. Under God the well-being of the families of Israel was paramount. When someone went into debt in order to survive, the key justice issue was not that the debtor should pay the creditor in full, but how to restore the debtor to a place of respect in the clan or tribe with dignity intact. More often than not, loans would be made to fellow clan members, so they were not to be seen by the creditor as an opportunity for personal or family gain, but as an opportunity to restore a brother in need. The ideal was not for some to become rich at the expense of others, but for all to enjoy their land inheritance in the presence of God. This relational emphasis is also the driving force in the law on interest.[9]

The ban on interest (Exod. 22:25; Lev. 25:35–38; Deut. 23:19–20)

In Exodus 22:25, the law that forbids charging interest on a loan is one of a series of laws dealing with the protection of defenceless and disadvantaged people. They are, as always in the OT, the immigrants, widows, orphans and the needy. God says, 'If you lend money to one of my people among you who is needy, do not be like a money-lender; charge him no interest.' God expected his people to have a strong social conscience and to care for one another. The verse presupposes a situation where some Israelites will have more than they need while others will find themselves in need. In such a situation, the money-lender sees the vulnerability of the needy as an opportunity for gain. This is not how God expects his people to behave towards each other. He expects the true Israelite to see a brother and do everything possible to help. As we have already seen from Deuteronomy, making a risky loan may be required to restore a brother with dignity. Here the Israelites with means to help are commanded to make interest-free loans to their needy brothers.

---

9. The Jubilee Centre in Cambridge, England, has many resources on its website, where the relational characteristics of the law are applied to various aspects of contemporary life. Many of the resources can be downloaded freely. See <http://www.jubilee-centre.org>, accessed 22 Mar. 2008.

The ban on charging interest in Leviticus 25:35–38 is found in the middle of the law of Jubilee that not only deals with the return of land to the families who had originally been granted it, but with how to help fellow Israelites who were sinking deeper and deeper into the mire of poverty. The 'countryman' or 'brother' in verses 35–36 is on the second step down from being able to hold his own on the inheritance given his family by God. The first step would have been to give up some land as security for a loan (vv. 25–28). In these verses, the brother has taken the next step down, lost his land and needs a loan to survive as a paid worker. The next step down would be to sell himself into bonded servanthood to a fellow Israelite, and the final step down would be debt slavery to a non-Israelite (vv. 39–53). It is interesting that the encouragement here is to treat the poor brother as well as 'an alien or a temporary resident' (v. 35).[10]

The aim of helping the poor brother was 'so that your countryman may continue to live among you' (v. 36). The idea was that he and his family would be able to preserve their place among the families of Israel. Since these verses come in the middle of the Jubilee laws, the ultimate aim was to preserve the countryman's family on the land that was God's inheritance to them. This idea of everyone having their place and dignity in society is striking. The well-being of the community was paramount and was to be put before any desire for personal profit and enrichment. To put profit before people by charging interest on a loan to a poor brother would be tantamount to both insulting and showing a total lack of respect for God (v. 36). Interest was not to be charged on loans of money or food (v. 37), and the law was backed up by the reminder of God's grace in rescuing his people from slavery in Egypt (v. 38). The God who rescued the Israelites from their profound bondage expected the better off among his people to be generous in their help to fellow Israelites in deep trouble.[11]

In Deuteronomy 23:19–20, the ban on charging interest to a fellow Israelite is unconditional because there is no indication that the ban applies only when the fellow Israelite is poor. This does not mean necessarily that the application of the law found in Exodus and Leviticus is being broadened. In an agrarian society with an originally equitable division of land, most loans would be made

10. Some idea of how they were to be treated can be seen in Exod. 22:21; 23:9, 12; Lev. 19:10, 33–34; 23:22; Deut. 10:19; 24:19–21.

11. There are many references to the exodus as an encouragement to obey God's laws; e.g. Lev. 19:36; 22:32–33; Deut. 5:15; 15:15; 16:12; 24:18, 22. Obedience to the law is a result of redemption, not its cause.

to relieve poverty. The thrust of the law here as in the other passages is probably to stop people exploiting the poor in their desperation. However, it is worth remembering that in response to these texts the Christian church for most of its history was very opposed to charging interest on loans.

Things changed during the Reformation and John Calvin is seen as the key figure in bringing about the change, so that he has been described by many as a father of modern capitalism. I am not competent to comment on the historical reliability of this charge, but we have easy access to Calvin's view on charging interest in his published works. For example, there is an extensive discussion of the topic in his *Harmony of the Pentateuch*.[12] The term Calvin used for charging interest is 'usury'. In the West, 'usury' has come to mean excessive or exorbitant interest, but in Calvin it is used in the older sense of charging any sort of interest at all. Calvin recognizes that there is an absolute ban on interest in the three passages already discussed, and that this ban is sustained throughout the OT. So the NIV is incorrect in translating a text like Proverbs 28:8 as

> He who increases his wealth by exorbitant interest
> amasses it for another, who will be kind to the poor.

'Exorbitant interest' is an incorrect translation because it implies that there is such a thing as non-exorbitant interest. That is not what the text is saying. The point is not that low-interest loans should be made, but that no-interest loans should be the norm.[13]

Calvin sees all the laws from Exodus 20:22 through to Deuteronomy as applications to every aspect of life of the fundamental principles of the Ten Commandments. Interestingly he deals with usury/interest under the heading of the Eighth Commandment, 'You shall not steal' (20:15).

Calvin deals with the above three passages together. He concludes that the main principle enjoined in the three cases is that 'the rich who has the ability,

---

12. John Calvin, *Commentaries on the Last Four Books of Moses Arranged in the Form of a Harmony* (Edinburgh: Calvin Translation Society, 1854), pp. 125–133.

13. Cf. Ezek. 18:8: 'He does not lend at usury or take excessive interest. He withholds his hand from doing wrong and judges fairly between man and man.' This verse (cf. Ps. 15:5) is part of a description of a righteous/just person. The NIV makes the same mistake as in Prov. 28:8. 'Excessive' is not in the original. What we have is another straight commendation of charging no interest. The NIV makes the same mistake again in Ezek. 22:12.

should uplift the poor man who is failing, by his assistance'.[14] That is, not to charge interest was an expression of charity. Calvin goes on to emphasize that while the Israelites were allowed to charge interest on loans to Gentiles, Christians do not have such a right and must be generous in their lending to the poor, whoever they are:

> It is plain that this was a part of the Jewish polity, because it was lawful to lend at interest to the Gentiles, which distinction the spiritual law does not admit. The judicial law, however, which God prescribed to His ancient people, is only so far abrogated as that what charity dictates should remain, i.e., that our brethren who need assistance, are not to be treated harshly. Moreover, since the wall of partition, which formerly separated Jew and Gentile, is now broken down our condition is different; and consequently we must spare all without exception, both as regards taking interest, and any other mode of extortion; and equity is to be observed even towards strangers . . . [T]he common society of the human race demands that we should not seek to grow rich by the loss of others.[15]

The reason why the Israelites were allowed to take interest from strangers, according to Calvin, was for the sake of equality. Since non-Israelites assumed that it was right to charge interest on loans, it was only right for Israelites to reciprocate. God 'accords the same liberty to His people which the Gentiles would assume for themselves; for this is the only intercourse that can be endured, when the condition of both parties is similar and equal'.[16]

But we are still left with the question 'whether usury is evil in itself'. Calvin admits that even the classical pagan traditions of Greece and Rome were against usury. He goes on:

> But if we come to an accurate decision as to the thing itself, our determination must be derived from nowhere else than the universal rule of justice, and especially from the declaration of Christ, on which hang the law and the prophets, – Do not unto others what ye would not have done to thyself. (Matt. 7:12).[17]

Having underlined again that charging interest of any sort to the poor is entirely forbidden, he says that 'if we would form an equitable judgement,

14. Calvin, *Last Four Books of Moses*, p. 127.
15. Ibid., p. 128.
16. Ibid., p. 129.
17. Ibid.

reason does not suffer us to admit that all usury is to be condemned without exception'.[18] He illustrates his point with two cases: (1) The case of someone who says he cannot pay back a loan within an agreed time while using the money he has to repay to profit somewhere else. Calvin thinks it is legitimate to charge for late payment in such a case. (2) The case of a rich man who borrows part of a sum needed to purchase land. Calvin believes it is just for the lender to receive a portion of the revenues of the land until he receives the principal in full.

What are condemned in the Bible are 'unjust exactions . . . whereby the creditor, losing sight of equity, burdens and oppresses his debtor. I should, indeed, be unwilling', Calvin continues,

> to take usury under my patronage, and I wish the name itself were banished from the world; but I do not dare to pronounce upon so important a point more than God's words convey. It is abundantly clear that the ancient people [of Israel] were prohibited from usury, but we must needs confess that this was a part of their political constitution. Hence it follows, that usury is not now unlawful, except in so far as it contravenes equity and brotherly union. Let each one, then, place himself before God's judgement-seat, and not do to his neighbour what he would not have done to himself, from whence a sure and infallible decision may be come to.[19]

As Chris Wright comments, 'This is hardly the capitalist's charter that Calvin is often accused of providing.'[20] Whatever conclusion is come to as to Calvin's significance in the appearance of a capitalist economic system, his understanding of the law against charging interest is sound. The OT absolutely forbids the rich from using their resources to increase their riches at the expense of the poor. Loans to the poor were always to be interest free.[21]

Jubilee (Lev. 25:8–55)

With the Jubilee we arrive at the pinnacle of the type of law we have already considered, because both the seventh-year sabbath of the land and the ban on

---

18. Ibid., p. 132.
19. Ibid.
20. Wright, *Deuteronomy*, p. 254.
21. For an interesting attempt to apply this law in our contemporary context, see Paul Mills, 'The Ban on Interest: Dead Letter or Radical Solution?', Cambridge Paper, Dec. 1993. Can be downloaded freely from <http://www.jubilee-centre.org/resources.php?page=6&catID=1>, accessed 22 Mar. 2008.

interest are incorporated into the Jubilee law. The beginning of Jubilee is timed precisely to the evening of the Day of Atonement, the most solemn day in the annual calendar, when Israel received forgiveness for all their sins. It was to be marked by the sounding of the ram's horn (*šôpār*) with heralds going throughout the country announcing that the year of Jubilee had come (vv. 8–13).

There is no certainty about the etymology of 'Jubilee', but what was meant to happen in the Jubilee year is clear. It was the seventh in a cycle of seven years that was to be characterized by two blessings: liberty from debt bondage and return to the original inheritance given to each family or father's house when Canaan was first possessed by the Israelites. *Liberty* or *freedom* and *return* or *restoration* are the key concepts of the Jubilee.

The Jubilee defined the method of buying and selling land in Israel (vv. 14–16). It made it impossible to sell land absolutely. What a purchaser bought when buying land was really a lease that gave him the right to use the land for a number of years, the maximum number being the number between the time of the purchase and the next jubilee. The maximum length of any lease would have been forty-two years, that is, the forty-nine years between Jubilees minus seven sabbath years of the land. Theoretically this system ruled out profiteering from the purchase of land because it made it impossible to take advantage of the poor by buying land cheaply and then selling at a higher price before the lease ran out. There would be a set value for a set number of crops, so if someone came along to redeem the land for the original owner, he would have to pay only the set value of the crops remaining on the lease. Here again the Israelites were encouraged to put the inclusive well-being of the whole clan before their own comfort, because that is what the Lord their God required of them: 'Do not take advantage of each other, but fear your God. I am the LORD your God' (v. 17).

What God demanded was very challenging, especially if the commentators who believe that the Jubilee year followed a sabbath year of the land are correct. That would mean almost three years without a harvest. God promises to provide enough in the year when cultivation took place before the Jubilee to last for three years (vv. 18–22). Keeping God's covenant would require real faith and trust in God's provision. The Jubilee meant a voluntary move in the direction of becoming poorer for the sake of the community and called for trust in God's ability to provide.[22] It called for the exercise of faith against reason.

---

22. As we shall see, the same pattern of divine demand is repeated in the new covenant teaching of Jesus in Matt. 6:19–34.

It was in the Jubilee law that God asserted his ownership of the land, as we noted earlier. What God did in the Jubilee year was to take possession of the land from his people and, as it were, give it back to them again on the basis of the principle of equity that had determined his giving of the land in the first place. In this way, he liberated those who were in bondage to debt and restored them to a place of dignity in the community of his people. In the context of the old covenant, God himself took on the role of the ultimate redeemer.

The right to redeem lost land and lost freedom is a key way to liberation and restoration in the remainder of the chapter on the Jubilee (vv. 25–55). The structure of the laws linked to the Jubilee is clearly determined by the repetition of 'If one of your countrymen becomes poor' (vv. 25, 35, 39, 47). The poverty of countrymen is to be the concern of all, but especially of fellow clansmen.

The first way of redeeming land leased because of poverty would be through a relative buying it back for his kinsman. The order of kinsmen-redeemers was brother, uncle, cousin and any other kinsman or clan member (v. 49; cf. Boaz in the story of Ruth). There is a debate as to whether the kinsman-redeemer bought back the land for the relative who had lost it or for himself. If the latter, the relative and his family would then become tenants of the kinsman-redeemer, but only until the Jubilee. The law of Jubilee would be very significant in this case because it would mean that large land holdings would be impossible even within tribes and clans, because land would have to be returned to the descendants of the original families at the Jubilee.

A second way to redeem would be for the one who had sold the right to use the land to prosper and acquire the means to buy it back. Strikingly a kinsman or an original owner had a right to buy back leased land and, in both cases, as stated above, the purchaser was not allowed to sell the land back at an inflated price. The kinsman or original owner was to pay only the value of the number of crops left in the lease. If neither a kinsman nor original owner had been able to redeem leased land, then, when the Jubilee came, God himself became the kinsman. He took the whole land of Israel into his possession and restored all the families of Israel to the inheritance that had been granted to them when the land was first settled.

Not only was the Jubilee law relevant to the loss of land; it was also relevant to the literal loss of freedom that often accompanies the slide into poverty. Without capital or land poor Israelites had only themselves to offer as payment to a creditor in return for their survival (see 2 Kgs 4:1–7). The lowest depth to which Israelites could sink would be to sell themselves into debt slavery to an immigrant (v. 47). Those who had sunk to such depths were to be well treated and were to be set free at the Jubilee when God intervened as their kinsman-redeemer (v. 54). There was an opportunity for debt slaves to be released in the sabbath year of the land (Deut. 15:12–18) but the offer of freedom in that year seems to have been only for heads of households, while wives and children had to be left in servitude. That is probably why the option of choosing to remain as a debt slave is highlighted in Deuteronomy. However, in the year of Jubilee the enslaved family could leave together to take possession of land and have the opportunity to live in freedom and dignity in Israel.[23]

John E. Hartley's final comment on the Jubilee legislation, which incorporates the law of the sabbath year of the land and the ban against interest as well, sums up the radical implications of these laws for Israel's economic life:

> The view of land ownership herein . . . is revolutionary. It does not promote the ownership of private property in a way that allows the rich to amass large tracts of land, displacing the poor, nor does it permit the speculative buying and selling of land that feeds inflation, which in turn increases poverty. Neither does this manifesto promote a social or common ownership of land. Instead, this legislation prescribes a classless society in which each family has an inalienable ownership of a plot of land. It promotes responsible work that attends ownership of property, and at the same time it promotes responsible brotherhood of all Yahweh's people arising from their faith in Yahweh. Those who are more prosperous assist their poorer brothers, raising them to their own level, because they fear Yahweh. Kinsman helps kinsman, neighbor helps neighbor to face and to overcome economic hardship. Greed and covetousness are broken.[24]

Protection for vulnerable groups

Up to this point the laws that have been considered provided structural mechanisms to stop the development of social stratification in Israel. There would be a large measure of equality in enjoying God's provision if these laws were observed. Obeying these laws would go a long way to ensuring that

23. Christopher J. H. Wright argues that the 'slaves' in view in Deut. 15 and Lev. 25 were different types of slaves. The former were landless 'Hebrew' ones, while the latter were Israelites who had lost their land. See *God's People in God's Land: Family, Land, and Property in the Old Testament* (Carlisle: Paternoster, 1990), pp. 249–257.

24. Final paragraph of 'Explanation' of Lev. 25:1–55, in *Leviticus*, Word Biblical Commentary on CD-ROM, vol. 4 (Dallas, Tex.: Word, 1998).

there would be no poor among the Israelites, as God had intended (Deut. 15:4). However, there were certain people who needed special legal protection. These were the orphans, widows and what the NIV unfortunately calls 'aliens'.

As in many countries still, the OT orphan (*yātôm*) was not necessarily a child who had lost both parents. The primary meaning of *yātôm* is 'fatherless'. This is why 'orphan' is more often than not coupled with 'widow' because children without a father would often mean that there was also a mother who was a wife without a husband. Because the whole system of land inheritance was based on the father's house the position of orphans and widows without fathers and husbands was very precarious. Unscrupulous close relatives and clan leaders could take advantage of their vulnerability to increase their wealth by taking over the dead father's land and neglecting to share any of its produce with orphans and widows. This type of exploitation would inevitably lead to the predicament of the widow and her two sons described in 2 Kings 4:1–7. Her husband was one of the company of the prophets, but when he died his wife and two sons were left without any support. To make matters worse, the dead husband had borrowed money and the creditor was demanding the two boys as bonded slaves in payment of the debt. Elisha's miraculous intervention saved the family, but the situation of the family was precisely what the law was meant to prevent. It would have been impossible to arrive at the situation of the prophet's widow without flouting God's law at many points.

The law strongly condemns the type of exploitation that must have happened to explain the widow's plight, and the prophets see it as one of the key reasons for Israel's expulsion from the land of Israel. Isaiah, for example, proclaims:

> Woe to those who make unjust laws,
> to those who issue oppressive decrees,
> to deprive the poor of their rights
> and withhold justice from the oppressed of my people,
> making widows their prey
> and robbing the fatherless.
> What will you do on the day of reckoning,
> when disaster comes from afar?
> To whom will you run for help?
> Where will you leave your riches?
> Nothing will remain but to cringe among the captives
> or fall among the slain.
> (Isa. 10:1–4)

Though often included with orphans and widows as a vulnerable group needing protection, 'aliens' (Hebrew *gēr*; plural *gērîm*) were in a very different place with regard to Israel's land laws. They were not Israelites but people who had chosen to live permanently among them. Rahab and her family from Jericho and the Gibeonites would be good examples from the time of the conquest. They realized that God was with the Israelites and preferred to make peace with them and submit to them, even if that meant being second-class citizens because they were not allowed to own land. As time went on, others would have come, fleeing famine or oppression or seeking an economic opportunity, and would have settled among the Israelites. 'Immigrants' would be a good word to describe this latter group and, like the first group, they would be well disposed toward the culture and customs of their adopted land. People who think it would be to their benefit to live among another people assume, initially at least, that they will assimilate with their host culture. So it is unsurprising that in the Septuagint *gēr* is almost always translated *proselytos* (proselyte, convert), although it cannot be assumed that the 'aliens' did actually always assimilate to the point of becoming Israelites.

That the *gērîm* were also clearly distinguished from another type of 'foreigner' (*nokrî*) is further evidence that they had gone some way in the direction of God. The *nokrî* was the foreigner who insisted on clinging to his/her gods. Some of the women Solomon married were *nokrî*, because they imported their idolatry with them to Jerusalem and insisted on having a provision for their idolatrous worship at the heart of Israelite government in Solomon's court. In this way, they caused Solomon to lead the people of Israel astray. Jezebel was the epitome of this type of foreigner, as were the Canaanite women whom Israelite men were strictly forbidden to marry because of the danger of slipping into idolatry.

Because they had moved some way towards God, the *gērîm* were to be given every encouragement to move closer.

1. *They were not to be mistreated*, but were to be seen as vulnerable people to be cared for like orphans and widows (Exod. 22:21–22; Lev. 19:33; Ps. 146:9; Zech. 7:10).

2. *They were to be loved.* Leviticus commands that 'the alien living with you must be treated as one of your native-born. Love him as yourself, for you were aliens in Egypt. I am the LORD your God' (19:34). This is a remarkable ancient command that must have been in Jesus' mind when he said that doing 'to others what you would have them do to you . . . sums up the Law and the prophets' (Matt. 7:12). God reminds the Israelites that they had been *gērîm* in Egypt and were eventually oppressed terribly by their hosts. He encourages them to remember how terrible that experience was and refrain from treating immigrants in the same way.

3. *They were to be included.* Like all other Israelites they were allowed to enjoy the rest and recreation of the sabbath and pilgrim festivals (Exod. 20:10; 23:12; Deut. 16:11, 14). At both the harvest festivals of Weeks and Tabernacles, which, with travel, lasted over a week, they were to be welcomed to join in the celebratory meals. With Levites, orphans and widows they were to participate in what had been produced from the land, through God's goodness, even though they, like the Levites, were not allowed to possess land. They were also included with the poor, orphans and widows in the right to glean (Lev. 19:10; 23:22; Deut. 24:19–21).

5. WELFARE LAW AND WHAT IT IMPLIES ABOUT BEING POOR

One of the most significant contributions of the liberal and socialist movements since the 1800s has been the general acceptance that governments have a responsibility to provide welfare services for their most deprived citizens. Heated debate continues about how much of its citizens' wealth a state can take to redistribute among the poor. Generally speaking, the left plead for higher- and the right for lower-welfare spending. The debate could be more profitable if both sides focused on how the welfare budget is spent rather than on its size.

There is much truth in the saying that the West has developed a culture that knows the price of everything and the value of nothing. Poverty is defined by level of income. Tremendous effort is put into finding the minimum level of income that people need in order to enjoy what would be regarded as the minimum level of goods. Relatively little attention is paid to the underlying philosophy that now conditions the way we live and the impact it has on the way social and communal relationships are viewed.

The prevailing philosophy in the West is that it is up to individuals to make the best of what they have to generate wealth for themselves. That is not to deny that there are many individuals and institutions in the West that are working hard to counter the spirit of individualistic materialism, but they are struggling against heavy odds. The statistics are clear: the more we have, the less we share. We should not be surprised that a culture based on the pursuit of individualistic self-interest should produce people with very weak social consciences.

What is striking about OT law is that it recognizes the very strong human bias to self-interest and provides a moral and legal framework to control it. That is why most of the law we have discussed up to this point has not focused on the poor but on putting limits on the rich and powerful. This is a fundamental thrust of all the laws concerning leaders as well as the laws on debt, interest and the release and restoration of land in the Jubilee. Underpinning all this was God's call to Israel to be an alternative type of community in the world that would testify through their being to the truth and justice of their God. 'Although the whole earth is mine', God had said to them at Sinai, 'you will be for me a kingdom of priests and a holy nation' (Exod. 19:5b–6). A holy nation would have no poor in it.

Old Testament welfare laws

God recognized that Israel would struggle from the start to be what he had called them to be, so the law does contain some welfare provision. There should be no poor, but the Lord also recognized that there would always be poor people in the land (Deut. 15:4, 11).

We shall look at just three laws that can be classed as welfare provision.

Generous lending (Deut. 15:7–11)

The context of this law is the law of debt forgiveness in the sabbath year of the land, considered earlier. This passage reminds us that lending to the poor is a positive thing. Being in debt is not evil. In fact, going into debt is often the means by which the poor can climb out of a hole with their dignity intact. The key is the proportion and terms of any loan. From the creditor's perspective loans to the poor were to be high risk. No interest was to be charged, and the possibility of losing the money lent because of the nearness of the year of release from debt was not to hinder giving a loan. The important thing was to give poor people the chance to re-establish themselves with dignity as contributors to Israel's economy.

These verses emphatically encourage this generous lending with two negative verbs in verse 7 (do not be 'hard-hearted'; do not be 'tight-fisted') being answered by two positive verbs in verse 8 ('be open-handed'; lend freely). 'Freely lend' in verse 8 and 'give generously' in verse 10 are double verb forms (literally 'lending you shall lend' and 'giving you shall give'), a Hebrew way of being very emphatic.

There is also an interesting use of 'body' language in the passage that underlines the strong encouragement given to generous lending. The command is not to be tight-fisted (v. 7) but to be open-handed (vv. 7, 11). The 'hand' is a symbol of power in the OT, indicating the ability to do something. Because the rich have the hand (power) to do something to bless the poor, they should be careful to do so. The 'heart' is the source of human thought and action. It is not to be hard (v. 7, 'do not be hard-hearted'), to think wicked things (v. 9, 'Be careful not to harbour this wicked thought') or be evil in the sense of being hesitant to reach out in mercy (v. 10, 'Give generously to him . . . without a grudging heart'). Finally the rich were not to 'give an evil eye' to the poor, which is the Hebrew underlying 'show ill will' in the NIV translation of verse 9.[1]

All this means that lending to the poor was really seen as welfare provision in Israel. The law had scant regard for the security of the creditor. It was totally focused on the well-being of the poor debtor.

Gleaning (Lev. 19:9–10; 23:22; Deut. 24:17–22)

This law stipulates that those who owned the produce of a piece of land should deliberately leave some of the harvest behind for the benefit of the poor. In both the Leviticus passages, the command is that gleanings were to be left for the poor in general with the aliens singled out for special mention. In the passage in Deuteronomy, it is the aliens, fatherless (orphans) and widows who are in focus as the groups most likely to be the poorest of the poor. Since these groups are in focus from verse 17 to 22 there is every reason to think that these verses should be seen as one block of teaching:

> Do not deprive the alien or the fatherless of justice, or take the cloak of the widow as a pledge. Remember that you were slaves in Egypt and the LORD your God redeemed you from there. That is why I command you to do this.
>
> When you are harvesting in your field and you overlook a sheaf, do not go back to get it. Leave it for the alien, the fatherless and the widow, so that the LORD your God may bless you in all the work of your hands. When you beat the olives from your trees, do not go over the branches a second time. Leave what remains for the alien, the fatherless and the widow. When you harvest the grapes in your vineyard, do not go over the vines again. Leave what remains for the alien, the fatherless and the widow. Remember that you were slaves in Egypt. That is why I command you to do this.

---

1. Cf. Matt. 6:22–23, where having a 'good' or 'bad' eye in Jesus' teaching has to do with being generous or mean, respectively.

Wright makes a strong case for reading this passage as a unit, so that not taking a widow's cloak and allowing aliens, fatherless and widows to glean becomes a matter of justice or rights rather than charity. To harvest in a way that left no gleanings would be to 'deprive the alien or the fatherless of justice', or, in other words, to deprive them of their rights. In God's sight, everyone in Israel has a right to essential necessities such as food and clothing. He underlines this by pointing out that

> the NIV's 'Leave it for . . .' is not quite what the Hebrew says (v. 20b). The Hebrew says, 'To the alien . . . it shall be' – an expression normally used to indicate ownership. The sense is therefore, 'Do not pick the forgotten sheaf, the remaining olives and the grapes, *they belong* to the alien, orphan, and widow.' The remainder of the harvest *is theirs*; they have every right to the final harvesting themselves.[2]

The right granted the poor is a right to participate in a harvest even though they themselves had no land to call their own. It is only right that those who have tilled the land and cared for the crop should have the bulk of the produce, but those who had no opportunity to till and tend must be allowed an opportunity to harvest. They must be able to go out and work to bring something into their storehouse. But, as with generous lending, this welfare provision also leaves them with their dignity intact.

Twice in the passage in Deuteronomy the people are told that the reason God is asking them to observe this law of gleaning is because they were slaves in Egypt. The strength to obey this law needed a strong theological motivation. It would be true to say that the strength to obey any of the laws examined in this chapter would need a strong theological motivation. Why should anyone obey any law that demands risky self-sacrificing behaviour, without strong moral and spiritual reasons for doing so? What we need is a memory of a God who redeems slaves – a God who saw our pitiful state and came at great cost to our rescue. 'Remember that you were slaves in Egypt . . . That is why I command you to do this' (Deut. 24:18; cf. v. 22).

The triennial tithe (Deut. 14:28–29; 26:12–15)

God commanded the Israelites to tithe all the produce of the land and herds as an offering to the Lord (Lev. 27:30–33). It seems that the primary purpose of this tithe was to support the Levites who were dispersed in many cities

---

2. Christopher J. H. Wright, New International Biblical Commentary, *Deuteronomy* (Peabody: Hendrickson, 1996), pp. 260–261; his italics.

throughout the land (Num. 18:25–26). Like the priests of the central sanctuary, the Levites were dedicated to God and, therefore, were not given a land inheritance. They were set apart to maintain the moral and ritual purity of the nation by supporting the administration of the cult of the central sanctuary, maintaining the system of ritual purity and teaching the moral and civil law.

The passages that deal with the tithe in Deuteronomy teach that the tithe was not exclusively for the use of the Levites. A part of it could also be used for celebratory feasts during the two pilgrim festivals of Weeks and Tabernacles (Deut. 14:23; cf. 16:11, 14). It seems that in the first two years of the cycle of farming years between sabbaths of the land, farmers would take a portion of their tithe to the central sanctuary, where it would be shared with those who had no means to produce food they could use for a party: orphans, widows, aliens and the Levites. It is likely, however, that most of the tithe even in these years was meant to go to the Levites. Then, in the third year of the cycle, the whole tithe was to be stored in the towns. As in other years, the Levites would be key beneficiaries of this tithe, but this triennial tithe was also to be used to support 'the aliens, the fatherless and the widows' (Deut. 14:29).

For the full seven-year cycle from one sabbath of the land to another, the system envisaged in Deuteronomy seems to have been as follows:

1. In the first two years, most of the tithe would go to the Levites, while some would be kept back for the feasting at the central sanctuary in which the main categories of poor people would be included.
2. In the third year, the tithe went into storehouses in the towns and was used to support the Levites and poor people over the next three years.
3. In years four and five, the poor could expect to join in the feasting at the sanctuary.
4. In the sixth year, the tithe was again stored in the towns and made available for the poor.
5. The seventh year was the Sabbath of the land when the land reverted to God and every Israelite was meant to be equal in that all, whatever their circumstances, were allowed to take of what grew on its own.

To operate this welfare system would clearly involve faith and restraint on behalf of the wealthier people. It also called for an administrative apparatus to provide good storage facilities and to make sure that the provision stored reached those who needed it. It was a faith-based, nationally organized welfare system. As Wright comments,

> care for the poor was structured into the regular economic life of the nation. It was not left to *private charity*. Rather it was a *public duty* that the weakest and poorest should also be enabled to 'eat and be satisfied' (Deut 14:29) from the blessing of Yahweh on the whole nation.[3]

What the law teaches about being poor

Where overcoming poverty is concerned, the focus of the OT is unquestionably on the rich and powerful within a framework of law that was meant to hinder inequality from becoming institutionalized. There is no emphasis on the suffering of the poor in order to stir the rich to show compassion. Even the key OT words for the poor, *'ānî* and *'ebyôn*, focus on the fact that the poor are the victims of the behaviour of others. *'Ānî* in particular refers to those without land, and for an Israelite to be without land implied an oppressive process of disinheritance because everyone had a right to land.

While the emphasis in the OT law is on giving the poor their rights, without dwelling on what it means to be poor the way in which their rights were to be secured does throw light on what poverty means for the poor. Without in any way wanting to draw attention away from the responsibility of the rich and powerful to address poverty, it is worthwhile focusing on what the OT strategy implies about what it means to be poor.

The law of debt release every seven years in Deuteronomy 15 gives us strong indications as what it means to be poor, if we think about how an Israelite would go into debt. Everyone was originally given enough land so that they could provide for themselves. So going into debt would likely be caused by some calamity or other.[4] A loan would be needed to see a family through a period of scarcity. But to repay the loan the debtor would have to use a part of future crops to repay, so would become more vulnerable to any future calamity. Poverty, therefore, means greater insecurity and vulnerability. What is interesting and significant about this law is that the poor and needy were to be helped by generous lending. A loan, rather than a gift, respects the dignity and abilities of the poor. It gives the poor an opportunity to claw themselves out of poverty by their own effort. This means that the poor are lacking in

---

3. Ibid., p. 184; his italics.
4. In view here are calamities that strike individual farmers, not the sorts of national calamities mentioned in Deut. 28, which would be God's sentence on the nation's apostasy.

opportunities to address their deficit. This passage emphasizes the need to be generous with our opportunities to the poor by not being obsessed with making sure that every penny of a loan is paid back – and in our case with interest. The Israelites, as we have seen, were strictly forbidden to charge interest on loans to the poor.

Gleaning is another example of giving the poor an opportunity to provide for themselves. The poor do have resources but no opportunity to use them. It is true that some people become poor because of laziness, bad management of resources or by becoming addicted to alcohol or other addictive substances. But even in many of these cases, laziness or addiction is as much the result as the cause of poverty. It is devastating for capable adults to have no opportunity to provide for themselves and their families when they long to do so. Even in the nineteenth century, William Booth, the founder of the Salvation Army, realized that drunkenness was as much a result as a cause of poverty: 'Let us never forget that the temptation to drink is strongest when want is sharpest and misery the most acute. A well-fed man is not driven to drink by the craving that torments the hungry; and the comfortable do not crave for the boon of forgetfulness.'[5] Poverty means frustration and a sense of helplessness that can lead to unimaginable despair.

The insecurity the poor experience is often the result of the abuse of power. This is powerfully illustrated by the prophet Nathan's parable to David because of David's terrible treatment of his faithful servant Uriah, whom he killed to hide his adultery with his wife Bathsheba:

> There were two men in a certain town, one rich and the other poor. The rich man had a very large number of sheep and cattle, but the poor man had nothing except one little ewe lamb he had bought. He raised it, and it grew up with him and his children. It shared his food, drank from his cup and even slept in his arms. It was like a daughter to him.
>
> Now a traveller came to the rich man, but the rich man refrained from taking one of his own sheep or cattle to prepare a meal for the traveller who had come to him. Instead, he took the ewe lamb that belonged to the poor man and prepared it for the one who had come to him. (2 Sam. 12:1–4)

It is only a story, but we can feel the frustration and sense of powerlessness of the poor man who could do absolutely nothing to defend himself against the rich man's unjust action. It is unsurprising that David, who was renowned for

5. *In Darkest England and the Way Out* (London: Salvation Army, n. d., c. 1890), p. 48.

his just rule, was furious before he was told that this is how he himself had acted towards Uriah.

It was too late to right the wrong done to Uriah when Nathan came to convict David of his sin, but Proverbs encourages those who have the ear of the powerful to speak up on behalf of the poor because they are unable to speak up for themselves:

> Speak up for those who cannot speak for themselves,
> for the rights of all who are destitute.
> Speak up and judge fairly;
> defend the rights of the poor and needy.
> (Prov. 31:8–9)[6]

Why are the poor often unable to speak up for themselves? What does it feel like not to have anyone listening to us? If no one listens, then nothing can be done about our plight. We are powerless, invisible, ignored and marginalized. That is what it means to be poor. That is why the poor need advocates.

Conclusion

The attempt at the end of this chapter to focus on the experience of poverty reflects the twenty-first-century Christian context, where the appeal to the powerful on behalf of the poor is made more often than not on the basis of compassion. The assumption is that if as rich Christians in our age of hunger we can begin to imagine what it is like to be poor, then we shall be stirred to do something about it. Furthermore if we understand poverty in the way described above, our intervention is much more likely to benefit the poor because we shall be concerned with their uplift rather than disempowering them with welfare benefits. However, in the context of the Torah that has been in focus up to this point, this is but a footnote to teaching on God's purpose in creation and redemption, which provides a framework for us for establishing just societies where there would be no needy people.

The laws on the seventh year release of the land, interest and the Jubilee considered in chapter 4 show that what God understands by economic growth

---

6. Derek Kidner comments on v. 8, 'The last phrase of the verse is lit. "sons of change", i.e., the insecure' (*Proverbs: Tyndale Old Testament Commentaries* [Leicester: IVP, 1964]), p. 183 (cf. Job 29:11–17; Ps. 72:12–14).

must not mean the enrichment of a few at the expense of others. In creation, God gave the earth and its resources to humanity as a whole, and in the redemption of Israel he gave the land of Canaan to Israel as a whole. His desire is that everyone should have access to resources with which to work in order to provide for themselves. God understands that human beings alienated from him will be inclined to use their ability to build up wealth way beyond what they need in a vain search for security and a name. Galbraith is right to contend that 'economics divorced from consideration of the exercise of power is without meaning and certainly without relevance'.[7] In the divine economy, self-interest must operate within limits. As Chris Wright states so powerfully, 'the right of all to *use* the resources of the earth seems morally prior to the right of any to *own*'.[8]

Obedience to laws such as the three considered in chapter 4 would ensure that there would be no needy persons in Israel, but the law is realistic enough to realize that obeying these laws would not be easy. So it also makes provision for the vulnerable and poor. God rules that the vulnerable are to be protected and the poor to be provided for in a way that preserves their dignity. Provision is not seen as something to be left to the charitable whims of the rich and powerful, but is more a matter of human rights.

---

7. J. K. Galbraith, *The Anatomy of Power* (Boston: Houghton Mifflin, 1983), p. xiii.
8. Christopher J. H. Wright, *Old Testament Ethics for the People of God* (Leicester: IVP, 2004), p. 148. This quote comes from ch. 5 of this fine book. The whole chapter is highly relevant to my conclusions here.

6. THE GLORY AND INADEQUACY OF THE MOSAIC COVENANT

There can be no doubt that if the law given to Israel through Moses had been observed, a just and equitable society as far as poverty was concerned would have been established on earth. It is also clear that the success of the project depended on the Israelites' faith and trust in God as the engine that would drive their obedience to his law. The faith that was required would mean living in a way that was radically different from the norm for human life lived in alienation from God as portrayed in Genesis 3 – 11. Being the people of God was a very risky business from the ungodly perspective that saw seeking security of goods for oneself, family and nation/ethnic group as the norm of human life, even if that meant denying such security to outsiders. The highest manifestation of this spirit is seen throughout history when nations grasp at world domination and divinity and build empires.

In the first place, Israel was called by God to challenge the power of this world's most powerful empire at that time with nothing but trust that God would intervene on their behalf. Then, having successfully escaped the clutches of empire, they were to take possession of land that was inhabited by peoples who had superior arms with which to defend themselves. Once the land had been possessed, they were then meant to manage it in a way contrary to the human desire for security in order to honour God and create an inclusive society in which there would be no poor people. And initially this had to be done without anything recognizable as a central government.

Once Joshua had died, leadership was provided by tribal and clan leaders and judges and priests diffused among the tribes. Israel's sense of national unity was provided by the centrally located tabernacle, representing the presence of God at the heart of the nation, where attendance was expected on a regular basis for the three pilgrim festivals. A priesthood faithful to God and well versed in the law was absolutely vital to the realization of the just and equitable community envisaged in the law. With such a priesthood and good judges, Israel would have consolidated its hold on the land and prospered in every sense and would have been a blessing to the nations.

Considerable power was vested in the hereditary position of chief priest, but, because the priesthood had no property, even the chief priest's power could not be consolidated into a significant coercive power. To put it simply, they had no way of making enough money to pay soldiers or police to impose their will on the nation. They could bully the people who came to the sanctuary as Eli's sons did but their power was severely limited. The chief justice was the other powerful central officer, but his power was circumscribed because he was essentially an elected servant of the tribal and clan leaders.

The age of the judges

Israel could have been a successful pluralistic state. It failed because the people and their diffused leadership struggled to trust God, despite all the amazing things he had done for them in saving them from slavery in Egypt, preserving them in the wilderness and bringing them into the Promised Land. Rather than assimilate the surrounding peoples into their Yahweh worship, they displayed a persistent tendency to assimilate into the surrounding peoples' Baal worship. So the story of the settled people recorded in the book of Judges is a story of decline into idolatry and immorality, leading to oppression by a foreign power that ultimately led to repentance and the emergence of a clan or tribal leader that mobilized tribe and nation to free the people from the oppressor. In most cases, the odds against Israel were heavy and victory was gained through divine intervention. Interestingly these leaders were called 'judges', and many of them were said to have 'judged' Israel for a number of years (Judg. 3:10; 10:2–3; 12:7–13; 16:31; 1 Sam 7:15).[1] They were a very mixed group of tribal leaders, a few of whom definitely acted as judges in the strictly legal sense. The most

1. The NIV in all these references consistently translates the Hebrew word that literally means 'judged' as 'led'.

intriguing is Deborah, described as a prophetess, but who also operated as an appeal court judge on a national scale because 'she held court under the Palm of Deborah between Ramah and Bethel in the hill country of Ephraim, and the Israelites came to her to have their disputes decided' (Judg. 4:5).[2]

As a woman Deborah was a very unlikely person to be called to lead Israel against an oppressor. This was true of others as well. Gideon was a younger son of an insignificant clan in the tribe of Manasseh, and Jephthah was a rejected illegitimate son in the tribe of Gilead. Samson and Samuel were born to childless mothers as a result of divine intervention and dedicated to God by their parents, but Samson more than proved that parental devotion is no guarantee of personal godliness. When Paul reminded the Corinthian Christians that 'God chose the weak things of the world to shame the strong' he was reminding them of a principle that had been embedded in the history of Israel from the beginning.

An obedient Israel needed the ordinary leadership of priests and judges; it was when disobedience had led them into captivity that they needed leaders especially endowed by God for the rescue operation. Deborah was already a prophetess when God used her to command Barak to lead the army of Naphtali against the more powerful army of the Canaanite king, Jabin. When Israel because of their idolatry was ravaged by nomadic Midianites, God first sent a prophet to convict Israel of their sin and then the angel of the Lord appeared to Gideon to call him. Like Moses, he was a reluctant leader and it took a lot of striking revelations before he led just three hundred men to complete victory. He was resolute in his faith in God and refused the offer from the leaders of Israel to become king and head of a dynasty, saying, 'I will not rule over you, nor will my son rule over you. The LORD will rule over you' (Judg. 8:23). Samuel, the last of the judges, was outstanding in that he combined an extraordinary prophetic calling with the ordinary calling of a judge and possibly of a priest as well. He was also a man of great integrity (see 1 Sam. 12).[3]

Jephthah had been driven away by his brothers because of his illegitimacy, but had built a reputation as an able commander of a mercenary force. It was this reputation that led the elders of Gilead to invite him and his followers to become commander of their army in a war against the oppressing Ammonites. His vow to sacrifice whatever came out of his house to meet him when he returned victorious as he marched to the war indicates rashness at best, or profound ignorance of the God of Israel at worst. Yet the Spirit of the Lord

---

2. Samuel also acted as an appeal judge (1 Sam. 7:15).
3. This whole chapter testifies to the wonderful integrity and deep spiritual intensity of Samuel's rule.

had come upon him shortly before he made his vow (Judg. 11:29–30). The Spirit of the Lord also came upon Samson on a number of occasions, and in his case that meant a manifestation of superhuman strength that had nothing to do with the moral quality of his personal life.

Interestingly the coming of the Spirit of the Lord to provide inspired leadership for Israel in a time of oppression is limited to the period of the judges and the early monarchy. For most of Israel's history the coming of the Spirit is associated with prophecy, beginning with the isolated reference to the Spirit of prophecy descending on the seventy elders in the time of Moses. The theme then re-emerges in the golden age of prophecy associated with Elijah and Elisha, and flows into the stream of the later writing prophets, especially Ezekiel (Num. 11:25; 1 Kgs 18:12; 2 Kgs 2:16; 2 Chr. 20:14; Ezek. 11:5; etc.).[4] As we have already seen, the Spirit of the Lord came upon Jephthah and Samson but also came upon Othniel, the first judge, and Gideon (Judg. 3:10; 6:34). The Spirit of the Lord also came upon the first two kings of Israel, Saul and David.[5]

As stated above, the context for the coming of the Spirit in the time of the judges and the early monarchy was the oppression of Israel by other nations, which was a threat to their security in the land that God had given to them. The threat was invariably the result of Israel's reluctance to obey the Lord and their tendency to assimilate the religion of the Canaanites and surrounding nations. Yet the Lord was very merciful in that he continued to hear the cries of his oppressed and sinful people, as he had heard their cries in Egypt, and came to their rescue. He did so in most cases by calling and equipping leaders with the vision and energy to galvanize the people to face their oppressors,[6] even though their cause was hopeless from the human perspective. Those leaders endowed with the Spirit of the Lord were full of vigour, vision, authority and an almost reckless bravery born out of a profound sense that the almighty God was on their side.

The transition to monarchy

As the time of the judges passed, even though the central sanctuary remained and the Levitical priesthood and judiciary must have continued to function to

4. This theme will be explored more fully in chapter 8.
5. In Saul's case, the Spirit of prophecy and of inspired leadership came upon him (1 Sam. 10:6, 10; 11:6; 19:23).
6. Samson as a maverick figure is the main exception.

some degree, the people sank ever deeper into ignorance, moral degeneration and disunity. Samuel was the last and greatest of the judges. He does not get as much credit as he should, probably because he was a very reluctant midwife of Israelite monarchy, but he was a great reformer of Israelite faith and morals who also led the people in defeating an oppressor simply through his prayer and worship (1 Sam. 7:7–11)!

At the end of his illustrious career, Samuel had the difficult task of overseeing a radical constitutional transition in Israel from the ad hoc charismatic leadership of the judges to dynastic monarchy. After his long and distinguished career, where he had seen God do amazing acts of reformation, revival and rescue, it is not at all surprising that when a request for a king came from the tribal leaders, Samuel was fiercely opposed to such a constitutional change. To be fair to Samuel, the reason they gave for wanting a king was appalling from his theological perspective on Israel's history. They wanted a king so that they could be like all the other nations around them! So Samuel spelt out to them what the kings of the nations were like. They were centripetal forces in nations that sucked in power, people, property and patronage that would inevitably weaken the authority of the tribes and clans that underpinned Israel's equitable distribution of land. The result would be the establishment of an aristocracy and the impoverishment of a large percentage of the people.

The elders could have asked for a king as described by Moses in Deuteronomy, but they did not, and, despite Samuel's warning, were insistent that they wanted 'a king to lead us and to go out before us and fight our battles' (1 Sam. 8:20).[7] At this point they reveal that national security was their main priority in asking for a king. From their observation of international relations they came to the conclusion that nations with kings were best able to defend themselves against external threats. For them security had become a constitutional, rather than a theological, issue. That God had rescued the nation from slavery, miraculously preserved it in the wilderness, established it in Canaan against heavy odds and then rescued it on many occasions did not provide a sufficient reason for trusting God for their security into the future. Neither did they appreciate that their security in the land was linked to their obedience to God. The key security issue they faced as

7. The account of the elders' request for a king and Samuel's response takes up the whole of 1 Sam. 8. They also pointed out the corruption of Samuel's sons as judges as another reason for requesting a king – probably not the most diplomatic way to ingratiate themselves with the old man!

tribal leaders was how to keep the people faithful to God, but this was clearly not in their list of priorities. It was not that they just had to trust God and do nothing. There was plenty they could do to make sure the legal framework put in place at Sinai was worked out in the nation's life. Their problem was that they focused on the powerful fighting machines the kings of the surrounding nations were able to build, so that they lost faith that a nation like theirs, with an equitable distribution of property and without a central focus of power, could resist an attack. Fundamentally, by losing faith in the sort of nation God had called them to be, Israel had lost faith in God himself.

Yet, despite their wrong motives and God's affirmation of Samuel's opposition, the time had come in God's purposes for Israel to have a king, and the beginnings of monarchical rule seemed full of promise. Saul seemed to possess one of the fundamental qualities of godly rulers: humility. He was reluctant to accept the responsibility, and his appointment was confirmed in the eyes of the people only when the Spirit of God came upon him in power and enabled him to muster Israel to repel the attack of Nahash the Ammonite on Jabesh-Gilead. When victory was secured, some of his followers wanted to kill those who had been initially hostile to his appointment, but Saul resisted them, saying, 'No-one shall be put to death today, for this day the LORD has rescued Israel' (1 Sam. 11:13). At this point his trust in God enabled him to forgive enemies, which made him a unifying figure in the nation. Sadly the good beginning was not sustained, and he found it increasingly difficult to restrain the power he had. Executive power, the ability to command people to do all manner of things, is an intoxicating brew, and few 'rulers' in any walk of life have been able to manage it well. Saul was not one of them and his failings led to his rejection and the anointing of David by Samuel to replace him.

David is a colossus in the history of God's covenant people, standing shoulder to shoulder with Abraham and Moses. It was under his leadership that the descendants of Abraham became the great nation fully occupying the Promised Land. The Spirit of the Lord came upon him in power the day he was anointed king by Samuel (1 Sam. 16:13) and hardly ever left him as he led God's people to victory after victory and united the nation in possession of the lands stretching from Egypt to the headwaters of the Euphrates. In executing God's judgment on the Canaanites, David conquered the fortress city of Jerusalem and established the city as Israel's capital. From there he 'reigned over all Israel, doing what was just and right for all his people' (2 Sam. 8:15). The deep piety that underlay his success as king is seen particularly in two aspects of his life. First as a gifted musician and poet he composed many songs that expressed his trust in God.[8] Secondly his desire to put the tabernacle and its worship at the heart of Israel's life. He brought the tabernacle to Jerusalem in order to exalt God's place at the heart of the nation, and would have built a magnificent temple to replace it had God not stopped him. It was at this point that God reaffirmed his covenant with Abraham by promising to make David's name great and make him the head of a dynasty that would endure for ever (2 Sam. 7:8–16). But the focus at this point in the history of redemption was on the blessing of Israel, and the ultimate purpose of blessing all the nations was very much in the background. Ironically for this to come into the foreground again David's line had to fail and the identification of God's people with one nation established in a specific land had to be broken.

Still it remains one of the great wonders of history that a just society something like the one envisaged in the law revealed at Sinai actually existed in Israel, even if only for relatively short periods. Even in the golden age of David and Solomon, the seeds of decline were in evidence when they are judged by the standard for kings set in Deuteronomy 17. Even David behaved like the kings of other nations by multiplying wives and even marrying one foreign wife (2 Sam. 3:3).[9] Otherwise he was close to the ideal king portrayed by Moses. Solomon on the other hand failed, as he had a very large harem with many foreign wives, some of whom insisted on importing their idolatrous practices into the very heart of Jerusalem. He also built Israel's military capacity, which included a large number of chariots with horses bought in Egypt. He sucked a substantial proportion of Israel's wealth to support his court and used forced labour extensively in his building projects. It is unsurprising that after his reign the kingdom divided and the nation began spiralling downwards towards unthinkable exile and the loss of both land and temple.

Israel's failure and the prophetic vision of a new covenant

Given the deep deception of the human heart, it is not that surprising that the nation of Israel formed by the covenant of Sinai and established in Canaan did not fulfil God's promise to make the descendants of Abraham a blessing to all nations. In a sense, the covenant of Sinai proved to be a failed covenant, as

8. Even the most sceptical scholars admit that David could have authored some of the psalms.

9. Maacah, daughter of the Aramean Talmai, king of Geshur, and the mother of Absalom, David's most troublesome son.

anticipated in Deuteronomy 29 – 32. God was not surprised by Israel's failure, but wove it into his mysterious sovereign purpose to open 'the door of grace and salvation to the nations'.[10]

From the latter years of Solomon's reign to the twin disasters of destruction and exile for Israel and Judah failure to keep the covenant was the predominant note in the nation's life. But even when the law was profoundly neglected, God had his prophets who consistently witnessed to rulers and ruled of their disobedience to God and the dire consequences that would inevitably ensue. The prophets' complaints focused primarily on the embracing of the idolatrous worship and the unjust ways of the surrounding nations. Sometimes unjust practice was coupled with apparent faithfulness to God, as expressed in careful observance of the temple cult, while at other times it was linked directly to open idolatry. The first chapter of Isaiah is a powerful example of the former, where the rulers of Judah are compared to the rulers of Sodom and Gomorrah despite their intense devotion to the temple cult. Addressing the rulers, God says he is sick of their sacrifices:

> Your hands are full of blood;
> wash and make yourselves clean.
> Take your evil deeds
> out of my sight!
> Stop doing wrong,
> learn to do right!
> Seek justice,
> encourage the oppressed.
> Defend the cause of the fatherless,
> plead the case of the widow.
> (Isa. 1:15c–17)[11]

If they do not repent, they will be judged and lose their position. But even in Isaiah 1, the judgment will be a prelude to a renewed people of God (Isa. 1:26).

The most devastating consequence of Israel and Judah's idolatry and injustice, according to the prophets, was going to be the destruction of the temple in Jerusalem and exile from the land. But the prophets also saw beyond the

10. See Christopher J. H. Wright, *The Mission of God* (Nottingham: IVP, 2006), pp. 341–344.
11. Amos was called to proclaim a very similar message to the northern kingdom, Israel (Amos 5:21–24).

exile to the establishment of a new covenant. As the prospect of Judah's exile drew nearer, it was revealed to Isaiah that one key ingredient of a new covenant was to be a very special king in the line of David. Isaiah prophesied that this king, upon whom the Spirit of the Lord would rest, was going to restore justice and peace to the whole earth and its creatures:

> A shoot will come up from the stump of Jesse;
> from his roots a Branch will bear fruit.
> The Spirit of the LORD will rest on him –
> the Spirit of wisdom and of understanding,
> the Spirit of counsel and of power,
> the Spirit of knowledge and of the fear of the LORD –
> and he will delight in the fear of the LORD.
>
> He will not judge by what he sees with his eyes,
> or decide by what he hears with his ears;
> but with righteousness he will judge the needy,
> with justice he will give decisions for the poor of the earth.
> He will strike the earth with the rod of his mouth;
> with the breath of his lips he will slay the wicked.
> Righteousness will be his belt
> and faithfulness the sash around his waist.
>
> The wolf will live with the lamb,
> the leopard will lie down with the goat,
> the calf and the lion and the yearling together;
> and a little child will lead them.
> The cow will feed with the bear,
> their young will lie down together,
> and the lion will eat straw like the ox.
> The infant will play near the hole of the cobra,
> and the young child put his hand into the viper's nest.
> They will neither harm nor destroy
> on all my holy mountain,
> for the earth will be full of the knowledge of the LORD
> as the waters cover the sea.
>
> In that day the Root of Jesse will stand as a banner for the peoples; the nations will rally to him, and his place of rest will be glorious. In that day the Lord will reach out his hand a second time to reclaim the remnant that is left of his people from Assyria,

> from Lower Egypt, from Upper Egypt, from Cush, from Elam, from Babylonia, from Hamath and from the islands of the sea. (Isa. 11:1–11)

This coming king was clearly going to rule with such great authority that he would drive the wicked from the face of the earth so that only the righteous would remain. As a consequence, violence and crying would be banished and peace would reign, symbolized by the transformed nature of the earth's most dangerous creatures. The banishment of evil essential to bringing about this wonderful transformation was to be achieved through powerful words rather than powerful weapons of war. In fact, this anointed servant of the Lord was going to establish justice through offering himself as a willing victim of suffering and death rather than by inflicting suffering on others. This is why there would be something radically different about what would happen to his words. After all, the law revealed at Sinai was full of true words that if obeyed would have led to a just society and peace. The true words were also accompanied by very clear warnings of the destruction and curse that would follow disobedience. But a powerful revelation of a law, accompanied by wonders and with severe sanctions attached could not make people obedient. If the coming king was to make a deeper impact so that the promise to Abraham could be fulfilled, he needed to represent a way of taking true words from the stone where they had been written by the finger of God and imprinting them on people's hearts. This is precisely what Jeremiah foresaw as the key characteristic of the new covenant:

> 'The time is coming,' declares the LORD,
> 'when I will make a new covenant
> with the house of Israel
> and with the house of Judah.
> It will not be like the covenant
> I made with their forefathers
> when I took them by the hand
> to lead them out of Egypt,
> because they broke my covenant,
> though I was their husband,' declares the LORD.
> 'This is the covenant I will make with the house of Israel
> after that time,' declares the LORD.
> 'I will put the law in their minds
> and write it on their hearts.
> I will be their God
> and they will be my people.

> No longer will a man teach his neighbour,
> or a man his brother, saying, "Know the LORD,"
> because they will all know me
> from the least of them to the greatest,' declares the LORD.
> 'For I will forgive their wickedness
> and will remember their sins no more.'
> (Jer. 31:31–34)

Jeremiah does not mention the Spirit in this prophecy, but the internalization of the law graphically described as writing the law on the heart is clearly a contrast with God's 'finger' writing the law for Moses on tablets of stone. What is in focus here is a divine, spiritual action effecting a radical change in the human heart, which is, biblically, the source of all human thought and action. It is also very significant that this divine process is intimately associated with the forgiveness of sins. Ezekiel, when describing the same process, refers explicitly to the Spirit:

> I will sprinkle clean water on you, and you will be clean; I will cleanse you from all your impurities and all your idols. I will give you a new heart and put a new spirit in you; I will remove from you your heart of stone and give you a heart of flesh. And I will put my Spirit in you and move you to follow my decrees and be careful to keep my laws. (Ezek. 36:25–27)

Both Jeremiah and Ezekiel witnessed the final defeat of Jerusalem and the exile to Babylon. They both proclaim the hope of a new covenant in the context of promising that the Jews will return to their land. The promise of return was fulfilled in the time of Ezra and Nehemiah and the Jews who returned were cured permanently of the sort of idolatry that characterized them before the exile. But the return did not signal the fulfilment of the prophecy to write the law on their heart; neither did it signal a secure hold of the land. The fulfilment of both had to wait until the coming of the Messiah Jesus, who now holds the key to the meaning of history. We shall return to the boon of the Spirit in due course, but we must first focus on Jesus Christ, who makes this greatest of gifts a reality. And, of course, Jesus was a descendant of Abraham and David.

PART TWO: JESUS AND THE FINAL REVELATION OF DIVINE GOVERNMENT

All that has been said about God's purposes and rule in the OT is viewed in the NT as preparation for the fuller revelation of the rule or kingdom of God in Jesus Christ. As the central figure in the biblical story, Jesus ends up towering above everyone and everything. The story ends with Jesus already in the place of highest honour, even though humanity was, and is, a long way from recognizing that this is the case. It is now generally agreed that Paul was quoting a piece of well-established Christian liturgy when he said in his letter to the Philippians that because of Jesus' willing humiliation,

> God exalted him to the highest place
> and gave him a name that is above every name,
> that at the name of Jesus every knee should bow,
> in heaven and on earth and under the earth,
> and every tongue confess that Jesus Christ is Lord,
> to the glory of God the Father.
> (Phil. 2:9–11)

This glorious destiny is not a creation of the early church but what Jesus himself expected. When asked directly by the high priest at his trial, 'Tell us if you are the Christ, the Son of God,' Jesus replied, 'Yes, it is as you say . . . But I say to all of you: In the future you will see the Son of Man sitting at the right hand of the Mighty One and coming on the clouds of heaven' (Matt. 26:63b–64; cf. Mark 14:61–62 and Luke 22:66–71). Hagner comments:

> Jesus' affirmation of being the Messiah, the Son of God . . . may not yet in itself have been sufficient grounds for the high priest to regard him as blaspheming. But when Jesus adds to his answer the quoted material from Dan 7:13 and the allusion to Ps 110:2, identifying himself as . . . the one who is 'given dominion and glory and kingship' whom all will serve and whose kingdom will see no end (Dan 7:13–14), the one who sits at the right hand of God (Ps 110:1), the high priest reacts to what he regards as horrifying blasphemy (cf. v. 65).[1]

For a Christian wanting to overcome poverty, there can be no better place to begin than at the feet of our humble and exalted Saviour, the Lord Jesus Christ. Who he is, what he has done, what he taught, what he is doing and what he will do should be the main sources of our inspiration and motivation. These questions can be answered only in the context of the OT revelation of God's purpose for his earth and its creatures and its outworking through his dealings with Israel. But, however significant God's revelation might have been through Israel, Jesus is seen as superior to anything or anyone that has gone before him.

---

1. Comment on Matt. 26:63b–64, in D. A. Hagner, *Matthew*, Word Biblical Commentary on CD-ROM, vol. 33b (Dallas, Tex.: Word, 1998).

7. JESUS THE SUPREME RULER

Jesus is presented in the NT as closely related to all the key figures and movements of the OT, but as superior to them.

Jesus superior to Adam

Luke, who uniquely in the Gospels traces the genealogy of Jesus back to Adam, is the evangelist who says most about his miraculous conception by the Holy Spirit. Whatever divine intervention was required for the eternal Word to become flesh, the result was a genuine son of Adam.

Jesus' preferred way of describing himself, especially in the Synoptic Gospels, is as the 'Son of man', a title most probably taken from Daniel 7:13. The context of the saying in Daniel is a dream-vision of a terrifying and frightening beast with large iron teeth that 'crushed and devoured its victims' (7:7b). In the interpretation,[1] the beast is said to be a powerful ruler of an empire that will oppress the saints until he is brought before the tribunal of the Most High. At that hearing,

1. The 'interpretation' is in Dan. 7:15–28, but it is an interpretation within the dream-vision. The same pattern is seen in Revelation, where characters in the vision explain to John the meaning of what he is seeing.

> his power will be taken away and completely destroyed for ever. Then the sovereignty, power and greatness of the kingdoms under the whole heaven will be handed over to the saints, the people of the Most High. His kingdom will be an everlasting kingdom and all rulers will worship and obey him. (7:26–27)

In this interpretation of the dream-vision, the human figure that appears from the heavenly realms is identified with the saints or those set apart to serve the Most High amid the cruelty and injustice of this world's empires. Much has been written about collective or corporate personality at this point – that the 'son of man' represents redeemed Israel or the saints of God. In the NT, this is precisely what Jesus sees himself as doing, so that he and those who belong to him become practically indistinguishable (e.g. Matt. 10:40–42; 25:40; John 15:1; Acts 9:4).

In many of the cases when Jesus uses the title 'Son of Man', the context is talk of his inevitable suffering, death and resurrection. He is clear that his glorification and consequently the glorification of his saints as well are to be by way of accepting, rather than inflicting, suffering. This is one of the key differences between the rule of the Son of man and the rule of the empires of this world.

This is precisely what Paul implies, also, when he describes Adam as 'a pattern of the one to come' in Romans 5:14. As the representative of humanity, Adam, by his rejection of God's command, introduced sin and death into the world. By the time of the flood much of the death in the world was a result of violence. Likewise, as a representative of humanity, by his obedience to death, Jesus Christ made it possible for many to be made righteous. While Adam was the fountainhead of death, Jesus is the fountainhead of life; and where life is, violence inevitably recedes. This is not to deny that the main theme of Romans 5:12–21 is the justification of sinners through the grace of God manifested in the death of the Lord Jesus Christ. But 'Christ the redeemer hero' justifies us so that we and our fellow human beings may have life, and that means rejecting violence, as Paul makes clear in Romans 12:9–21. The 'eternal life' Jesus brings is a matter of quality as well as quantity, and the quality of his rule is fundamentally non-violent. With Jesus at the helm of government no one will be crying for justice.

Jesus superior to Abraham

God made a promise to Abraham that he would bless all peoples/nations on earth through him. In the NT, Jesus is the descendant of Abraham (Matt. 1:1) who makes this promise a reality. Peter in his second sermon reminds his Jewish hearers of God's covenant with Abraham, that he would bless all peoples (Acts 3:25) on earth through his offspring.[2] He then goes on to say that 'When God raised up his servant [Jesus], he sent him first to you [Jews] to bless you by turning each of you from your wicked ways' (Acts 3:26). Like Paul, Peter believed that the promise made to Abraham was fulfilled by one particular descendant or seed of Abraham (Gal. 3:16). Jesus' resurrection proves that he is that seed. The indestructible life of Jesus means that his life-giving impact is far superior to that of his ancestor Abraham, just as the well from which a river springs has very limited life-giving value when compared to an inexhaustible lake into which the river eventually flows.

In Hebrews, Jesus is seen as superior to Abraham because he is a priest after the order of Melchizedek. The argument sounds a little strange, to Westerners in particular, but is based on the concept of representative persons. While Abraham represents the priesthood that arose in the line of Jacob's son Levi, Melchizedek represents a priesthood that is not dependent on belonging to one branch of a particular family and is, as a result, timeless. When the mysterious figure of Melchizedek, King of Salem, came to bless Abraham on his return from a successful military campaign to rescue Lot, Abraham recognized him as his superior and gave him a tenth of the spoils. The point of the extended section on Melchizedek in Hebrews is that the priesthood of Jesus is superior to the priesthood that arose from Abraham, because Jesus lives for ever and 'is able to save completely those who come to God through him, because he always lives to intercede for them' (Heb. 7:25).[3] The key concept is a life that has absorbed and conquered suffering, violence and death.

The argument between Jesus and representatives of the Jewish religious establishment in John 8 also focuses on Jesus' claim to be able to give life, which means he is greater than Abraham. When Jesus says, 'if anyone keeps my word, he will never see death' (v. 51), the Jewish religious leaders respond, 'Abraham died and so did the prophets, yet you say that if anyone keeps your word, he will never taste death. Are you greater than our father Abraham?' (vv. 52–53). This argument ends with the startling declaration about the pre-existent and indestructible life of Jesus that is seen by the

2. The Greek translated 'peoples' as *patriai*, which originally meant a group descended from one individual, which was smaller than a tribe but larger than a household or fathers' house – a clan. Here it has developed the wider meaning of 'a people', an 'ethnic identity' or even a 'nation'.
3. For the section on the priesthood of Melchizedek, see Heb. 6:16 – 7:28.

Jewish authorities as a claim to divinity: 'Before Abraham was born,' Jesus declared, 'I am' (v. 58).[4]

Jesus superior to Moses

For the Jew, Moses, as the giver of the law (*tôrâ*), was unquestionably the greatest man who had ever lived, towering over everyone else. The author of the letter to the Hebrews, writing to Jewish Christians, is in no doubt that Jesus is superior to Moses. 'Jesus has been found worthy of greater honour,' he says, 'just as the builder of the house has greater honour than the house itself' (3:3). Moreover even a very faithful servant in the household of God, as Moses was, is inferior to a faithful son who has ultimate authority over the household (3:1–6). This passage is in no doubt that Moses was a faithful servant of God and must, therefore, have a significant place in the story of redemption; but Jesus is superior to Moses. The big question in the context of this book is whether what Moses said about just government has any continuing validity now that Jesus Christ his superior has come. This will be the focus when discussing the teaching of Jesus.

Jesus superior to Israel

That God rescued his people Israel from slavery in Egypt and brought them through the Red Sea to Sinai, where they received his law, indicated that he was giving them a very special and exalted position among the nations of the world. When they arrived at Sinai, God told Moses to tell the people:

> You yourselves have seen what I did to Egypt, and how I carried you on eagles' wings and brought you to myself. Now if you obey me fully and keep my covenant, then out of all nations you will be my treasured possession. Although the whole earth is mine, you will be for me a kingdom of priests and a holy nation. (Exod. 19:4–6a)

If, in the light of what he had done for them, the Israelites responded to God in love and obedience, they would affirm that they were his special possession. As such they would be

---

4. Cf. vv. 24 and 28 in the same chapter, and the OT background in Isa. 41:4; 43:13; Ps. 90:2.

> a servant nation instead of a ruling nation. Israel as a 'holy people' then represents a third dimension of what it means to be committed in faith to Yahweh: they are to be a people set apart, different from all other people by what they are and are becoming – a display-people, a showcase to the world of how being in covenant with Yahweh changes a people.[5]

A vine or vineyard is a common picture in the OT of this special role God intended for his people.[6] God had lavished his love and care on this special vine or vineyard so that it would produce an abundant crop of good fruit; but as it matured, all it produced was wild grapes. The wild grapes were idolatry and its outworking in social injustice. The rulers of Israel were particularly culpable in this production of bad fruit. As a result:

> The LORD enters into judgment
> against the elders and leaders of his people:
> 'It is you who have ruined my vineyard;
> the plunder of the poor is in your houses.
> What do you mean by crushing my people
> and grinding the faces of the poor?' declares the Lord, the LORD Almighty.
> (Isa. 3:14–15; cf. Jer. 12:10; Ezek. 19:10–14)

Jesus takes up the theme of the vineyard in the parable of the wicked servants (Matt. 21:33–46; cf. Mark 12:1–12; Luke 20:9–19). The fact that the vineyard planted by the landowner in Jesus' parable is described in precisely the same way as the vineyard in the Septuagint translation of Isaiah 5 shows that Jesus is applying to Israel in his day what God said to Israel in the days of Isaiah. Just as the prophets tended to focus on the rulers of Israel when comparing Israel to a vine or vineyard, Jesus does the same. What is new is that Jesus says that the fate of Israel in his day will be determined by the leaders' reaction to him. In the parable, they decide to kill the beloved[7] son of the vineyard owner when he comes to claim the fruit he has every right to expect. They kill the son, thinking they can then lay claim to the vineyard for themselves. The result of their action is that the vineyard, described as

---

5. Comment on Exod. 19:6 in John I. Durham, *Exodus*, Word Biblical Commentary on CD-ROM, vol. 3 (Dallas, Tex.: Word, 1998).
6. For 'vine', see Ps. 80:8–16; Jer. 2:20–22; 8:13; Ezek. 19:10–14; and for 'vineyard', see Isa. 3:14; 5:1–7; Jer. 12:10.
7. In Mark's version of the parable, the son is described as 'beloved' (12:6).

the kingdom of God, will be taken from them 'and given to a people [or 'nation', *ethnos*] who will produce its fruit' (Matt. 21:43). Here again we have strong echoes of the language of Exodus 19, where the covenant people are described as a kingdom of priests and a holy nation. What is new about this people who have come under the rule of God and are set apart for his service and the service of humankind is that they are focused on Jesus Christ. Jesus is the cornerstone, the foundation on which their individual and corporate lives are built. It is difficult to avoid the conclusion that *ethnos* here refers to the church. The use of *ethnos* is suggestive of the incorporation of the *ethnoi*, nations or Gentiles, into the people of God so that the fulfilment of God's purposes for Israel will be a people drawn from all nations – including the mainly Jewish Christians for whom Matthew wrote his Gospel.

Not only did Jesus teach that he is the foundation of the new 'Israel' but he also taught that in one sense he *is* the new Israel. It is certain that Jesus was thinking of the way in which Israel was compared to a vine in the OT when he declared, 'I am the true vine and my Father is the gardener [or 'vinedresser']' (John 15:1). Having pointed to the frequent comparison of Israel to a vine in the OT, D. A. Carson comments on this striking claim:

> whenever Israel is referred to under this figure it is the vine's failure to produce fruit that is emphasized, along with the corresponding threat of God's judgment on the nation. Now, in contrast to such failure, Jesus claims, 'I am the *true* vine', *i.e.* the one to whom Israel pointed, the one that brings forth good fruit. Jesus has already in principle, superseded the temple, the Jewish feasts, Moses, various holy sites; here he supersedes Israel as the very locus of the people of God.[8]

Since, as we have already seen in the comparison between Jesus and Adam and Abraham, Jesus' superiority is located in his endowment with indestructible life, he cannot fail to produce good fruit. What is amazing for us as fallen human beings is that this Vine's fruit is produced in us when we are united with Jesus by faith through the power of the Holy Spirit. The key word to describe this Vine's fruit is love, which is manifested in the integral communion and community with Jesus and each other that its 'branches' enjoy. Some of the implications of this will be discussed in the section on the church.

---

8. D. A. Carson, *The Gospel according to John* (Leicester: IVP, 1991), p. 513.

Jesus as prophet, priest, king and judge

Moses described the different types of leader/ruler Israel needed in order to establish the just society envisaged in the covenant and provided a good example of each role himself. Jesus is presented in the NT as the supreme example of these various leadership roles.

Prophet

Abraham is the first person to be called a prophet in the Bible (Gen. 20:7), but Moses sets the standard for all subsequent prophets. In the OT, a prophet was a messenger called by God to speak the words of God to his or her generation. When Moses and all the prophets God subsequently called to serve his people under the old covenant spoke as prophets, the focus was not so much on detailed legislation but on speaking the word of God into specific historical circumstances with prescient knowledge sometimes confirmed by supernatural divine acts.

In Deuteronomy 18, Moses prophesied that in the future God would raise a prophet like him to speak God's word to his people (Deut. 18:15). The immediate context of this statement is a statement about the way the nations sought guidance through 'sorcery or divination' (v. 14). The contrast is between the divine call and revelation that came to Moses and the general idolatrous quest for supernatural guidance by occult means that is so common among human beings alienated from God.

In his second sermon in Acts, Peter argues that Jesus is the prophet promised by Moses. The implication is that Jesus is a pioneering prophet like Moses and that he establishes a new and superior phase in the story of redemption. Having been crucified, raised from the dead and exalted to the throne of God, Jesus has sent his apostles to proclaim forgiveness of sins to all who repent as preparation for his return from heaven to restore everything. Moses as God's prophetic servant saved the Israelites from slavery in Egypt and led them to the land of Canaan; Jesus saves God's people from sin and leads them to the renewed heaven and earth (Acts 3:17–23).

Priest

As a Levite, Moses was also a priest. If he had lived to enter the Promised Land, like all the Levites, he would have had no right to land and would have lived off the tithes of the other eleven tribes. As for the crucial task of the high priest and his family in the tabernacle, it was Moses who had been used by God to establish the whole sacrificial system that was meant to ensure the continuing presence of God with his people Israel.

There are strong hints in the teaching of Jesus that he believed he had come to fulfil the tabernacle/temple and become the 'place' where all human beings can be reconciled with God. In the letter to the Hebrews, we have an extended and detailed description of this fulfilment process. One of the most striking contrasts between the tabernacle/temple of Moses and Jesus is that the latter is located in 'heaven' because Jesus was exalted to the right hand of God after his resurrection. One profound implication of this is that access to God has become universal because it is not tied to any place on earth.

This has profound implications for the place of land in the new, as compared to the old, covenant. A holy place by definition needs a holy land. A divine person transcends place and land. So, as Wright says, 'There is no "holy land" or "holy city" for Christians. We have no need of either – we have Christ.'[9] So management of land in accordance with God's law is now overarched by what it means to be in Christ. God's law that conditioned Israel's possession of land is not annulled by Jesus but is included in a greater and more wonderful revelation of the meaning and purpose of humanity's management of the whole earth.

King

Moses ruled Israel justly and describes the key characteristics of a just king in Deuteronomy 18. David was the historical king who approximated most closely to this Mosaic ideal. As the line of David came to an end with the exile to Babylon, the prophets proclaimed that this was not the end of God's promise to David that his house and kingdom would endure for ever (2 Sam. 7:16). A king would yet arise in the line of David:

> For to us a child is born,
> to us a son is given,
> and the government will be on his shoulders.
> And he will be called
> Wonderful Counsellor, Mighty God,
> Everlasting Father, Prince of Peace.
> Of the increase of his government and peace
> there will be no end.
> He will reign on David's throne
> and over his kingdom,

9. Christopher J. H. Wright, *Old Testament Ethics for the People of God* (Leicester: IVP, 2004), p. 193. On p. 187 he quotes W. D. Davies's striking phrase that Christianity 'has Christified holy space'.

establishing and upholding it
with justice and righteousness
from that time on and for ever.
(Isa. 9:6–7; cf. 11:1–4)

Such prophecies were responsible for the post-exilic conviction that developed among the remnants of Israel/Judah that they should expect a Messiah, an anointed king in the line of David, who would restore the fortunes of the Jews and establish a worldwide empire where justice would prevail. The birth narratives of both Matthew and Luke emphasize that Jesus was this long-awaited son of David.

Matthew's Gospel begins with 'A record of the genealogy of Jesus Christ the son of David' (Matt. 1:1). Jesus is the Christ, the Messiah, so long expected by the Jews. This is then affirmed by the story of the astrologers who have travelled a great distance to pay homage to the newborn king of the Jews (Matt. 2:1–2). The story is meant to underline the conviction that Jesus was no ordinary king but a highly exalted figure who would command the allegiance of people way beyond the boundaries of Israel. It also emphasizes the contrast between the unassuming, humble nature of this king and the cruel and violent Herod, so typical of the kings of this world.

In Luke, the angel's message to Mary when he announces the conception of Jesus also emphasizes that he is the long-awaited Messiah in the line of David. Gabriel says of Jesus, 'He will be great and will be called the Son of the Most High. The Lord God will give him the throne of his father David, and he will reign over the house of Jacob for ever; his kingdom will never end' (Luke 1:32–33).

After the birth narratives, the kingship of Jesus does not come into sharp focus again until the final week of his ministry leading up to his passion. The kingdom of God is a central theme in his teaching, and he implies that the coming of the kingdom is intimately linked to what he says and does; but there is a reluctance to proclaim himself openly as the long-expected king. When Peter on behalf of the disciples declares that Jesus is the Messiah (Matt. 16:16), Jesus warns them to keep this realization to themselves. The reason for his reluctance becomes clear in John's account of the feeding of the five thousand: 'Jesus, knowing that they intended to come and make him king by force, withdrew again to a mountain by himself' (John 6:15). He was going to be king on his own terms and in a totally counter-cultural way.

The final week of Jesus' earthly ministry begins with a public declaration of kingship, for he deliberately fulfils Zechariah's prophecy concerning the Messiah by riding into Jerusalem on the colt of an ass:

Rejoice greatly, O Daughter of Zion!
Shout, Daughter of Jerusalem!
See, your king comes to you,
righteous and having salvation,
gentle and riding on a donkey,
on a colt, the foal of a donkey.
(Zech. 9:9)

Before the final crisis of his arrest and trial, Jesus challenges the religious authorities in Jerusalem to think again about the nature of Messiah by referring them to Psalm 110, where David addresses the victorious Messiah as his Lord. Jesus' question Would David call a son of his, Lord? is meant to push them to realize that the Messiah's kingship is very different from that of his forefather as well as being far superior (Matt. 22:45). Sadly, rather than thinking through the implications of Psalm 110, the Jewish authorities use Jesus' claim to be king in his triumphal entry into Jerusalem as the cornerstone of their case against him before the Roman authority represented by Pilate. The case is that in claiming to be King of the Jews, Jesus is directly threatening the rule of the Roman emperor in Palestine. Pilate does not believe that Jesus is what the Jewish authorities say he claims to be, but out of political expediency condemns him to death and has written on his cross in Hebrew, Latin and Greek, so that it is crystal clear to all who can read, that he is being executed as the King of the Jews (Matt. 27:11; cf. Mark 15:2; Luke 23:3; John 18:33–37; Matt. 27:37; cf. Mark 15:26; Luke 23:38; John 19:19).

In John's extended account of his interrogation by Pilate, Jesus' view of the nature of his kingship is explained more fully than in any other part of the Gospels. As in the Synoptic Gospels, Pilate asks Jesus if he is the King of the Jews. Before answering this question in the same way as he does in the Synoptics, Jesus uses the opportunity to describe the nature of his kingship: 'Jesus said, "My kingdom is not of this world. If it were, my servants would fight to prevent my arrest by the Jews. But now my kingdom is from another place"' (John 18:36). Jesus is not saying that his kingdom or kingship has nothing to do with the earth when he says it is not 'of this world'. In John's Gospel, 'this world' is the natural and supernatural sphere opposed to God. The sphere of opposition to God and his ways on earth has always been extensive, as witnessed by Satan's claim to be able to offer all the kingdoms of the world with their authority and splendour to Jesus if he worships him (Luke 4:5–7). Of course Jesus knew that Satan was and is a liar (John 9:44c) and that his authority has been nothing like as extensive as he would have us believe among the governments of the world. That apart, there can be no doubt that there is plenty of evidence of injustice and violence in the way governments rule. What Jesus fixes on as the most distinctive characteristic of his rule, as compared to the rule of 'this world', is that violence is ruled out as a means to defend or expand its interests. This above all else proves that his kingdom is 'from another place' as the NIV translates the simple negative 'not from here' (*enteuthen*) of the Greek.

The fact that his kingship is not exercised through the power of the sword does not mean that it is powerless. In fact, it wields a far more powerful weapon than the sword – TRUTH: 'Jesus answered, "You are right in saying I am a king. In fact, for this reason I was born, and for this I came into the world, to testify to the truth. Everyone on the side of truth listens to me"' (John 18:37b). In John's Gospel, Jesus has claimed to be the truth, so the truth in view here is not something only said, but is a way of being human in all its fullness. Jesus is the full embodiment of truth in this sense, so that being prepared to listen to his voice in preference to any other becomes the test of whether we are on the side of truth or not. When this is coupled with the rejection of violence as the means for asserting kingship, then we have a strong echo of the prophetic expectation of the Messiah as one who

> will strike the earth with the rod of his mouth;
> with the breath of his lips he will slay the wicked.
> (Isa. 11:4b)

The supreme evidence that he is able to do this is that, having tasted the violence of this world to death, he rose again!

Judge

In Moses' description of the different types of leader/ruler in Israel in Deuteronomy, the role of judges is described first because they had a crucial role in keeping the people faithful to the God who had redeemed and given them the law by which they were to live in the Promised Land. With the coming of the new covenant written on the heart by the Spirit, the Promised Land is desacralized and the people of God called from every nation do not need to observe the specific law given to ensure the continued occupation of a specific piece of earth. It is unsurprising, therefore, that Jesus while on earth rejects the role of judge in its OT sense.

In Luke 12, a man comes to Jesus with the request that he act as an arbitrator or judge in a dispute he has with his brother over an inheritance (Luke 12:14). Jesus rejects the request, saying, 'Man, who appointed me a judge or an arbiter between you?' In this response, Jesus echoes and inverts the statement made to Moses by a Hebrew who was ill-treating a fellow Hebrew (Exod. 2:14). It is possible that Jesus is ironically suggesting that if the man making the request wants to recognize Jesus as a new Moses, he should not use him for his own ends but subject his life to his authority at a deeper level.[10] This is what Jesus does when he goes on to challenge the man who makes the request, together with the whole listening crowd, with a deep problem of the human heart that underlies the man's request. The problem is greed or covetousness, the desire to possess without reference to one's own needs or the needs of others that flows from the deep insecurity of the human heart alienated from God. The parable of the rich farmer that Jesus tells to drive home his point shows clearly that we are in a new covenant context in this passage with its emphasis on heart transformation bearing fruit in compassionate action. People at peace with God would not consider senselessly hoarding God's bounty for themselves, but would use it to bless God and the needy.

Jesus also rejected the role of judge in the ultimate sense during his earthly ministry. Like John the Baptist Jesus saw his coming as bringing imminent judgment on the Jewish religious establishment who were focused on the temple. But for the ordinary Jewish people and also the Gentile outsiders he saw his coming in terms of God's mercy and grace. When he declared that he was the one anointed by the Spirit to proclaim good news to the poor, prophesied by Isaiah, he stopped short of saying he had come to proclaim 'the day of vengeance of our God' (Isa. 61:2b; Luke 4:16–19). Jesus was not in the world in order to condemn but to save (John 3:17; 12:47; Matt. 9:13; 15:24; Mark 1:38; Luke 4:18, 43). That does not mean setting aside the judgment of God on human unrighteousness and injustice. The perspective, in John's Gospel in particular, is that the world is already under the judgment of God but Jesus comes into the world as light coming into the darkness. Those who gravitate to the light are saved, but those who shrink from him remain in darkness. At the final judgment the ultimate destiny of all will be determined by their response to the light. Even in this day of grace and mercy, in which humans have lived since the ascension of Jesus, his presence in the world has

---

10. 'Jesus declines to intervene, and says so by means of an allusion to Exod 2:14. The tone is ironical, and Jesus seems to challenge the petitioner to recognize whether he is trying to make use of a perceived status and authority in Jesus without facing the claim upon his own life implicit in that status and authority. If Jesus is some kind of "new Moses," then he needs to be heard and obeyed (Deut 18:18–19)' (para. 3 of the 'Explanation' of Luke 12:13–21, in John Nolland, *Luke 9:21–18:34*, Word Biblical Commentary on CD-ROM, vol. 35b [Dallas, Tex.: Word, 1998]).

been a judgment in that he divides those who are of the light from those of the darkness simply by their response to him. But when he comes again in glory, he will become the judge who will determine the final destination of every human being (John 5:24–30; Acts 10:42; 17:31; Rom. 2:16; 2 Tim. 4:1).

In John 12, Jesus says that

> the person who hears my words but does not keep them, I do not judge him. For I did not come to judge the world, but to save it. There is a judge for the one who rejects me and does not accept my words; that very word which I spoke will condemn him at the last day. For I did not speak of my own accord, but the Father who sent me commanded me what to say and how to say it. (John 12:47–49)[11]

It is time to turn to what Jesus did.

---

11. Carson comments on this passage, 'The reason why the Son's words are so final . . . is that they are the words of the Father . . . Many Jews saw the law of Moses as the source of life . . . But now the law of Moses, as gracious a gift of God as it was, is being replaced, or, better, fulfilled, by Jesus the incarnate Word. All that Jesus says . . . has been commanded by the Father . . . , and God's command, which

8. WHAT JESUS DID: THE ACTS OF THE SUPREME RULER

John ends his Gospel by saying that 'Jesus did many other things as well' as the ones recorded in his Gospel and 'If every one of them were written down . . . the whole world would not have room for the books that would be written' (John 21:25)! The world is now full of books on the limited number of Jesus' actions recorded in the NT, so this brief reflection on his actions will be very selective. The overriding control, as with everything in this book, is relevance to overcoming poverty.

Jesus' actions are ultimately focused on the profoundest level of our fallenness as human beings. He did indeed perform many amazing miracles of healing and deliverance, which had a dramatic impact on the physical life of those who were healed and delivered, but his ultimate aim was to transform the life of the whole person. He was lavish with his power to heal and deliver, so that many who had been unable to function economically and socially were wonderfully restored. But all this was indicative of something much deeper that was happening. Resurrecting the dead only-son of a widow, for example, had profound economic implications for the grieving mother, and healing a man with leprosy had profound social implications. This is significant when we consider the actions of Jesus or the impact of his actions when we think about how we should act as his disciples. But this was not the whole story, as the stories of miraculous deeds themselves sometimes force us to consider.

As the founder of the new covenant, Jesus' deepest objective was heart transformation, which means transformation at the deepest level of our human existence, the source of our feeling, thinking and willing. It is uncleanness at this level that he has come to address:

> 'Are you so dull?' he asked. 'Don't you see that nothing that enters a man from the outside can make him "unclean"? For it doesn't go into his heart but into his stomach, and then out of his body.' . . . He went on: 'What comes out of a man is what makes him "unclean". For from within, out of men's hearts, come evil thoughts, sexual immorality, theft, murder, adultery, greed, malice, deceit, lewdness, envy, slander, arrogance and folly. All these evils come from inside and make a man "unclean".' (Mark 7:18–23; cf. Matt. 15:16–20)

This profound statement is the conclusion to a debate with the Pharisees and teachers of the law about the ritual washing of hands before meals. Jesus contrasts their focus on ritual cleanliness as demanded by the 'tradition of the elders' with the moral cleanliness demanded by the 'command of God'. Jesus concentrates on moral uncleanness and its deep root in the depravity of the human heart. One is reminded here of the bleak picture of humanity before the flood when 'every inclination of the thoughts of [their] heart[s] was only evil all the time' so that the earth was corrupt and 'full of violence' (Gen. 6:5, 11). Jesus affirms here that the root of poverty, as one of the great evils in the world, is depraved human hearts from whose warped thinking come theft, murder, greed and envy. 'Envy' translates 'an evil eye' in Greek and, as we shall see when we come to examine Jesus' teaching about the eye in Matthew 6:22–23, it probably means a lack of generosity towards the poor in particular. Whether or not Jesus is abrogating the ritual purity laws of the OT in this passage may be put to one side as a matter for debate, but what he says is totally consistent with his insistence that humanitarian and ethical concerns are far more important than ritual purity (Matt. 9:12–13; 12:7; 23:23).

Jesus' compassion for those who suffered deeply because they were considered ritually unclean also shows that his priority was the well-being of the needy. The OT ritual purity laws were based on the premise that impurity is contagious, so that those who were guilty of making themselves impure and those who were involuntarily inflicted with an impurity were to be excluded from the presence of God, which was manifested in the tabernacle/temple, and from the society of his people. In most cases, restoration was possible; but in some cases, such as prolonged bleeding or serious 'leprosy', the alienation was profound. On a number of occasions, Jesus does not hesitate to touch those considered beyond cleansing and, in so doing, not only heals a devastating illness, or even raises someone from the dead, but also brings wholeness into their lives.

In this context, Christians throughout the centuries have seen the actions of Jesus as an example for them to follow in serving the needy. If Jesus was prepared to go to the margins and touch or be touched by the pollution of the needy and the suffering, then his followers could do no less. The following testimony of a theological student who did an internship with a Christian organization working with the neediest in Mumbai, India, testifies to the contemporary reality of this response to Jesus:

> I had a very memorable incident that I will always treasure in my heart. It was giving bath to an old man who was lying on the street suffering from paralysis. He had no food, shelter and also without clothes. Since all his family members died he had no one to care for him. The condition of the person was very bad and I found it very difficult to touch him in order to give him bath. But with the help of the staff we could give him bath and dressing.[1]

I was told that the sight of the old man's filthy condition, which included an open sore with maggots in it, paralysed the young student until a colleague took hold of his hand and brought it into contact with the sufferer.

The filth that comes out of the human heart generates an enormous amount of pollution, which is evidenced by the suffering and need in societies everywhere. At the margins of every society, we find the untouchable, those who are considered so polluted and polluting that they are shunned. In countries with a high level of poverty, such people are often the literal poor who live on the streets or in slums. In the rich countries, an example would be people with mental health problems who, in relative terms, are also often very poor. Jesus did not shun pollution but faced up to it and, in touching the untouchable, drove the pollution away and cleansed them.

Touching the untouchable

An example of this was the healing of the woman who had been subject to bleeding for twelve years (Mark 5:21–34). The impact of this type of ailment on this woman would have been catastrophic. For twelve long years she would have been excluded from a normal social and marital life because of her ritual

1. This is an unedited copy of the student's report.

uncleanness. On top of this she was impoverished because she had spent everything she had on futile medical care and had to contend with the debilitating physical weakness caused by her condition. Then she heard about Jesus. The more she heard, the more she felt that if anyone could help her, he could. But how could she, an unclean outcast, go to him with her need? She decided to risk it and pushed her way through the crowd until she could touch his cloak. She had faith, believing that by touching Jesus she would not make him unclean, but on the contrary her touch would make her clean. She was right: the instant she touched him she knew that she had been healed, but in her act of desperate faith she had not imagined Jesus would want everyone to know that he had been touched by an unclean woman. So when he did, she fell at his feet and told her whole story. She would never forget his response. He called her 'daughter', which meant that he loved her and she now belonged to him. She already knew her ritual uncleanness was a thing of the past, but, more than that, Jesus told her she could now enter a life of peace and wholeness. She returned to her family and community enriched economically (no more doctor's bills), psychologically (no more sense of failure), and socially (no more isolation). Everything had been made new!

The incident with the haemorrhaging woman happened while Jesus was on his way to the home of Jairus, a synagogue leader, who had pleaded with him to come to the aid of his desperately sick daughter. We can imagine Jairus' frustration as Jesus stopped to deal with the woman, and then his despair when news came that his daughter had died. Jesus pressed on to Jairus' house. There he went to where the daughter lay and, having thrown everyone out of the room except for the parents and three of his disciples, took the young woman by the hand and commanded her to get up – which she did! Even the uncleanness of death had to yield to Jesus' touch (Mark 5:25–43). Ignoring the rules of ritual purity again, Jesus touched the coffin of the widow of Nain's dead only-son before raising him from the dead (Luke 7:14).

At the end of chapter 4 of his Gospel, Matthew gives a summary of Jesus' ministry as *teaching*, *preaching* and *healing* and this summary is repeated almost word for word at the end of chapter 9 (Matt. 4:23; cf. 9:35). Between these two summaries, Matthew first includes a large block of teaching in the form of the Sermon on the Mount (chapters 5–7), and then a block of narrative focusing on Jesus' miracles of healing (chapter 8–9). Nine miracles of healing are described in this narrative block, and some have argued that they can be divided into three groups of three, focusing on different aspects of Jesus' healing work. The first cluster of three miracles focuses on Jesus' readiness to touch people who were marginalized and excluded for various reasons.

Matthew begins with the account of healing a man with leprosy (Matt. 8:1–4). There is a dispute among scholars as to whether biblical leprosy is the same disease as that which is now called leprosy, or Hansen's disease. Biblical 'leprosy', as described in Leviticus 13 – 14, included a number of skin diseases. People could recover from some of them, while others were incurable. The incurable form was greatly feared, and this was the condition with which this man was afflicted.

Even worse than the physical pain and disfigurement caused by skin disease was the spiritual and social banishment. A person with leprosy became ritually unclean as well as sick and had to live in isolation from family and community. Added to this, according to Leviticus, people with leprosy had to leave their hair unkempt, wear mourning clothes, cover the bottom half of their faces and shout 'Unclean! Unclean!' wherever they went (Lev. 13:45–46). The fact that Miriam and Uzziah were afflicted by leprosy as a judgment from God on their sin also led to the belief that leprosy was always a judgment for a specific sin (Num. 12:12; 2 Chr. 26:20). Being rejected by God and the community, people with leprosy were in a terribly pitiful condition. They represented the deepest depth of human despair because of sin. It is significant that this is where Matthew chooses to begin his account of the mighty deeds of Jesus the Messiah.

Matthew tells the story of the healing/cleansing very simply and graphically. A man with leprosy approaches Jesus and kneels before him to ask for cleansing. He is already convinced that Jesus can cleanse him. What he is concerned about is Jesus' willingness or not. 'Lord,' he says, 'if you are willing, you can make me clean' (Matt. 8:2). What happens next is both amazing and shocking. The man with leprosy has probably knelt at a safe distance from Jesus to make his request. Jesus now very deliberately 'reached out his hand and touched the man' (v. 3). To those watching, this simple act would make Jesus unclean. Jesus is putting himself outside the community with the man with leprosy. To them the contagion of leprosy is unstoppable. But Jesus knows that his touch and willingness will drive the contagion into reverse. It is not Jesus who will become unclean, but the man with leprosy who will become clean! 'Immediately,' the man with leprosy, 'was cured [Greek: cleansed] of his leprosy' (v. 3).

From the perspective of the unclean man the touch of Jesus must have been an electrifying experience. Ever since his leprosy was confirmed he would have been untouchable, except by other untouchables. We know that in our world, so full of sin and wickedness, touching is not always good, but the touch of Jesus represents everything that is good about touching. For the man with leprosy the touch of Jesus would have meant much. Supremely it would have meant acceptance by God and the community. It would have meant that his life was no longer to be defined by the terrible disease that had made him unclean. He was no longer a reject. From the unclean man's perspective, what happened after the touch was inevitable. In one sense, there was no need for Jesus to say that he was willing, because the touch had already more than proved that he was. The man was cleansed immediately. He was then told by Jesus to keep the miracle quiet and go through the normal procedure of ascertaining that he had been cleansed so that he could officially take his place in society again.

We are not told whether any of the people mentioned above, whose lives were so dramatically turned around by the touch of Jesus, responded to him in faith and love. His ultimate aim was heart cleansing and transformation, but he was not afraid of making real contact with those considered unclean at the margins of society in order to achieve his end and, in the process, make a massive difference to the economic, psychological and sociological aspects of their lives as well. Jesus touched the untouchable who presented themselves to him and made them clean.

Driving out unclean spirits

Not only did Jesus touch the untouchable, but he also delivered those who were in bondage to demons. In Mark's Gospel, demons are often called 'unclean spirits'.[2] Dealing with this type of uncleanness was not the most common miraculous activity in which Jesus engaged. There are only four detailed accounts of exorcism in the Gospels,[3] and of the four only one is focused entirely on the person being delivered or cleansed, the Gadarene/Gerasene demoniac (Mark 5:1–17).

There is some debate as to exactly where this miracle of delivering the Gadarene/Gerasene demoniac was performed, although there is agreement that it was in an area adjacent to the Sea of Galilee populated mainly by Gentiles. Nothing is said about the ethnic origins of the tormented man, but the fact that he calls Jesus 'Son of the Most High God' (Mark 5:7) suggests that he may be a Gentile. His condition is absolutely pitiful. He is endowed with

2. Mark's phrase *en pneumati akathartō* is translated by 'with an evil spirit' in the NIV.
3. (1) The possessed man in the synagogue (Mark 1:23–26; Luke 4:33–35); (2) the Gadarene demoniac (Mark 5:1–20; Matt. 8:28–34; Luke 8:27–35); (3) the Canaanite woman's daughter (Mark 7:24–30; Matt. 15:21–28); and (4) the boy at the foot of the mount of transfiguration (Mark 9:17–19; Matt. 17:14–18; Luke 9:38–43).

supernatural strength that makes him unable to be restrained, and he wanders naked in the hills, where there are cave tombs, and continually shouts loudly and harms himself with stones. Yet, as soon as he sees Jesus, he comes running to him and falls on his knees before him. As in his dealing with others who have an unclean spirit, Jesus does not touch the sufferer. Jesus' authority over the unclean spirit/s is expressed by his command. In this case, there seems to be a bit more 'negotiation' than in the other cases, but the outcome is not in doubt: the spirits will have to leave their victim. They are allowed to enter a large herd of pigs, which they drive headlong over a precipice into the sea, where they drown. The loss of the pigs is a big economic loss to the district, but in Jesus' mind it is worth the loss for the people of the district to be able to see the poor tormented man sitting quietly with Jesus, 'dressed and in his right mind' (v. 15). And not only is the possessed man released from his bondage but he also becomes a disciple of Jesus. He wants to leave his area and go with Jesus, but Jesus sends him home to his family 'to tell them how much the Lord has done for you, and how he has had mercy on you'. The man obeys and becomes the first 'Christian missionary' in the Decapolis in the sense of being a thankful advocate for the transforming power of Jesus (vv. 19–20).

Without denying the reality of this man's bondage to demons in any way, he is also a graphic illustration of the universal bondage of sin. This man's heart had been taken over by unclean spirits because his heart, like every other human heart, had been polluted by evil. In his powerful act of cleansing, Jesus showed that he was able to cleanse hearts from the pollution of evil and in the process restore the man to sanity and the possibility of a fruitful life in his society as witness and worker. This is Jesus as victor over the contagion of evil. But evil is also 'sin'. It is not mere pollution but an offence against God, and where there is an offence there is need for forgiveness.

Forgiving sins

In one case, a healing is offered by Jesus as proof of his ability to touch life at this deepest level of the offence to God caused by the evil in our hearts. A paralytic is brought by some faithful friends who overcome all hindrances to lay him at the feet of Jesus. Impressed by their faith Jesus says to the paralytic, 'Take heart, son; your sins are forgiven' (Matt. 9:2). By saying this, Jesus is not directly linking the man's physical condition with a particular sin. The Bible is consistent in denying that 'sin equals suffering' is a simple equation. Job and other passages that recognize the suffering of the righteous and the well-being of the unrighteous represent the default biblical approach. However, it is also clear that the existence of sickness and suffering in the world is ultimately a consequence of sin. The fall in Genesis 3 casts a long and deep shadow on human life. Here Jesus claims authority to deal with the root as well as with the consequences of sin.

The teachers of the law who heard Jesus saying that the paralytic's sins were forgiven were inwardly outraged by the blasphemous claim to be able to do something only God can do. Knowing their thoughts, Jesus asks, 'Which is easier: to say, "Your sins are forgiven," or to say, "Get up and walk"?' (Matt. 9:5). The implication is that it is easier to say, 'Your sins are forgiven'; but to prove that he has authority to forgive sins he not only tells the man to get up and walk but the man actually does so. As the man stands and picks up his bed to walk home, as well as realizing the wonderful truth that there is someone who can forgive his sins, it must also dawn on him that there is no need for him to depend any more on the charity of others for his livelihood.

This story emphasizes that the mighty cleansing acts of Jesus that bring such amazing transformation into broken lives point towards his most significant work, which is the forgiveness of sins. Hagner's 'Explanation' of the story of the healing of the paralysed man makes this point powerfully:

> Here again the authority of Jesus stands at the center of the passage. The one who can heal has also the power to attack the very root of all sickness and suffering, namely, sin. There can indeed be no ultimate healing, well-being, or *shalom* unless the evil power opposed to these things is defeated. The healings performed by Jesus are signs of the imminent defeat of sin and the power of evil. This is the true work of Jesus, and any attempt to put the healings at the center of his purpose is to misunderstand the centrality of the cross in Jesus' ministry. When this passage is seen within the context of the whole book, it is clear that for Matthew there can be no forgiveness of sins without the cross, just as there can be no healing without the cross. This theological connection cannot be broken. But the healing of sickness and suffering, like death, the fruit of sin, depends on the prior and greater work of Jesus. So in this narrative with the forgiveness of sins we are, as at many key junctures in the Gospel, brought to the central necessity of the cross. It is from the cross that the Son of Man ultimately derives his authority in word and deed, and with it the possibility of the proclamation of the dawning of the kingdom of God.[4]

Before launching into a discussion of the cross of Jesus, it may be helpful to summarize briefly how we have arrived at this point. We have seen that,

4. Ibid.

because of our alienation from God, there is an inevitable tendency in us to use the great abilities with which we have been endowed by our creator to satisfy our own desire for security at the expense of others. This is the ultimate source of all the oppression, cruelty and poverty with which our history is littered. The way we use our power has more often than not caused poverty. But running through much of our history there is also a divine revelation of an alternative way to use our power that brings blessing rather than cursing in its wake. This way is defined by righteousness/justice and we can see what it could look like in the image of the type of government and law revealed through Moses in the covenant of Sinai. However, this covenant was inadequate because it could not bring about the renewal of the human heart so profoundly infected with evil. The prophets foresaw the coming of one who would establish a covenant that would make possible the cleansing of the human heart from sin, and the NT teaches that Jesus was the fulfilment of their prophecies. We have considered something of his impact on broken lives that has inspired his followers into selfless service through the ages, but his followers have always believed that it was on the cross that Jesus performed the greatest of his miracles. It was here that the power of sin, and therefore the sinful use of power, was broken. It was the cross that made possible the actual rule or 'kingdom' of God in human lives, so that the use of our power to bless becomes a reality. Thus the cross must be central in any truly Christian view of how to overcome poverty.

The death of Jesus: breaking the power of sin

Every major Christian tradition believes that the death of Jesus is at the heart of the Christian faith, so it is appropriate that the cross is the symbol of Christianity. What will be said on this central topic is rooted in the evangelical understanding of the cross, but I would be surprised if Christians from other traditions did not share my conviction that if our efforts to overcome poverty cannot be rooted in an understanding of the cross, then the attempt will have no roots in Christian tradition at all.

Doctrinally the evangelical view of what the death of Christ means, the doctrine of atonement, is rooted in the Protestant Reformation, while its experiential roots are in the Great Awakening or Methodist Revival of the eighteenth century. There have been times since the eighteenth century when this doctrine has been hotly debated even within the evangelical family, and it has also been severely attacked from outside. The heaviest external criticism was seen at the beginning of the twentieth century, and ironically at the beginning of the twenty-first century it is being attacked from within in terms that seem to echo the earlier external attack. It is not within the scope of this book to address the issues being raised in the current debate. What will be attempted is a brief outline of the doctrine that is adequate to justify the contention that the atonement is the crucial foundation provided by the triune God for renewing human beings both socially and individually.[5]

When calling Saul of Tarsus, Jesus said his task was to open the eyes of the Gentiles so that they would be transferred 'from darkness to light, and from the power of Satan to God, so that they [would] receive forgiveness of sins and a place among those who are sanctified by faith in me' (Acts 26:18). There are three aspects to the task the risen Lord gave Saul/Paul. The first has to do with *authority* (*exousia*) or *rule*. Paul will be an agent of the immigration of people from the rule or kingdom of darkness into the rule or kingdom of light. The second aspect is the *forgiveness of sins*. This is the way into the kingdom of God. The third aspect has to do with *becoming a member of the new covenant people of God*, the church, which is expressed as gaining 'a place among those who are sanctified by faith'. If forgiveness was so vital as the key to the kingdom and membership of the covenant people of God, why does Paul say to the Corinthians that 'I resolved to know nothing while I was with you except Jesus Christ and him crucified'? (1 Cor. 2:2). The answer is that by the time Paul was writing to the Corinthians, he had, with other leaders in the early church, come to see clearly that it is the cross that makes forgiveness possible. So the doctrine of atonement is a description of how the apostles understood the way in which the cross makes possible the forgiveness of sins.

If to make forgiveness of sins possible the incarnate Son of God had to die on the cross, then sin must be taken very seriously. As we have already seen in the section on the OT, sin is not easily rooted out from the human heart. The pattern of rejection of God's authority, leading to evil deeds towards others, soon became deeply ingrained in our human nature after the fall. This is a persistent theme running through the OT. By the time of the flood, the deep depravity of the human heart had led to a world so full of violence that the destruction of all humanity, except for righteous Noah and his family, was justified. But the bitter root of sin remained in the heart of Noah and his progeny.

---

5. For the outline I am indebted to John Stott, *The Cross of Christ* (Leicester: IVP, 1986). Though written well before the current debate about the atonement, this excellent volume deals thoroughly with the objections of authors like Steve Chalke and Brian McLaren, who would benefit from pondering Stott's balanced and profound study of the subject.

Even God's intervention in establishing his covenant with Abraham, which led to the rescue of his ancestors from slavery in Egypt and the establishment of the Sinai covenant, floundered because of the incorrigibility of the Israelites. This is not to say that the Israelites were particularly sinful. If God had chosen another people to be the people through whom all nations would be blessed, the result would have been the same. At their worst the Israelites only desired to be like everyone else! Israel was very privileged, but experiencing God's mighty works and hearing his commands was not enough to counter the source of sin in the heart. It is unsurprising that as Judah was about to be sent into exile for its sins, God spoke of a new covenant that would involve renewal from within. But for this deep renewal to be possible, sins had to be dealt with. There had to be a way to remove the pollution of sins so that God could get a foothold in our heart.

Sins are such a deep problem because they are an expression of our rebellion against God and our rejection of his rightful authority over us as our creator. The five words for sin in the NT all express the concept of missing or breaking a standard that has been set by God.[6] Every sin makes us guilty before God, a serious situation because he is unspeakably holy. And what is more, there is something in us, even as fallen human beings, that makes us appalled when people who have perpetrated the most awful crimes seem to get away with it. The psalmist expressed this feeling many centuries ago:

> But as for me, my feet had almost slipped . . .
> For I envied the arrogant
> when I saw the prosperity of the wicked . . .
> they clothe themselves with violence . . .
> Their mouths lay claim to heaven,
> and their tongues take possession of the earth . . .
> They say, 'How can God know?
> Does the Most High have knowledge?' . . .
> When I tried to understand all this,
> it was oppressive to me
> till I entered the sanctuary of God;
> then I understood their final destiny.
> (from Ps. 73:2–17)

6. These are *hamartia* (missing the mark), *adikia* (unrighteousness), *ponēria* (wickedness of a vicious and degenerative kind), *parabasis* (trespass, transgression) and *anomia* (lawlessness).

The psalmist was perplexed by the way the powerful seem to be able to oppress the poor violently at will and then enjoy their wealth as if there was no one capable of bringing them to justice for their wickedness. But then he went into the presence of God and understood that these particularly heinous human actions are known to the all-knowing and holy God, who will finally call their perpetrators to account and punish them. But if he knows about these great and obvious sins, he also knows about the little sins, which also render us guilty before a holy God; and what human beings are there who could claim to be without sin or never to have done anything less than love God with all their mind, soul and strength and their neighbour as themselves?

Jesus makes it clear that a sense of guilt before God is a prerequisite to receiving forgiveness. It is the tax collector who in desperation cries to God to have mercy on him, a sinner, goes home having been heard by God, rather than the Pharisee who congratulates himself on his goodness and ends up talking to himself (Luke 18:9–14; cf. Mark 2:17; Luke 15:17–21).

Being guilty of rejecting God's right to rule over us, we are banished from his presence. From the spiritual and moral point of view it becomes impossible for us to be where he is, because of his holiness. His presence becomes fatal to us. Seeing God and continuing to live our ordinary sinful human life are totally incompatible. As the OT expresses it on numerous occasions, to 'see' God really would mean death (Exod. 3:6; 33:20–23; Judg. 13:12; Isa. 6:5). God's holiness is not only a passive quality of his essential being, but is also an active quality. The reason why seeing God would be fatal for us is that his holiness opposes as well as exposes sin. God's active opposition to sin is his wrath.[7] Many Western evangelicals in particular seem to have become uneasy with the idea that God is full of wrath towards evil; but it is impossible to retain a high respect for the authority of the Bible without respecting its clear teaching on the wrath of God. Even Jesus will say to many on the Day of Judgment, 'I never knew you. Away from me, you evildoers!' or 'Depart from me, you who are cursed, into the eternal fire prepared for the devil and his angels' (Matt. 7:23; 25:41).[8]

Because God is holy he cannot but be angry with sinners, and that anger will be satisfied unless something intervenes to turn it away from us. As Stott concludes, 'There is within God a holy intolerance of idolatry, immorality and

---

7. Stott, *Cross of Christ*, p. 106: 'God's holiness exposes sin; his wrath opposes it.'
8. That God's anger against sin is like an all-consuming fire is a very popular image in the NT (especially on the lips of Jesus) of the wrath of God finally destroying sinners: Matt. 7:19; 13:40–43; 18:8; Mark 9:43–48; Luke 16:24; John 15:6.

injustice . . . If evil did *not* provoke his anger he would forfeit our respect, for he would no longer be God.'[9] But God has revealed himself in the OT as well as the NT as a God of love and mercy. This is seen in his great patience with the wicked. If there had been just ten righteous people in Sodom and Gomorrah, God would have spared the cities despite their gross sin (Ezek. 16:49). God had patiently suffered the wickedness of the Canaanites for centuries before he visited them in judgment with the invasion of his chosen people. When God revealed something of his glory to Moses upon renewing the covenant after the sin of the golden calf,

> he passed in front of Moses, proclaiming, 'The LORD, the LORD, the compassionate and gracious God, slow to anger, abounding in love and faithfulness, maintaining love to thousands, and forgiving wickedness, rebellion and sin. Yet he does not leave the guilty unpunished . . .' (Exod. 34:6–7)

God did not become a God of love when he gave his one and only Son for us; neither did he cease being a God of justice. He has always been a God of love and justice.

The character of God as both loving and just is expressed in the biblical tradition of sacrifice. Sacrifice is ubiquitous among ancient peoples and is usually seen as a human attempt to buy the favour of the gods; but among God's chosen people it developed a different meaning. From the appearance of the ram that took the place of Isaac on the altar on Mount Moriah many sacrifices among God's people have been substitutionary. The sacrificial animal God provides takes the place of a human being who would have suffered judgment and death had it not been for the intervention of the shed blood of the sacrifice.

The Passover lamb can also be viewed as a substitutionary sacrifice. God declares that the land of Egypt is going to be judged with the death of every firstborn in the land because of wicked treatment of God's people. It is difficult to deny that this sentence was just, because the Egyptian authorities with the acquiescence of the people had cruelly enslaved the Israelites and, in order to control their numbers, had murdered their baby boys by throwing them into the river. So that the angel of death would distinguish between Egyptian and Israelite homes the latter needed to be protected by the blood of a sacrifice, because, although they were victims, they were also guilty before God. The sacrifice was a lamb without blemish, whose substitutionary blood

9. Stott, *Cross of Christ*, p. 124.

smeared on the doorposts would cause the angel of death to pass over. Israelite firstborn males were spared by the blood of a firstborn male shed in their place.

With the four bloody sacrifices of the tabernacle/temple cult the person making the offering laid his hands on the head of the animal before it was killed. This can only be symbolic of the transference of the offerer's life, including his sin, to the animal. The animal was then sacrificed instead of or on behalf of the one making the sacrifice. In the ritual of the Day of Atonement, two goats were taken as representative of the whole nation of Israel. The first was killed and its blood taken by the high priest into the holy of holies, where the blood was sprinkled over the mercy seat. On the second the high priest laid his hands as a symbol of the transference of the whole nation's sin on to the goat. This goat was then taken into the desert and left free in as isolated a place as possible. The whole ritual symbolized the removal of the nation's sin by a substitutionary death.

The tabernacle, and later the temple, was the place where God in his grace chose to be present with his people. We have already seen that the presence of God would prove fatal to sinful human beings. The whole tabernacle cult was clearly meant to stop this happening. The point of the sacrifices was to provide substitutes so the people would not suffer the just punishment for their sins, and so the presence of God with them would be a blessing and not a curse.

As the temple cult was being swept away and God's wrath was unleashed on the Jews in the form of Babylonian invaders, a new sacrifice for a new covenant came sharply into view in the form of the Suffering Servant of Yahweh:

> Surely he took up our infirmities
>   and carried our sorrows,
> yet we considered him stricken by God,
>   smitten by him, and afflicted.
> But he was pierced for our transgressions,
>   he was crushed for our iniquities;
> the punishment that brought us peace was upon him,
>   and by his wounds we are healed.
> (Isa. 53:4–5)

From the NT perspective Isaiah 53 is unquestionably the most significant OT passage for understanding the meaning of Jesus' death, and therefore for understanding what Jesus meant when he claimed to fulfil the Law and the Prophets. The plain meaning of the text of Isaiah 53 quoted above is that the

Suffering Servant was punished as a substitute for transgressors. In this context, it is also fair to conclude that when Jesus says he is going to give his life as a ransom for many, or that the cup in his supper represents his blood poured out for many, he is thinking of penal substitution (Mark 10:45; 14:24). This also seems to be the reasonable way to understand the following statements by the apostles:

> [Paul:] But God demonstrates his own love for us in this: While we were still sinners, Christ died for us. (Rom. 5:8)
>
> Christ redeemed us from the curse of the law by becoming a curse for us, for it is written: 'Cursed is everyone who is hung on a tree.' (Gal. 3:13)
>
> All this is from God, who reconciled us to himself through Christ and gave us the ministry of reconciliation: that God was reconciling the world to himself in Christ, not counting men's sins against them . . . God made him who had no sin to be sin for us . . . (2 Cor. 5:18–19b, 21)
>
> For God was pleased to have all his fullness dwell in him, and through him to reconcile to himself all things, whether things on earth or things in heaven, by making peace through his blood, shed on the cross. (Col. 1:19–20)
>
> [Peter:] [Jesus] himself bore our sins in his body on the tree, so that we might die to sins and live for righteousness; by his wounds you have been healed. (1 Pet. 2:24)
>
> [Hebrews:] So Christ was sacrificed once to take away the sins of many people; and he will appear a second time, not to bear sin, but to bring salvation to those who are waiting for him. (Heb. 9:28)

So, as Stott concludes, the biblical and evangelical doctrine of atonement means that

> the sinless one 'was made sin for us', which must mean that he bore the penalty for our sin instead of us, and he redeemed us from the law's curse by 'becoming a curse for us', which must mean that the curse of the law lying upon us for our disobedience was transferred to him, so that he bore it instead of us.[10]

10. Ibid., p. 148.

What this means is that our sins can be forgiven. We do not have to account for them any more because we can go to God and ask to be covered in the righteousness of Christ, knowing that anyone who asks will indeed be cleansed and become indwelt by the Spirit of the living God. What we need is to have our spiritual eyes opened so that we see who Jesus is and what he has done, supremely in his death, so that we can trust that he really does have authority to forgive our sins and that he can cleanse us from within and make us acceptable to God through the work of the Holy Spirit within us. This is the heart of the good news, the gospel, which human beings everywhere need to hear.

Since we have already established that the root cause of poverty is sin, it follows that the evangelical doctrine of atonement I have tried to describe must have something to do with overcoming poverty. All the apostles are clear that the forgiveness we receive through the Lord's death is not only a door into the presence of God but also a door into a new type of life. Paul develops this theme in Romans 6 – 8. He explains that what happens when we believe in Jesus for forgiveness of sins is that we symbolically die with him; and just as Jesus was raised from the dead we are also raised with him to live a new type of life. Now that we are forgiven and indwelt by the Spirit, we can offer the various aspects of our physical life to righteousness, that is, to do what is right by God and our fellow human beings. This is not an easy matter. Though we have been freed from the power of sin as forgiven people, as long as we live as physical beings in this world that is organized in its opposition to God, we remain vulnerable to sin's influence. This can lead to profound inward conflict in which we can be driven almost to despair at times, but we are assured that Jesus can and will rescue us by the power of his indwelling Spirit.

The Spirit brings us into what theologians have called a mystical union with Jesus in his death, resurrection and ascension, so that in our intimate relationship with him we come to want to do those things he would have us do. As Paul puts it in Ephesians, 'we are God's workmanship, created in Christ Jesus to do good works, which God prepared in advance for us to do' (Eph. 2:10). But what are the good works that forgiven sinners do? Paul and the other apostles go on to describe them in many of their letters, but Jesus also tells us what they are in the Gospel accounts of his teaching ministry. So we shall go on to consider the way of life characteristic of the kingdom of God, as described in the Sermon on the Mount, before returning to consider the power of the Holy Spirit that has been unleashed as a result of Jesus' resurrection and ascension.

9. WHAT JESUS TAUGHT: THE BEATITUDES

What is in view here is the ethical teaching of Jesus. Focusing on his person and work before coming to his ethical teaching has been deliberate. Jesus is the sun of our moral universe because of what he is and what he did. Without him we can do nothing of any moment in this world, including significantly overcoming poverty, although we may be able to alleviate some.

Because the Sermon on the Mount is the best-known block of ethical teaching in all the teaching of Jesus, we shall concentrate on it and particularly on those aspects that have implications for overcoming poverty.

To write a brief and coherent account of the Sermon on the Mount's teaching that is relevant to overcoming poverty is a daunting task. This is unquestionably the most famous account of a sermon ever written, and endless words have been produced to explain its meaning. Added to this are radically different ideas about the nature of the ethics of the sermon as a whole. Some see it as a *house of the future*. The ethic of the sermon is not one by which people can live now, but is going to be the ethic by which people will live during the millennial rule of Jesus. Others see it as a *law court*. It is the place to go to understand the impossible standard God has set us, so that we shall despair of ourselves and run to God for forgiveness. Yet others see it more like a *church building*. The righteousness in view in the sermon is the righteousness we get as a gift of God's grace in Christ. The sermon is primarily about how we sort out our personal relationship with God.

I believe that though these pictures may contain grains of truth, they are inadequate because they either cancel out or water down the sermon's relevance for everyday living. The sermon is actually more like a *Christian family home* where real people seek to live in a counter-cultural way among others who do not share their beliefs or ethics. It was a common practice in the past for Christian homes to have a plaque on the wall declaring that 'Christ is the head of this home, the unseen guest at every meal, the silent Listener to every conversation'. The implication is that if Jesus is there, then how we speak and how we act will be conditioned by his presence. That is exactly what the Sermon on the Mount is about. It is the description of a way of living in the presence of Jesus the Messiah and Revealer of the kingdom of God.

It is very difficult to avoid the conclusion that the kingdom or rule of God is the central theme of the sermon. Immediately before the sermon, Matthew has summarized the ministry of Jesus as teaching, proclaiming the good news of the kingdom and healing. It is also clear from the teaching of John the Baptist that the kingdom of God being inaugurated by Jesus was inextricably entwined with who he was. The person of Jesus was as significant to the coming kingdom as what he would say or do.

The sermon itself begins with a sort of prologue describing the characteristics of kingdom people in the Beatitudes, with the first and final beatitude eliciting the promise that 'theirs is the kingdom of heaven' (Matt. 5:3b; cf. 10b).[1] The main block of the sermon is introduced by the section on Jesus' relationship to the Law and the Prophets, which ends with the statement that a righteousness surpassing that of the Pharisees and teachers of the law is needed for entrance into the kingdom of heaven (Matt. 5:17–20).[2] In the section on prayer, we are instructed to pray for the coming of the kingdom; and in the section on our attitude towards material things, to seek God's kingdom and righteousness before anything else (Matt. 6:10, 33). Then, in the concluding section, Jesus says that entrance into the kingdom is conditional on doing the will of the Father, which is explained as putting the words of the Sermon on the Mount into practice (Matt. 7:21, 24). This final reference is

1. When referring to the kingdom, Matthew sometimes uses simply 'kingdom', as in 4:23. Usually, though, he has 'kingdom of heaven', as here, which reflects the contemporary reluctance to use the divine name. On some occasions, he has 'kingdom of God', as in Matt. 12:28. However, the three expressions are synonymous.
2. V. 20 forms an inclusio with 7:12 to form the main body of the sermon.

conclusive proof that the Sermon on the Mount is meant to be an ethic by which kingdom people are expected to live in their everyday lives.

It may be stating the obvious, but we need to be reminded that kingdom language is political language. On view in the Sermon on the Mount is a method of government characteristic of the 'realm' of God. We have already seen that there should have been no poverty in an Israel obedient to the rule of God; and we shall see that when the kingdom of God is finally revealed in all its glory, there will be no poverty. Described in the Sermon on the Mount are the character and actions of kingdom people and the inevitable impact they must have on poverty in the here and now.

The Beatitudes (Matt. 5:3–10)

It is interesting that the best-known statement of the ethics of the kingdom Jesus came to establish begins with a declaration of blessing, just as the establishment of the old covenant with Abraham was also steeped in 'blessing' (Gen. 12: 2–3). Blessedness is promised to those who have a number of inward dispositions worked out in specific actions. Before turning to the individual beatitudes, it is important to emphasize that the various dispositions and actions that lead to blessedness do not describe different individuals but the rounded character of kingdom persons.

The poor in spirit

The Beatitudes begin by declaring the blessedness of the poor in spirit. It is now popular to argue against spiritualizing this reference to the poor. The beatitudes found in Luke, where Jesus simply says 'Blessed are you who are poor' are referred to as evidence. But it is clear that Jesus is making a different point in Luke's account (Luke 6:20).[3] In Luke, Jesus is directly addressing his disciples in the second person because they had chosen the path of voluntary poverty in forsaking their means of earning a living when they followed him. There Jesus is saying that those who have responded to his call

3. The relationship between Matthew's 'Sermon in the Hills' and Luke's 'Sermon on a Level Place' is complex. It is possible that both evangelists record material from the same occasion. There is also the possibility that as a very busy itinerant preacher Jesus used the same material on different occasions and that Matthew's and Luke's material comes from memory of the use of similar material on different occasions.

to forsake all to follow him are truly blessed. Here in Matthew, Jesus is making a more general point about the attitude of the truly blessed. They are those who see that they are impoverished within and that they need God to lift them up. They are the opposite of the proud. This is certainly a way of understanding the meaning of poverty that had become common in the OT, especially in the Psalms. This more 'spiritual' understanding of poverty is also more consistent with the OT, because it never views poverty as a blessing but as an evil result of sin. It so happens that the majority of people who have confessed their inward poverty before God throughout the ages have not been the wealthy and powerful of the world, but the poor.[4] However, it is also the case that not all the physically poor are poor in spirit. To be poor in spirit is to be in a spiritual state that transcends literal poverty and wealth, but that has an impact on both. The poor are raised up in their spirit, which more often than not marks the beginning of a journey away from literal poverty; the rich when they become poor in spirit are humbled and begin to move in the direction of divesting themselves of their wealth for the benefit of the poor. The key point that needs to be made is that both the poor and the wealthy need to become poor in spirit, and that their doing so is a crucial step in the direction of literally blessing the poor. This will become clearer as we go through the sermon.

Those who mourn

A common perspective in commentators who live in rich countries is that they are not people who are sad because of bereavement but are repentant. They are people sorrowing because of their own sin and the sin of others that is causing such a lot of pain and grief in the world (see Ps. 119:136; Ezek. 9:4; Luke 19:41–42; Phil. 3:18). Leon Morris comments:

> Perhaps we should bear in mind that typically the worldly take a light-hearted attitude to the serious issues of life, a fact that is very evident in our modern pleasure-loving generation . . . Because they do not grieve over what is wrong in themselves, they do not repent; and because they do not grieve over the wrong they share with others in the communities in which they live, they take few steps to set things right. Because

4. In his 'Comment' on this phrase, Hagner argues that 'poor' is to be taken literally. See Donald A. Hagner, *Matthew 1–13*, Word Biblical Commentary on CD-ROM, vol. 33a (Dallas, Tex.: Word, 1998). That king David thought of himself among the righteous poor suggests that Hagner's position is not watertight: see Ps. 40:17; cf. 70:5.

they are not moved by the plight of the poor and the suffering, they make no move to help the world's unfortunates.[5]

I am very conscious that I am in danger of representing only the perspective of the oppressor here. In the quotation from Leon Morris, the focus is entirely on the repentance of those who have the means to do something about the sin of poverty. But what about the mourning of the poor who are always going to be in the majority in the kingdom of God, if my understanding of poverty of spirit is correct? What does it mean for them to mourn? Even the poor need to repent of their rebellion against God, but the sorrow they feel because of their poverty is different from the sorrow rich people feel because of the poverty of the poor. The poor mourn their condition while looking to God for justice with the assurance of the long revelatory tradition that he will vindicate their cause. Mary gives powerful expression to this OT hope as an integral aspect of the rule of the Messiah when she becomes assured she is to be his mother:

He has brought down rulers from their thrones
  but has lifted up the humble.
He has filled the hungry with good things
  but has sent the rich away empty.
(Luke 1:52–53)[6]

Other beatitudes and subsequent passages in the Sermon on the Mount will show how this sorrow that the poor feel should be expressed.

The meek

To be meek is to be self-effacing. Here again the perspective of the poor and powerful differs. This is not to deny that there is self-promotion among the poor. The sin of self-aggrandizement is universal. Neither can we deny the reality of self-loathing among the rich and powerful. The overflowing psychiatric clinics of the West witness to the contrary. But many of the poor do not have to become invisible, because they already are. This is probably true

5. *The Gospel According to Matthew* (Leicester: IVP, 1992), p. 97. Cf. John R. W. Stott, *The Message of the Sermon on the Mount* (Leicester: IVP, 1978), p. 41: 'It is not the sorrow of bereavement to which Christ refers, but the sorrow of repentance.'
6. These verses are full of OT allusions; see e.g. 1 Sam. 2:5–8; Job 5:11; 12:18–25; Pss 34:17–18; 73; 107:9; 113:7–8; 146:6–9; Jer. 5:26–29; 17:11; 31:10.

particularly of a great many poor women in the world. For such people to be meek is to come to the conviction that they matter to God, even if they are treated as nonentities by their husbands and male-dominated society. They look to God to lift them up, and trust in his willingness and ability to do so.

Though coming from a very different starting point, the privileged and powerful likewise become meek when they depend on God to make a difference. Moses, although he had spent forty years in exile before God called him to his great task, had a very privileged upbringing. His education and grooming for the exercise of power contributed to making him one of the greatest leaders in history. Yet he is described as the meekest man on earth (Num. 12:3).[7] Meekness is the opposite of self-assertion, but does not preclude strong assertion of the truth and justice of God. Moses was very strong on what God wanted. His will was subjected to God's will, but he was also an unwilling leader. He did not push himself forward but almost had to be forced into prominence by God. For those who are privileged and have access to power, this is one of the most important lessons to learn when engaging in a struggle to overcome poverty. The crucial factor is not gaining control of power but dependency on God. Those who seek power in order to help the poor end up being corrupted by any power they may acquire. Those who seek to bless the poor in dependence on the power of God really succeed. This is not an excuse for refusing to confront injustice but a challenge to do so in God's strength as the only way to make a significant difference: '"Not by might nor by power, but by my Spirit," says the LORD Almighty' (Zech. 4:6).

Poverty of spirit, mourning and meekness describe the humble person. Poverty of spirit drives us to God, mourning drives us to God with the evils of the world, meekness is the attitude that makes it possible to do something about it in God's strength.

Those who hunger and thirst for righteousness

Righteousness (*dikaiosynē*) is a key concept in the Sermon on the Mount and is closely linked with the concept of the kingdom (see Matt. 5:10, 20; 6:33).[8] But what exactly does it mean. Earlier in Matthew when Jesus went to be baptized, John initially refused him. Jesus persuaded him to go ahead by saying that his baptism was necessary 'to fulfil all righteousness' (Matt. 3:15). It is

7. 'Humble' is used in the NIV.

8. We have also seen that it is central to the concept of the rule of God in the OT.

very unlikely that 'righteousness' means moral goodness in this instance. It is more likely to mean everything Jesus needed to do in order to fulfil his mission of establishing the kingdom of God. Crucial to this fulfilment was Jesus' identification with sinners that reached its climax in his substitutionary death on the cross. This is the source of the common Christian understanding of righteousness as something that we lack but which is given us freely by God when we trust in Jesus. This is right, but does not exhaust the meaning of righteousness that encompasses the wider purpose of establishing the kingdom. Significantly this wider purpose is clearly indicated in Greek by the fact that there is only one term for 'righteousness' and 'justice'. There is certainly nothing in the context of Matthew 5:6 to suggest that righteousness in the sense of the imputed righteousness of Jesus is the exclusive meaning of *dikaiosynē* in this instance. In fact, those commentators who believe that the reference to the poor in verse 3 should be taken literally argue that it must mean 'justice' in this instance. The truth is probably more subtle and reflects the Hebrew roots of the NT. Hebrew does distinguish between being just/righteous (*ṣedeq*) and executing justice/righteousness (*mišpāṭ*), although the two terms are treated as synonyms in Hebrew parallelisms (Pss 36:6; 72:1–4). What this suggests is that it is possible to distinguish conceptually between being righteous and doing justice but that the two concepts are essentially inseparable, so that it is impossible to be righteous without doing justice, and vice versa.

So to hunger and thirst for righteousness is to long for the comprehensive blessing the kingdom of God will bring. It is to long for people to be made righteous through the blood of Christ and that justice will be done for the poor. One cannot be more important than the other: both are kingdom priorities because the kingdom means the reign of righteousness/justice. The new heaven and earth are 'the home of righteousness/justice' (2 Pet. 3:13), and it is ridiculous even to suggest that those who have been transplanted into it from the kingdom of darkness through the sacrifice of Christ should act other than justly as they await their consummation. We love justice now because we shall love it for ever.

The merciful

Up to this point the Beatitudes have focused on states of mind, but here the focus is on action. There is a clear echo of the Septuagint of Proverbs 14:21 here, which reads 'blessed is the one who has mercy on the poor' (*eleōn de ptōchous makaristos*). In Jewish society by the time of Jesus, giving to the poor had become the most exalted way of showing mercy. This can be seen in Matthew 6:2, where the words translated 'give to the needy' originally meant 'to do an act of mercy' but had 'by the intertestamental period . . . become a technical expression for almsgiving'.[9] There is no need to limit showing mercy to showing mercy to the poor here, but it is good to remember that poverty provides the best forum for being merciful.

The pure in heart

The heart in the Bible is not the seat of the emotions but the centre of what we are as human beings. It controls the way we think, the way we act and the way we feel. Poverty of spirit creates the possibility of cleansing at the centre of our personality because it recognizes that there is much cleansing to do within. Jesus came to call those who knew that they were sinners so that the recognition of the need for inward cleansing became an absolute prerequisite for benefiting from his grace. Faith in Jesus' offer of forgiveness cleanses the heart and creates the possibility that good things will flow from within. Here again we are dealing with the very essence of the new covenant. If there is purity in the heart, then God is at the centre and his life can flow out to others. We cannot be blessed or a blessing unless we give attention to our heart relationship to God. This does not mean immediate perfection, but it does mean that we can be channels of God's blessing to others and that we can begin to be single minded in our pursuit of God and the good of our neighbours. If we do this, we are assured we shall see God not in a way that will prove fatal but as the ultimate experience of bliss.

The peacemakers

Peace is a very comprehensive concept in the OT. It is the opposite of everything the world has become as a result of sin. By the time of the flood the world was full of violence and, sadly, that is still a valid description of the world today. Brief extracts from a news report published by the Church Mission Society (CMS) about the impact of inter-ethnic conflict on Christian ministry and the community in Nyankunde in the Democratic Republic of Congo (DR Congo) in September 2002 vividly illustrate the destructive impact of violence:

> The hospital, orthopaedic centre, pharmacy, schools, churches, shops, nursing schools . . . were systematically looted . . . The dead include Revd Henri Basimake, the HIV/AIDS coordinator for the Anglican Province of Congo, as well as four other colleagues, medical students recently qualified from the . . . College in

9. Comment on Matt. 6:2, in Hagner, *Matthew 1–13*.

> Nyankunde . . . The only water pipe has been cut by the attackers, and cholera has broken out in Nyankunde and Bunia. There is now no hospital or medical care for the region.[10]

It takes little imagination to picture the impact of such senseless violence on the quality of people's lives. As a conflict within a state the civil war in DR Congo, which is estimated to have claimed more than 3 million lives, is now typical of most conflicts in the world. At the beginning of 2006 the United Nations High Commission for Refugees (UNHCR) estimated that such conflict had caused the internal displacement of 23.7 million people in 52 countries. The combined suffering of people fleeing their homes in terror while everything they have is looted and destroyed is unimaginable to us in the peaceful West, but this is the reality of conflict and violence. Peace in the sense of the cessation of conflict would be a precious gift in these situations.

But peace in the OT is not simply a lack of violence, conflict and war. It is what happens when people live their life in the way God always intended they should. Fundamental to this is restoration of our broken relationship with our creator. This is pictured prophetically in Isaiah, who sees the beautiful feet of the herald coming over the mountains to proclaim peace because the Lord has redeemed his people (Isa. 52:7–10). John the Baptist proclaimed the dramatic return of the Lord himself to his people, so that he could reveal his glory to all humankind because the sin of his people had been paid for (Isa. 40:1–5). This is the kingdom that has come, is coming and will come in Jesus the Messiah bringing glory to God and peace on earth (Luke 2:14). Real peace is peace with God, peace between people and peace with the rest of creation.[11]

The world in which we live is full of conflict that is the cause of an immense amount of poverty. Nations, tribes and families fight each other. Quarrels abound in every community. In the midst of this, the followers of Jesus are called to be making peace between people as well as between people and God through the good news of the gospel. Peace and poverty cannot coexist. We are actively and deliberately to bring conflict to an end by reconciling enemies, and in the process create one of the essential conditions for people to flourish

---

10. See <http://webarchive.cms-uk.org/news/2002/press11_09_02.htm>, accessed 19 Mar. 2008.
11. See Isa. 65:17–25 for a wonderful poetic picture of this peace in the new heavens and earth that God promises to create for his people.

in every sense and thus overcome poverty.[12] It is peacemakers in this comprehensive sense that are known as the children of God.

Those persecuted because of righteousness

This beatitude is somewhat unexpected. From the human perspective, kingdom people do not seem to be people the powerful need to fear. Paul reminds the congregation of Christians in Corinth, 'Not many of you were wise by human standards; not many were influential; not many were of noble birth' (1 Cor. 1:26), and this could probably be said about most Christian congregations since. Yet the history of the church is drenched in the blood of martyrs, and there were more Christian martyrs in the twentieth century than the previous nineteen centuries added together. So what do the powers that be find so threatening about Christians? Very simply it is kingdom people's concern for righteousness/justice, which Jesus says is synonymous with their love for him. 'Blessed are you', he says, 'when people insult you, persecute you and falsely say all kinds of evil against you because of me' (Matt. 5:11).

The powers of this world will find us threatening in the same way they found Jesus threatening. The teachers of the law and Pharisees were threatened by Jesus because he challenged their preoccupation with their own goodness, which led to a lack of compassion for ordinary people struggling in their sins, sorrows and sufferings. The high priest's family, who controlled the lucrative temple cult in Jerusalem, were threatened by Jesus' reminder that the cult was not meant to benefit them but the ordinary people and even Gentiles. Herod Antipas was threatened because he felt that Jesus, like John the Baptist, would condemn his immoral lifestyle. Pilate, the colonial governor, was persuaded that Jesus was a threat to the power of the divine Caesar in Palestine.

In other words, the righteousness/justice Jesus embodied was a threat to the religious, economic, moral and governing powers of this world! They thought they had put an end to the threat when they nailed him to the cross, but he rose from the grave and his threatening Spirit lives on in the hearts and lives of his kingdom people. Everything we are and do should speak of his peaceable kingdom that by its nature undermines the injustice perpetuated by the powerful rulers of this world. But we should expect to by persecuted and

12. Cf. Leon Morris, *The Gospel According to Matthew* (Leicester: IVP, 1992), p. 101: 'There is a quality of peaceableness, a disinclination to engage in disputes, that is admirable, but Jesus is talking about more than that. He refers not to peace-*keepers* but to peace-*makers*, people who end hostilities and bring the quarrelsome together.'

should rejoice when it happens, because our reward in heaven will be great (Matt. 5:12).

Salt, light and a city on a hill (Matt. 5:13–16)

Having described the character of kingdom people, Jesus gives his disciples three pictures of the impact of their lives on the world. Here again it is important to emphasize the primacy of the kingdom. The disciples may not have seen themselves particularly clearly in Jesus' description of kingdom people, but Jesus knew that their adherence to him would eventually make them those types of people. This is why he could say that the way they were going to live would make them salt and light to the world and a visible community of love that would be impossible to hide. Jesus is very emphatic on this point. 'You yourselves', he says, meaning 'you really are' going to be the salt and light of the world and a city that cannot be hidden. Being in the kingdom is the source of doing kingdom works, but there is no being without doing good works. The good works to be done that will cause people to give praise to their heavenly Father are described in the main body of the sermon.

The old and the new righteousness/justice (Matt. 5:17–20)

Before describing the good works of the kingdom, Jesus explains how they are related to the revelation of God's will in the OT. He emphasizes the continuing validity of the OT and states that the great in the kingdom will be those who obey and teach its commands. But their continuing validity is now founded on the fact that they have been fulfilled by Jesus. In Jesus, and only in Jesus, has the entire law continuing value. In Jesus, a righteousness/justice superior to that of the Pharisees and teachers of the law has been revealed. This superior ethic is expounded in Matthew 5:21 – 7:12 and we shall focus on its implications for overcoming poverty.

10. WHAT JESUS TAUGHT: STRATEGIES FOR KINGDOM LIVING

Actions that break the cycle of sin (Matt. 5:21–48)

In the six cases dealt with by Jesus in this section, he generally follows the pattern of stating a law, describing the human problem that makes the law necessary and commanding actions that deal with the problem. Three of the six cases deal with aspects of the human condition at the root of our violence and have, therefore, a strong bearing on the perpetuation of poverty.[1]

Murder

The command in the first case 'You shall not murder' is amplified to include the traditional conviction that a murderer deserves to be judged (Matt. 5:21–26). In dealing with this case, Jesus focuses on the judgment that is the inevitable consequence of murder. In describing the human predicament in the context of this law, he emphasizes that we shall be judged or condemned for a lot more than actual acts of murder. All murderous thoughts and

1. Glen H. Stassen and David P. Gushee, *Kingdom Ethics: Following Jesus in Contemporary Context* (Downers Grove: IVP, 2003), pp. 133–141. I have found this book immensely helpful in grasping the relevance of the Sermon of the Mount for our lives today.

intentions also make us culpable before God's law and deserving condemnation. But kingdom people are not helplessly caught in the web of hatred and accusation that will bring people to judgment. So Jesus commands us to do everything in our power to remove the inward hatred that will cause those who harbour it to be condemned. He assumes that the sorts of persons described in the Beatitudes will not harbour hatred against others, so that they are free to try to deal with the hatred directed against them. If a fellow believer has something against us, we are to go to that believer to sort out the problem. Our calling is to reconciliation, which means stemming the flow of God's wrath towards a brother/sister who may be nursing the roots of hatred towards us. Our responsibility to do this extends even beyond the boundaries of God's family to unbelievers who resort to the law of the land to express their hatred towards us. In this case by doing everything in our power to settle out of court, however unsatisfactory such reconciliation often is, we shall save ourselves as well as our adversaries a lot of trouble. Our calling as kingdom people is to do everything in our power to change the hearts of our enemies.

Everything the disciples who heard this radical teaching knew about the rule of God would remind them that this is not something we can do in our own strength. Even in the OT it was God who established his rule over Israel. He redeemed them from slavery by his mighty acts; he preserved them in the wilderness and enabled them to take possession of the Promised Land; he saved them from the power of invading armies until their sins became so great that he allowed them to be conquered and exiled; he brought them back from exile. So when Jesus commands us to do something that seems so difficult from our human point of view, he is not mocking us but calling us to trust in his power to change people when we obey and do what is totally contrary to our sinful human nature. We must not forget that his command now comes with the promise of his presence in the power of the Holy Spirit. The glory of such commands is that we are not left helpless in a world torn apart by hatred and violence. We can and must do something as kingdom people to stem the tide of evil.

An eye for an eye

The fifth case dealt with by Jesus is the law of proportionate retribution: an eye for an eye and a tooth for a tooth (Matt. 5:38–42). Even in the OT this was a principle for limiting the severity of punishment so that it fitted the crime. If someone lost an eye as a result of an unjust action, punishment would probably not be the removal of the guilty person's eye but compensation that would reflect the value of an eye. This is still a fundamental principle of any just legal compensation system. This law was revealed because of the common human desire for revenge when someone does something that hurts us and our interests. The desire to hit back is deeply ingrained in our sinful nature, as is our inability to control our revengeful response once it is unleashed. Lamech's boast is still typical:

> If Cain is avenged seven times,
> then Lamech seventy-seven times.
> (Gen. 4:24)

Kingdom ethics begin from a different premise to just satisfaction for evil perpetrated against me. Their fundamental premise is, What strategies can be used to respond to unjust action that could influence for good those who are perpetrating the injustice? Paul had clearly absorbed this radical teaching of Jesus, for he says, 'Do not be overcome by evil, but overcome evil with good' (Rom. 12:21). So when someone sets out to insult us by striking us with the back of their hand on our right cheek, we offer them our other cheek, thus giving them the opportunity to treat us as an equal by striking us with an open hand on our left cheek! When we are sued for our shirt, we declare our freedom and dignity by freely giving our adversary our coat as well. When we are bullied by an oppressive regime to serve their servants against our will, we offer out of the goodness of our heart to help them freely and go the extra mile. With this type of generous spirit, when asked by the needy for gifts or loans, we respond positively, although we know we shall have nothing to gain for ourselves by doing so.

Giving to the one who asks may not mean giving exactly what is asked for. It may be better to offer to take alcoholics for a meal than to give them money to feed their addiction, and it would be sensible to assess whether a person asking for a loan would use it well. The key point is that kingdom people are generous people who seek the well-being of those who ill treat them and make demands on their resources. The reason for our existence is to do good and bless, to give of ourselves to others, as our Lord gave of himself for us. Doing this will inevitably mean that we move from giving to the poor and needy to asking why those we are serving are in their present condition. We shall not be able to avoid socio-structural issues. Loving the young girl in prostitution in a city is bound to lead us to sex trafficking and the poverty that so often feeds this desperate evil. The impoverishment of the Ghanaian rice grower will lead us to the International Monetary Fund and its structural adjustment programme, which means that Ghanaians are buying subsidized Californian rice in their shops and market stalls.

Love for enemies

The sixth and final case drives home this principle of generosity in the most radical way possible by commanding love for enemies (Matt. 5:43–47). The traditional teaching was that neighbours, probably meaning fellow Jews, were to be loved, while enemies, probably meaning Gentiles, could be hated. Jesus exposes the vicious human propensity that underlies this false understanding of God's law. As we saw from the early chapters of Genesis, fallen humans sought to deal with their insecurity because of their alienation from God by forming solidarity groups where they would find affirmation, meaning and protection from external threat. Families, cities and nations came to serve this purpose early in the history of our race. In a fallen world perceived to be full of uncertainty, we need some group to embrace so that we can feel secure from the threat of those who are excluded.[2] Our desire for security drives us to seek solidarity with others, while our fundamental insecurity means that there are always the excluded who threaten us. So we love our neighbours and declare outsiders as enemies we can legitimately hate. Jesus refers to two groups despised by religious Jews: tax collectors and Gentiles. Tax collectors were collaborators with the Roman oppressor and had a very bad reputation for exploitation. Being despised by their own people, it is unsurprising that they looked after each other's interests. They loved each other even if they hated those who despised them. The Gentiles were the soldiers, civil servants and opportunists from different ethnic groups who took advantage of the Roman occupation of Palestine to make a living. Despite their diversity, they supported each other in the face of hostility from many Jews. What Jesus is saying is that it is deeply ingrained in our sinful nature to love or feel solidarity with those with whom we have common interests in order to defend ourselves from the hostility of those who despise our particular group of neighbours. Since we become neighbours for protection in a context of hostility, we believe there is every justification to hate those who are hostile towards us.

Jesus dramatically cuts across this universal human propensity rooted in our alienation from God, and commands us to love our enemies and pray for those who persecute us. What Jesus has already said about stemming murderous intent and responding to oppressive action has laid the foundation for this climactic command to love enemies. This type of love is the only way to stem the flow of hatred and exclusion that blights human life. Justice cannot do it alone.

---

2. There is an echo here of Miroslav Volf's excellent book *Exclusion and Embrace: A Theological Exploration of Identity, Otherness, and Reconciliation* (Nashville: Abingdon, 1996).

The cry of the oppressed for justice if not tempered by love always ends up with the oppressed, when they succeed, becoming the oppressor.

The theological justification given by Jesus for this command to love enemies is his heavenly Father's covenant with creation after the flood. Knowing that the flood had done nothing to change the evil inclination of the human heart, God covenanted with himself to ensure that the regular cycle of seedtime and harvest would persist as long as the earth endured (Gen. 8:21–22).[3] God's loving provision does not depend on whether those for whom he is providing reciprocate or not. His sun and rain that sustain all living things are provided unconditionally even to his enemies.[4] To be the children of our heavenly Father we must love in this unconditional way.

Nelson Mandela is not known as a devout Christian, but it is clear from his autobiography that this section of the Sermon on the Mount took root in his heart during his Methodist upbringing, grew into a strong plant during his long and unjust imprisonment and bore amazing fruit in the process of forming a new, democratic South Africa. Mandela's actions bear witness to the integrity of the following testimony:

> I knew that people expected me to harbour anger towards whites. But I had none. In prison, my anger towards whites decreased, but my hatred for the system grew. I wanted South Africa to see that I loved even my enemies while I hated the system that turned us against one another . . .
>
> I was often asked how I could accept the (Nobel Peace Prize) jointly with Mr de Klerk after I had criticized him so severely. Although I would not take back my criticisms, I could say that he had made a genuine and indispensable contribution to the peace process. I never sought to undermine Mr de Klerk, for the practical reason that the weaker he was, the weaker the negotiations process. To make peace with an enemy, one must work with that enemy, and that enemy becomes your partner . . .
>
> It was during those long and lonely years that my hunger for the freedom of my own people became a hunger for the freedom of all people, white and black. I knew

---

3. Cf. the comment on the promise in this passage in the context of climate change on p. 25.
4. Jesus is stating a general truth here. It is true even today in a world with an enormously expanded population that God provides adequately for all and that hunger is a matter of poor distribution and not poor provision. This general truth is not undermined by specific circumstances where God's provision is influenced by people's behaviour, so that he was able to use drought and famine as a rod to chastise his disobedient people Israel.

> as well as I knew anything that the oppressor must be liberated just as surely as the oppressed . . . The oppressed and the oppressor alike are robbed of their humanity.[5]

The radical teaching of Jesus in this passage mercilessly exposes the depth of our depravity, but does not leave us without hope. We are given clear directions on how to stem the tide of evil in our hearts and communities. The way of the world and Satan has ever been to divide and oppress, while the way of the kingdom is to unite and bless. The sorts of kingdom people described in the Beatitudes, who live lives of humility and meekness before God, who long for righteousness/justice and peace, who are merciful and pure in heart and who are persecuted for being who they are can but make an impact on poverty when they obey their Lord's commands in Matthew 5:21–48.

The standard pious acts of kingdom people (Matt. 6:1–18)

The three standard pious acts discussed by Jesus (giving alms to the poor, prayer and fasting) are described as 'righteousness' (*dikaiosynē*). The key point Jesus emphasizes for all three acts is that they should be done to please God rather than other people. In the section on prayer, there is additional teaching that includes the Lord's Prayer.

In all the discussion there has been among evangelicals since the 1950s about the relative importance of evangelism and social action, it has been easy to forget that our Lord Jesus Christ assumed that his disciples would share what they have to relieve the needs of the poor. He says, '*when* you give to the needy', and not, '*if* you give to the needy', and the 'when' here does not point 'to an occasional happening, but to . . . regular practice'.[6] There is a temptation at this point just to repeat this statement over and over again so that it will sink in that Jesus actually said it. Jesus expected his disciples to share their possessions with the poor.

The term that underlies 'give to the needy' in the NIV is *eleēmosynē*, which is derived from the verb *eleeō*, meaning 'to have compassion, show mercy'. It acquired the technical meaning of 'alms' when used by the Jews in their Greek (Septuagint) translation of Daniel (see Dan. 4:27). This reflects the obvious

---

5. Nelson Mandela, *Long Walk to Freedom* (London: Abacus, 1995), pp. 680, 734, 751.
6. Leon Morris, *The Gospel According to Matthew* (Leicester: IVP, 1992), p. 136. N. 4 on the same page says, '*hotan* is employed "Usually of an iterative action, indefinite, in the past or future" (J. H. Moulton, *Syntax*, p. 112).'

fact that giving resources to relieve the suffering of the poor is a prime expression of mercy and compassion. A link with the proclamation of blessing on the merciful in the Beatitudes is also obvious.

Ignoring the assumption of Jesus here is probably a far more serious issue than whether evangelism is more important than social action in Christian discipleship. That we have ignored this assumption as rich Western and Westernized Christians is unquestionable. The following paragraph from Ron Sider's *The Scandal of the Evangelical Conscience* may focus on all who claim to be Christians in the US, but a large proportion of them are evangelical and recent research has shown that they are only marginally more generous than other Christians:

> American Christians live in the richest nation on earth and enjoy an average household income of $42,408. The World Bank reports that 1.2 billion of the world's poorest people try to survive on just one dollar a day . . . [I]f American Christians just tithed, they would have another $143 billion available to empower the poor and spread the gospel. Studies by the United Nations suggest that just an additional $70–$80 billion a year would be enough to provide access to essential services like basic healthcare and education for all the poor of the earth. If they did no more than tithe, American Christians would have the *private* dollars to foot the bill and still have $60–$70 billion more to do evangelism around the world.[7]

The potential impact of generous Christian almsgiving in overcoming poverty is immense, but that is not the main point of Jesus' teaching. He is indeed concerned that we give alms, but in this section of the Sermon on the Mount is more concerned with how we do it. The key point is that it should be done integrally or holistically. It should be done as an expression of love for God and neighbour and not to boost our own ego. Almsgiving should be God-conscious and neighbour-conscious, rather than self-conscious, action. To give alms as an ostentatious show of religious devotion to boost our own image is to use God and our needy neighbour for our own ends. Our aim should be to honour our Heavenly Father and bless our needy neighbour. We should use neither God nor the poor to boost our own image. Self-interest has no place in the Christian effort to overcome poverty.

The same altruistic principle applies to prayer and fasting – that as disciples of Jesus we are called to honour our heavenly Father and bless our needy neighbour, not to attempt to impress others with our piety.

---

7. Ronald J. Sider, *The Scandal of the Evangelical Conscience: Why Are Christians Living Just Like the Rest of the World?* (Grand Rapids: Baker, 2005), pp. 21–22; his italics.

The beginning of the Lord's Prayer makes this crystal clear:

> Our Father in heaven,
> hallowed be your name,
> your kingdom come,
> your will be done
> on earth as it is in heaven.
> (Matt. 6:9b–10)

The prayer is focused on God because it is the honour of *his* name, the coming of *his* kingdom and the doing of *his* will we are to request. But the prayer is corporate. The honour of God's name is the joint longing of the disciples of Jesus, who together long for the full manifestation of the rule of God over a renewed humanity in a renewed earth, and who pray that this glorious reality will cast its shadow on earth now as God's will is done. But this is not an abstract request on behalf of others; we are asking that we as disciples together will hallow our heavenly Father's name, submit to his rule and do his will in our daily lives, and it is clearly our Father's will that we should give alms to the poor.

Biblical fasting is essentially about humbling ourselves before God. It is about the priority of being in tune with God and seeking his blessing on people, projects and plans and on the process of mastering our physical appetites. But it is also about choosing, in submission to God, to deny ourselves the legitimate enjoyment of some of our goods in order to bless those who have nothing. Commenting on Matthew 6:16–18, Stott says that

> when through Isaiah God condemned the hypocritical fasting of the inhabitants of Jerusalem, his complaint was that they were seeking their own pleasure and oppressing their workers *on the very day of their fast.* This meant that partly there was no correlation between the food they did without and the material need of their employees. Theirs was a religion without justice or charity. So God said: 'Is this not the fast that I choose . . . Is it not to share your bread with the hungry, and bring the homeless poor into your house?' Jesus implied something similar when he told of the rich man feasting sumptuously every day while the beggar lay at his gate, desiring to be fed with the crumbs which fell from his table.[8]

8. John R. W. Stott, *The Message of the Sermon on the Mount* (Leicester: IVP, 1978), p. 138; his italics. The passages referred to are Isa. 58:1–7 and Luke 16:19–31.

The disciples' reason for living (Matt. 6:19–34)

Having taught that his disciples' pious acts should flow from love for God and neighbour, Jesus goes on logically to discuss what drives the way we live. Jesus teaches that ultimately we have only two alternatives: we can be driven by the desire to accumulate earthly treasure, on the one hand, or heavenly treasure, on the other (vv. 19–21). Put another way, we can serve either God or Mammon/money.

This is one of those parts of our Lord's teaching that profoundly challenges the Western consumerist lifestyle. The constant message of consumerist advertising is that accumulating material treasure is the way to a life worth living. Jesus says a resounding 'NO!' to this message. The treasure worth having cannot be found in this present age that is passing away, but in the kingdom that will be fully revealed when Jesus comes in glory. It is not the proverbial 'pie in the sky when you die' but is much closer to that 'pie' than the 'pies' that can be accumulated in this world. To be in heaven is to be where our Father God is. Throughout the Sermon on the Mount, Jesus has been teaching us what it means to live in the presence of God. The wonder of the sermon is that it lays before us what it means to live kingdom lives in our fallen and sinful world. The heavenly treasure built up as we live such lives is superior because it cannot be lost, for the heavenly kingdom is eternal. Moreover the treasure we value shows clearly to everyone what really motivates us. People who say they are Christians, but spend much of their time and energy hoarding all the things this world can offer, show clearly that their heart is not in the heavenly kingdom. This is the message of Matthew 6:19–21.

In Matthew 6:24, Jesus drives his point home by saying that God and Money – what Jesus calls Mammon – are incompatible, alternative masters. Jesus gives us a stark choice. We must serve either God or Money, and 'Money' includes everything money can buy.

What Jesus says about alternative treasures and masters raises the question of how we can know which treasure we are seeking and which master we are serving. We are given the answer in the mysterious section about 'eyes' in Matthew 6:22–23.

What does having 'good' or 'bad' eyes mean in this passage? Jesus is clearly not talking about a physical disability here. Looking first at what Jesus meant by 'bad' eyes is probably the best way to reach understanding. Jesus' original hearers would have heard him talk about 'evil eyes', a perfectly familiar idea to them as Jews with their roots in the OT and rabbinic traditions.

Deuteronomy 15:1–18 contains the law of release from debt and debt slavery in the seventh year. Having to forgive debts in the seventh year could inhibit lending to the poor, especially, as we have seen, if the seventh year was near. So God says through Moses, 'Be careful not to harbour this wicked thought: "The seventh year, the year for cancelling debts, is near," so that you do not show ill will towards your needy brother and give him nothing' (Deut. 15:9). 'Show ill will' is a dynamic equivalent translation of the 'give an evil eye' that is in the Hebrew text. Again, in the section on freeing debt slaves in the same chapter, those who had enslaved fellow Israelites in lieu of debt repayment are encouraged, 'Do not consider it a hardship to set your servant free' (Deut. 15:18). Here 'consider it a hardship' translates 'it must not be hard in your eyes'. To have a hard, evil eye in this passage is to refuse to be generous towards the poor and needy. The evil eye is a *mean* eye.

So if the 'bad' eye is a mean eye, is the 'good' eye a generous eye? The word translated 'good' (*haplous*) in Matthew 6:22 occurs only here in the NT and in the parallel passage in Luke 11:34. The prime meaning is 'simple' or 'single'. It refers to that 'in which there is nothing complicated or confused', something that operates in the way it should. But the way words from the same root are used points to 'generous' as a legitimate translation, even without the strong circumstantial evidence of Deuteronomy 15. James 1:5 says, 'If any of you lacks wisdom, he should ask God, who gives generously [*haplōs*] to all without finding fault' (cf. also Rom. 12:8; 2 Cor. 8:2; 9:11, 13). A simple eye is an eye that responds generously when it sees someone in need. No questions are asked. Things are seen as they really are and the response fits the seeing. God responds to our request for wisdom in the same way. There is nothing complicated about it. He responds 'simply, openly, frankly, sincerely', motivated 'solely by his desire to bless'. In the same way, when teaching about exercising the gifts of the Spirit in Romans 12, Paul says that the gift of contributing to the needs of the poor is to be done in 'simplicity, sincerity, [with] mental honesty' and 'an openness of heart',[9] leading to generous gifts.

So how do we know that desire for heavenly treasure drives us and we are serving God not money? By having simple rather than evil eyes – eyes that see the suffering of the poor in all its stark reality, and hands that respond generously without quibbling. For those of us who have been blessed with access to the Western way of life, with its high income and excellent benefits, it means living more simply so that others may simply live. The extent of our commitment to overcoming poverty is the evidence of the extent of our commitment to God and his heavenly kingdom.

---

9. Quotes in this paragraph are from J. H. Thayer (ed.), *A Greek–English Lexicon of the NT*, 4th ed. (Edinburgh: T. & T. Clark, 1901), p. 57.

Throughout the ages there have been some who have given up their source of income entirely in order to follow Jesus the Messiah. Some of the first apostles were in this category. But even they needed shelter, food and clothing! In Matthew 6:25–34, Jesus reassures such disciples that God will provide for the needs of those who commit to living for the kingdom. Towards the end of this section, Jesus returns to the fundamental motivation for living and tells his disciples that living for food and clothing, which represent all material things, is characteristic of nations who have not been privileged like Israel to receive God's revelation of the true motivation for living. As we have seen, Israel knew what it meant to be called into risky living in obedience to God, with what was done for the poor and marginalized as the test of obedience. What Jesus does is to fulfil this OT principle when he calls his disciples from all nations to 'seek first [the Father's] kingdom and his righteousness' (Matt. 6:33).

What does it mean to seek first our Father God's kingdom and righteousness/justice? In the OT heritage Jesus was consciously fulfilling, God's kingdom meant his rule over the whole earth, over his covenant people Israel by electing grace and the prospect of his rule over a renewed Israel that would be joined by an innumerable host from all the nations. God delegated his rule or dominion over the earth to human beings at the beginning, but we rejected the privilege of ruling under God's authority and sought to rule in independence of our creator. The result was a world full of injustice and violence. God then took steps to re-establish his rule by saving a people from slavery and giving them a small part of the earth that they could rule over under his authority. Like their original human ancestors, these people also rejected God's authority and eventually managed the estate God had given them in a way totally contrary to God's revealed will. The result was an Israel and a Judah filled with idolatry, injustice and violence. In his incarnate Son, Jesus the Messiah, God found a man totally subject to his rule and prepared to give himself up to death as a sacrifice for his fellow human beings. Having been raised from the dead, the power of the Holy Spirit was unleashed in the world to recreate sinful human beings from within so that by faith in Jesus they would have renewed hearts from which would spring transformed minds, reconstructed wills and redirected passions. These are the people who make the kingdom or rule of God the highest priority in their lives.

The character of the kingdom that is to dominate the lives of Jesus' disciples is defined by its righteousness/justice. First, in the context of the whole story of God's revelation, righteousness means being in a right relationship with God. From the time of Abraham it was clearly revealed that the only way to be right with God is to believe that he can deal with the sin that alienates us from him. Secondly obeying his revealed will is the basis for living out God's righteousness/justice in our lives. For anyone to claim to be justified by faith while manifesting no just action in their lives is impossible. Justification without the fruit of just living is impossible. Just living is the only conclusive proof of justification.[10] Thirdly just living involves personal and social ethics. In this sense, making righteousness/justice our priority means living personally in a way consistent with God's justice and seeking to ensure that others also live in a way consistent with his justice. Biblically, poverty is seen primarily as the result of injustice. So seeking justice for the poor must feature somewhere in our quest for righteousness/justice in this third sense.

In a sermon by Christopher J. H. Wright on Matthew 6:33, which I was privileged to hear in September 2005 at the time when the 'Make Poverty History Campaign' was at its height in the United Kingdom, his application contained the following challenge:

> The Bible does not make a great distinction between kindness, generosity and compassion, on the one hand, and righteousness and justice, on the other. In . . . Matthew 6:1–4, Jesus calls giving of alms to the needy acts of righteousness. So it is a justice issue. The simple fact is that justice for the poor and needy is one of the defining marks of biblical righteousness.
>
> Psalm 112 is written about the person who fears the Lord:
>
> He is generous and lends freely and conducts his affairs with justice.
>
> *He has scattered abroad his gifts to the poor, and his righteousness endures for ever.*
> (Ps. 112:5, 9)
>
> Proverbs says:
>
> *The righteous person cares about justice for the poor, but the wicked have no such concern.*
> (Prov. 29:7)
>
> Nine years ago, John Stott preached from [this] text [in Proverbs] . . . He said that when, at the age of 42, he first confronted that text and was struck by it, he realised

---

10. The more traditional term 'sanctification' could have been used here, where it would be clear that justification and sanctification can be theoretically distinguished but are also inseparable.

that by the standard of that text he was a wicked person. The righteous care about justice for the poor; the wicked have no such concern.[11]

To whom do we entrust the good news of the kingdom? (Matt. 7:6–11)

Jesus' saying about giving what is sacred to dogs or pearls to pigs is unquestionably the most obscure saying in the sermon on the Mount. Commentators agree that 'what is sacred' and 'pearls' must mean the good news of the coming of the kingdom in Jesus Christ. They also agree that Jesus' hearers would immediately have thought of Gentiles in the reference to 'dogs' and 'pigs'. However, most argue that the 'dogs' and 'pigs' cannot mean 'Gentiles' here, but those who have viciously rejected the gospel. Contrary to the teaching in verses 1–4 about not judging, disciples should judge that some people are so hardened that they do not deserve to be offered the gospel any more. But there is a way of understanding the passage that can accommodate the understanding of 'dogs' and 'pigs' as 'Gentiles'. According to this interpretation the passage is not about proclaiming the gospel or evangelism but about whom we trust to bring in the kingdom. From this perspective verse 6 is not an exception to the non-judgmentalism taught in verses 1–4 or an obscure isolated saying but an introduction to the teaching on prayer in verses 7–11. Disciples are not to entrust the sacred task of bringing in the kingdom into the hands of the Gentile powers represented by Rome in the time of Jesus.[12]

History amply testifies to the truth of our Lord's warning if this is the right understanding of the passage. When Christians have entrusted the coming of the kingdom to the powers of this world, the sacred pearl has all too quickly been trampled underfoot. Rather we should look to our heavenly Father to bring in the kingdom. He is the one we can trust, so, with zeal and passion, we should ask of him, seek him and knock at his door. What we desire of him are the good things of his kingdom and righteousness/justice, and we ask, seek and knock in the knowledge that he wants to give us these good things. In Luke, this greatest gift God can give his suppliants is equated with the Holy Spirit (Luke 11:13). This is appropriate because it is only in the power of the

11. Sermon preached at All Soul's, Langham Place, London, 18 Sept. 2005. The sermon can be found at <http://www.allsouls.org/ascm/allsouls/static/sermons/515d364f0616762c28177b1b81521a1950350144.kont?pageNo=3>, accessed 26 Mar. 2008.
12. Stassen and Gushee, *Kingdom Ethics*, pp. 457–458.

Holy Spirit that we are able to make any significant change in people's lives, whether it be bringing people under the rule of Jesus (evangelism) or seeing justice established in the way people relate to one another (social action).

This understanding of Matthew 7:6–11 does not support the sort of pietism that says Christians should have nothing whatsoever to do with the powers of this world as represented by state governments and international intergovernmental and commercial institutions. What it says to us is that as we work for the kingdom and justice, it is not the powers of this world we trust to bring in the kingdom but the power of God. A Christian involved in advocacy with and on behalf of the poor will achieve nothing significant for the kingdom of God without the dependence on God that is the fountainhead of prayer.

The Golden Rule (Matt. 7:12)

With this verse Jesus brings the section of the Sermon on the Mount that began in 5:17 to a close. The section began with his declaration that he had not come to 'abolish the Law or the Prophets' and ends with a brief statement that 'sums up the Law and the Prophets'. This statement also clearly sums up the essence of Jesus' fulfilment of the OT revelation. The brief statement is an ethical statement showing that Jesus' focus in the whole sermon has been on the way we relate to each other as human beings. It is a statement of how kingdom people are meant to live in the world: *In everything do to others what you would have them do to you.*

The following testimony from Ray Bakke is a powerful illustration of the meaning of the Golden Rule for rich Western and Westernized evangelical Christians who are suspicious of those who spend their lives in service of the poor:

> Some years ago I was in the Billy Graham Centre, Wheaton College – a real evangelical Mecca. The discussion of the day was how can that college do urban ministry. A very wealthy man in the meeting said, 'Ray, when you and others talk about urban evangelism I get very excited. When you talk about social justice, social action, social involvement I get very, very nervous. Isn't that the social gospel?' I could feel myself becoming a little defensive but for some reason I didn't respond at that level. I said, 'Clayton, where do you live?' Well, Clayton lives in a very nice suburb. I asked him why he lived there and he told me all the good reasons: good schools, safe, clean, nice housing value. Finally I said, 'Clayton, if anybody believes in the social gospel it's you. Every reason you've given me for where you live is a social reason. You've committed your whole life to it. If those systems weren't working you

> wouldn't live there.' I said, 'You are living where those systems function . . . Me and my church live where those systems don't function . . . We are trying hard to bring our social systems up to what you already enjoy.' It's hypocritical for people to say I shouldn't be concerned about these things when they have already committed their whole life and family to live where those systems exist.[13]

The conclusion of the Sermon on the Mount

Jesus' final word in the sermon is that only those who do 'the will of my Father who is in heaven' who will enter into the eternal kingdom on the Day of Judgment (7:21). What Jesus does in the sermon is give us the ultimate revelation of the Father's will for the way we should live as human beings that is going to be used to determine whether we belong in God's kingdom or not. Our ability to live the sermon comes from God, but living it is the only proof that we have been touched by grace.

Therefore, in the context of this book there can be only one conclusion: those who claim to follow Christ and belong to the kingdom of God for whom overcoming poverty is not a priority are making an empty claim. They would do well to attend to the foundations on which they are building their lives (Matt. 7:24–27).

---

13. Testimony taken from J. Steward, *Biblical Holism* (Melbourne: World Vision, 1994), p. 153.

11. WHAT JESUS IS DOING: THE WORK OF THE HOLY SPIRIT

Jesus is not dead. When he appeared in glory to John on the island of Patmos, he reassured him, saying, 'I am the Living One; I was dead, and behold I am alive for ever and ever' (Rev. 1:18). Since his ascension, the reality of this indestructible life of Jesus and the significance of his redemptive work as the incarnate Son of God is mediated to humankind by the Holy Spirit. In the context of this book, the question is how what Jesus is now doing through the Holy Spirit is linked to the old and new covenant teaching about power and poverty. In brief, does the Holy Spirit have a role in overcoming poverty?

As already stated, the gift of the Holy Spirit is the greatest blessing resulting from the life and work of our Lord Jesus. John the Baptist had said that while he baptized with water, Jesus would baptize with the Spirit. Just before his ascension, Jesus affirms the truth of John's prophecy 'He [Jesus] will be baptize you with the Holy Spirit and with fire' (Matt. 3:11; cf. Mark 1:8; Luke 3:16; Acts 1:5). This baptism with the Holy Spirit was not the beginning of the Spirit's work in creation or in human lives, but it did mark a new phase in the history of redemption. To appreciate what was new, we need to understand something of the Spirit's work under the old covenant.

The Spirit in the Old Testament

After the reference to the Spirit, or Wind, of God hovering over the dark chaos of the original creation poised to execute the creative Word in Genesis 1:2, there is silence about the Spirit until the period of the exodus. When the time came to build the tabernacle, the design for which had been revealed to Moses, the Lord said about Bezaleel, the chief craftsman, that he had 'filled him with the Spirit of God, with skill, ability and knowledge in all kinds of crafts – to make artistic designs for work in gold, silver and bronze, to cut and set stones, to work in wood, and to engage in all kinds of craftsmanship' (Exod. 31:3–5; cf. 35:31). The Spirit is here associated with an unusual creative ability in handling different materials that was required to execute the purpose of God.

The next reference is in Numbers 11. The complaints of the Israelites led Moses to despair of carrying the burden of leadership. God instructed him to choose seventy elders to whom God would give a portion of the Spirit in Moses so that the burden of leadership would be shared. The elders were chosen and commanded to appear before the tabernacle, where the transference of a portion of the Spirit who rested on Moses was evidenced by their prophesying. There is no description of this 'prophesying', but it was clearly some sort of ecstatic utterance not normal to the elders. In this case, it was an isolated incident because none of the elders ever prophesied again (Num. 11:25b). Two of the seventy elders who had been summoned had remained in the camp, but they also started prophesying where they were. When Joshua heard this, he wanted to stop them, but Moses said, 'Are you jealous for my sake? I wish that all the LORD's people were prophets and that the LORD would put his Spirit on them!' (Num. 11:29). This sentiment is echoed in Joel's prophecy, fulfilled at Pentecost (Joel 2:28–29; Acts 2:17–21).

The link between the Spirit and prophetic utterance is affirmed in the mysterious story of Balaam. Despite the fact that he was not an Israelite, Balaam clearly had some knowledge of the Lord God of Israel. It was the Lord who told him not to go and curse Israel when he was first invited to do so by Balak, the king of Moab. It was also the Lord who told him to go with Balak's messengers when he was invited the second time – and then, in the incident of the talking ass, condemned him for going. The key to this mystery is probably Balaam's desire to use his prophetic gift for material gain. He was the archetype of those who use their religious expertise to make money.[1] However,

1. Peter warns against 'the way of Balaam son of Beor, who loved the wages of wickedness' (2 Pet. 2:15).

Balaam was thwarted by the Spirit of God, who took charge of his tongue and used him to proclaim blessings on Israel instead (Num. 24:2). The case of Balaam shows clearly that there is no essential link between prophetic utterance from the Spirit of God and the state of the prophet's heart in relation to God. This is true although a general outpouring of the Spirit of prophecy is seen in Joel as a mark of the messianic age and affirmed by Peter in his sermon on the day of Pentecost (Joel 2:28–32; Acts 2:16–21).

In Judges, it is the Spirit coming upon various leaders who gives them the ability to lead the way in rescuing the people of God from oppression. The Spirit came upon Othniel, Gideon, Jephthah and Samson (Judg. 3:10; 6:34; 11:29; 13:25; 14:6). The presence of the Spirit in the lives of these leaders was generally evidenced in their ability to muster, inspire and lead the people of Israel against superior enemy forces. In the case of Samson, it was seen in his superhuman strength in resisting the Philistine oppressor. Of the four, only Gideon explicitly opposed the idolatry that was the cause of Israel's oppression by the Midianites, although even he succumbed to idolatry after his victory (Judg. 8:25–27). In Jephthah and Samson's case, the presence of the Spirit does not seem to have had much influence on their profoundly flawed characters. They may have been inspirational leaders, but they were not good men.

In the transition from the era of the judges to the monarchy in the time of Samuel, the Spirit of the Lord was also active. Samuel tells Saul that one of the confirmations of his call to the monarchy would be the coming of the Spirit of prophecy upon him. This happened when he joined a procession of prophets in Gibeah. Prophesying in this case, as with the elders in the time of Moses, was a type of ecstatic utterance during which the prophets lost control of their mind and will. Saul also experienced the type of Spirit influence experienced by the judges, which enabled him to inspire Israel to resist the oppressive challenge of Nahash the Ammonite. Saul, because of his pride and disobedience, also knew that the Spirit of God had left him, for he became tormented by an evil spirit from the Lord (1 Sam. 10:10; 11:6; 16:3). Saul is a truly tragic figure. He was torn apart by his knowledge of what was of God and his insatiable pride and jealousy. That the Bible says God was responsible for the evil spirit that tormented Saul is perhaps another way of saying that to know God's will and yet resist it and pander to the lust of the flesh will certainly disturb the mind's balance.

As the Spirit of God departed from Saul, Samuel was instructed to anoint David as the next king of Israel. David was the first leader of Israel for whom the act of anointing was linked with the coming of the Spirit. 'So Samuel took the horn of oil and anointed him in the presence of his brothers, and from that day on the Spirit of the LORD came upon David in power' (1 Sam. 16:13). As with the judges and Saul, the Spirit enabled David to unite and lead the people of Israel to freedom from their enemies. But unlike his predecessors, there was a strong religious and moral emphasis to David's leadership. He decisively led the people back to God and believed that the presence of the Spirit in his life, evidenced by the success of his kingship, was in some way linked to his heart obedience to the law of God. This became clear to him in his bitter repentance when convicted by Nathan the prophet of his terrible sin in causing the death of his faithful servant Uriah, so that he could cover up his adultery with Uriah's wife Bathsheba. He verbalized this bitter experience in Psalm 51:

> Against you, you only, have I sinned
>   and done what is evil in your sight . . .
> Surely I was sinful at birth,
>   sinful from the time my mother conceived me.
> Surely you desire truth in the inner parts;
>   you teach me wisdom in the inmost place.
>
> Cleanse me with hyssop, and I will be clean;
>   wash me, and I will be whiter than snow . . .
> Hide your face from my sins
>   and blot out all my iniquity.
>
> Create in me a pure heart, O God,
>   and renew a steadfast spirit within me.
> Do not cast me from your presence
>   or take your Holy Spirit from me.
> Restore to me the joy of your salvation
>   and grant me a willing spirit, to sustain me . . .
> You do not delight in sacrifice, or I would bring it;
>   you do not take pleasure in burnt offerings.
> The sacrifices of God are a broken spirit;
>   a broken and contrite heart,
>   O God, you will not despise . . .
> (Ps. 51:4–17)

David was convicted of his sin by the inspired words of Nathan, his prophet friend and adviser. The relationship between the groups of ecstatic prophets we get a glimpse of here and there in the OT and the sort of prophet represented by Nathan, or the great writing prophets like Isaiah or Jeremiah, is unclear, but the utterances of both types are attributed to the Spirit of God.

Azariah, Jehaziel and Zechariah, who prophesied in the reigns of Asa, Jehosaphat and Joash respectively, did so because the Spirit of the Lord came upon them. In the time of Nehemiah, when the Jewish remnant came to renew their covenant with God, the Levites, recounting in prayer their sad history of disobedience, said that God had admonished them by his Spirit through his prophets. Paul, in dialogue with the Jewish leaders in Rome, said, 'The Holy Spirit spoke the truth to your forefathers when he said through Isaiah the prophet' that they would not accept the truth even when they heard it (Acts 28:25; 2 Chr. 15:1; 20:14; 24:20; Neh. 9:30).

As well as being inspired by the Spirit, the prophets whose writings complete the OT also say a number of things about the Spirit. In Isaiah, the Spirit is closely associated with various representations of the Messiah. In Isaiah 11, where the Messiah is a descendant of David ('A shoot will come up from the stump of Jesse', v. 1), there is a wonderful description of the messianic reign, with the Spirit of the Lord at its heart:

> The Spirit of the LORD will rest on him –
>   the Spirit of wisdom and of understanding,
>   the Spirit of counsel and of power,
>   the Spirit of knowledge and of the fear of the LORD –
>   and he will delight in the fear of the LORD.
>
> He will not judge by what he sees with his eyes,
>   or decide by what he hears with his ears;
> but with righteousness he will judge the needy,
>   with justice he will give decisions for the poor of the earth.
> He will strike the earth with the rod of his mouth;
>   with the breath of his lips he will slay the wicked.
> Righteousness will be his belt
>   and faithfulness the sash round his waist.
>
> The wolf will live with the lamb,
>   the leopard will lie down with the goat,
> the calf and the lion and the yearling together;
>   and a little child will lead them.
> The cow will feed with the bear,
>   their young will lie down together,
>   and the lion will eat straw like the ox.
> The infant will play near the hole of the cobra,
>   and the young child put his hand into the viper's nest.

They will neither harm nor destroy
on all my holy mountain,[2]
for the earth will be full of the knowledge of the LORD
as the waters cover the sea.
(Isa. 11:2–9)[3]

What is most striking about this Spirit-endowed kingly Messiah is the peaceableness of his kingdom. He will establish justice for the poor and needy, which will inevitably mean judgment on their wicked oppressors. But he will not establish his rule with the usual violence of the kings of this world, because he comes armed with words, not weapons of mass destruction. His power will be embodied by the Spirit of wisdom, understanding, counsel, knowledge and fear of the Lord. The result of his peace coming among human beings will be peace in the whole creation. The cessation of human violence will mean that the whole of nature will cease to be 'red in tooth and claw'.[4]

In Isaiah 32, the complacent rich women of Jerusalem are told to prepare for the judgment coming upon their luxurious living, which is the fruit of injustice. They will be taken as slaves into exile, and their beautiful homes, pleasant fields and fruitful vines are going to be laid waste, because their enjoyment of them has been bought with the blood of the poor. Where they once enjoyed their unjust luxury will remain a wasteland until

the Spirit is poured upon us from on high,
and the desert becomes a fertile field,
and the fertile field seems like a forest.
Justice will dwell in the desert
and righteousness live in the fertile field.
The fruit of righteousness will be peace;
the effect of righteousness will be quietness and confidence for ever.
(Isa. 32:15–17)

---

2. Cf. Isa. 2:2, where 'the mountain of the LORD's temple' (Mount Zion) will become the focus for the peaceful unification of all the nations. Here 'it is not that peace is restricted to one place but rather that a dramatic change has come over the whole earth. When the true order of creation is restored the whole earth is the Lord's hill, indwelt by his holiness' (J. A. Motyer, *The Prophecy of Isaiah* [Leicester: IVP, 1993], p. 125).
3. This wonderful passage was quoted in full on p. 91. It bears repeating.
4. Alfred Tennyson, *In Memoriam*, §56.

Here the Spirit brings life where there was only death and destruction. Again the link between the establishment of justice and righteousness in human society and the establishment of a comprehensive peace that includes the whole of creation is emphasized.

In the first Servant Song in Isaiah 42, the Lord says he will put his Spirit on the Servant, with the result that he 'will bring justice to the nations' (Isa. 42:1). What is the 'justice' (*mišpāṭ*) this Spirit-endowed Servant will bring? Motyer says that

> in the light of the foregoing court scene it must retain its meaning of 'judgment at law', the result of the trial between the Lord and the idols. The servant thus carries to the world the message that there is only one God. Another shade of meaning follows automatically: 'justice' summarizes those things which the Lord has authoritatively settled. It is a summary word for his revealed truth . . . and its requirements . . . The third appropriate shade of meaning is the righting of wrongs, the establishment of a just order.[5]

The striking thing about this prophecy is the totally counter-cultural way in which the Servant is going to establish justice. Rejecting the pomp and violence of worldly rule, his focus will be on restoring the weak and vulnerable. It is unsurprising that Matthew believed that the way Jesus behaved was a fulfilment of this prophecy (Matt. 12:17–21).

In Isaiah 59:21, the new covenant, the Spirit and the Messiah are brought together. The covenant is that God's '"Spirit who is on you [the Messiah], and my words that I have put in your mouth will not depart from your mouth, or from the mouths of your children [Hebrew 'seed'], or from the mouths of their descendants from this time on and for ever," says the LORD.' Through the Spirit or life of God with which the Messiah is endowed, he is able to give birth to children of God. This process will go on from one generation to the next and be evidenced by the passing on of the words or truth of God.

Finally in Isaiah we have the passage Jesus explicitly applied to himself when he spoke in his home synagogue in Nazareth at the beginning of his public ministry:

> The Spirit of the Sovereign LORD is on me,
> because the LORD has anointed me
> to preach good news to the poor.

5. Motyer, *Prophecy of Isaiah*, p. 319.

He has sent me to bind up the brokenhearted,
 to proclaim freedom for the captives
 and release from darkness for the prisoners,
 to proclaim the year of the LORD's favour . . .
(Isa. 61:1–2)

As with David, the anointing of the Messiah signals the coming of the Spirit to equip for the great task of ruling. The fundamental characteristic of this rule is that it is going to be good news to the poor. The poor 'are the downtrodden, the disadvantaged, those held back from progress and amelioration by people or circumstances'.[6] When the prophecy was uttered, the poor were the exiled Jews brought low because of their sin. In the light of Jesus, they have become representative of all that is wrong with human life on earth. The 'poor' must not be spiritualized or literalized. Poverty as both a literal and spiritual condition is ultimately undesirable to God, although ironically a consciousness of poverty is essential in order to benefit from the Spirit-endowed Messiah. But there will be no poverty in any sense in his glorious kingdom (Isa. 65:17–25).

For some reason that remains a mystery there is no mention of the Spirit at all in Jeremiah. He has a clear vision of a new covenant in which the law of God would be written on the heart of his people, but there is no mention of the Spirit having a role in this wonderful new phase of God's redemptive action (Jer. 31:31–34). It is left to Ezekiel, in whose prophesying the Spirit has a central role (e.g. Ezek. 3:12, 14, 24; 8:3; 11:1; etc.), to attribute heart obedience to God's will to the action of the Spirit: 'I will give you a new heart and put a new spirit in you; I will remove from you your heart of stone and give you a heart of flesh. And I will put my Spirit in you and move you to follow my decrees and be careful to keep my laws' (Ezek. 36:26–27).

Finally there is a reference to the Spirit in Zechariah that makes a very significant point about the presence of the Spirit in the life of God's people. Zerubbabel was faced with the very difficult task of rebuilding the temple in Jerusalem after the Babylonian exile. Not only were the remnant who returned economically and socially weak, but they carried the weight of the sin and glory of their predecessors. The Lord's word of comfort was, 'Not by might nor by power, but by my Spirit' (Zech. 4:6). What is done by the Spirit cannot be claimed as a human achievement. This did not mean that Zerubbabel and his workers were to down tools, but it was an encouragement to them to offer their weakness to God so that they could rejoice at seeing what the Spirit of God

6. Ibid., p. 500.

can do with weakness. The presence of the Spirit points to the unpredictable divine plus that happens when we come to the end of our feeble human attempts to control what happens in the future. The Zechariah passage also reminds us that the action of the Spirit is contrary to the way of the world that so often entails physical violence.

The Spirit in the Gospels and Acts

The atmosphere of the birth narratives and the account of John the Baptist's ministry are consistent with what was said about the Spirit in the OT. It is as if the Spirit of prophecy that had been dormant since Malachi was stirring again. Elizabeth and Zechariah are filled with the Spirit, and Simeon is moved by the Spirit, to make their prophetic utterances (Luke 1:41, 67; 2:25). John the Baptist is filled with the Spirit from birth and speaks powerful prophetic words (Luke 1:11). Jesus is conceived by the Spirit and symbolically filled by the Spirit at his baptism; he is led by the Spirit to be tempted and then, full of the Holy Spirit, launches into his healing and teaching ministry (Matt. 1:18, 20; 3:16; cf. Mark 1:10; Luke 3:22; John 1:32; Matt. 4:1; cf. Mark 1:12; Luke 4:1, 14). That he was able to drive out demons by the Spirit of God is clear evidence, according to Jesus, that the kingdom of God had come upon his generation (Matt. 12:28). But the influence of the Spirit was not to be limited to Jesus and his actions.

First the twelve apostles and then seventy-two disciples are sent out with power to proclaim the coming of the kingdom and to prove it by healing and casting out demons. The disciples were also warned that doing kingdom work would lead to persecution such as being hauled before the courts; they were assured that when this happened, there would be no need to be overawed, because the Holy Spirit would give them the right words to say (Matt. 10:20; cf. Mark 13:11; Luke 12:12). In teaching his disciples about prayer, Jesus assures them that the heavenly Father will give the Holy Spirit to all who ask for him (Luke 11:13). Finally the risen Jesus commissions his disciples to go and make disciples of all nations and baptize them in the name of the Father, the Son and the Holy Spirit (Matt. 28:19).

Given this background in the Synoptic Gospels, what happens in the book of Acts is what we would expect. The risen Lord Jesus tells his disciples to wait in Jerusalem for an outpouring of the Holy Spirit that will equip them to be his witnesses in Jerusalem, Judea, Samaria and to the ends of the earth. Then, on the day of Pentecost, the Spirit comes upon all 120 disciples and they begin to praise God ecstatically for his mighty works. Amazingly the ecstatic praise is understood by the visitors to Jerusalem from many countries in their own languages. Peter, now endowed with power to speak, explains that Joel's prophecy that all God's people, young and old, male and female, would be filled with the Spirit of prophecy is being fulfilled. He then goes on to declare that Jesus, who was killed by the Romans at the instigation of the Jewish authorities, has risen from the dead and has thus been declared Lord and Messiah. It is because he is the Messiah that Jesus has poured out the Spirit. Thousands believe, repent and are baptized in water and the Spirit (Acts 1:2, 5, 8; 2:4, 17, 33, 41).

Peter and the apostles were also given the power to heal, and the dramatic healing of a lame beggar at one of the gates to the temple leads to their arrest and appearance before the Jewish high court. There they fearlessly give a good account of themselves in fulfilment of Jesus' promise of the presence of the Spirit when such events occur. Persecution eventually caused the church to be scattered; everywhere they went they gossiped the good news of Jesus and the church continued to grow (Acts 3:1–10; 4:1–22; 8:4).

It is unnecessary to tell the whole story of Acts at this point. Enough has been said to prove the validity of the common evangelical understanding that it is a work of the Holy Spirit to empower the disciples of Jesus against all odds to be effective verbal witnesses to the good news that he is the Saviour of sinners who trust in him. The evidence evinced so far also supports the emphasis among Pentecostals and charismatics that the verbal witness is bolstered by signs and miracles. But that is not the whole story.

The fact that all the disciples on the day of Pentecost were given the gift of prophetic utterance by the Spirit was no guarantee of their entrance into the kingdom of God. The fact that the Twelve and the seventy-two had healed the sick and cast out demons, and that the apostles also did so after Pentecost, was no guarantee that their names were written in heaven (Luke 10:20). I have already referred to the sobering words of Jesus at the end of the Sermon on the Mount:

> Not everyone who says to me, 'Lord, Lord,' will enter the kingdom of heaven, but only he who does the will of my Father who is in heaven. Many will say to me on that day, 'Lord, Lord, did we not prophesy in your name, and in your name drive out demons and perform many miracles?' Then I will tell them plainly, 'I never knew you. Away from me, you evildoers!' (Matt. 7:21–23)

What the OT concludes about the new messianic covenant and the testimony of Jesus witness loudly that even powerful verbal testimony backed by signs and wonders is not the deepest and most significant work of the Holy

Spirit. The deepest work of the Spirit is the inward renewal of sinful people so that the will and purpose of God comes to be written on their hearts.

This is an emphasis that needs to be heard among the Pentecostals and charismatics who lay a heavy emphasis on 'power evangelism' and 'power encounters' with the spirits of darkness. It is not to deny the reality of the powers of darkness or that some people may be commissioned to reveal the power of the risen Lord through signs and wonders. However, the crucial test of such manifestations of extraordinary power is whether they cause people to repent, believe in Jesus for forgiveness and begin to follow him along the path of servanthood. Sadly this is often not the case. As John Stott has written:

> I confess to being frightened by the contemporary hunger for power, even the quest for the power of the Holy Spirit. Why do we want to receive power? Is it honestly power for witness (as in Acts 1:8), or power for holiness, or power for humble service? Or is it in reality a mask for personal ambition, a craving to boost our own ego, to minister to our self-importance, to impress, to dominate or to manipulate?[7]

There is no doubt that Jesus was primarily concerned with heart renewal, which means renewal at the source of what we are. He proclaims the pure in heart blessed and his strategies for kingdom living, as we have seen, have to do with what flows out of us towards God and our fellow human beings. What we really value is what we value in our heart. In his conflict with the religious authorities, he emphasizes that what we say and do are merely the evidence of what we are in our hearts. So if evil words and evil deeds flow from our hearts, the most important thing that can be done to any human being is to effect a change for good at this most profound level of our being. It is doing the will

---

7. Quoted in Keith J. Hacking, *Signs and Wonders Then and Now: Miracle-Working, Commissioning and Discipleship* (Nottingham: Apollos, 2006), p. 17. This book is a thorough analysis of the teaching of Matthew, Mark and Luke-Acts on the place of signs and wonders in the ministry of Jesus and his disciples in view of the claims of Third Wave theology. Hacking's conclusion is that 'the models of discipleship presented to us in the Synoptic Gospels and Acts do not encourage the expectation that the manifestation of signs and wonders is to be considered normative in the experience of all who seek, through the leading and presence of the Spirit in their lives, to follow Jesus and to model his teaching and example' (p. 258). I have also dealt with this issue from a very different angle in Dewi Hughes with Matthew Bennett, *God of the Poor: A Biblical Vision of God's Present Rule* (Carlisle: Authentic, 2006), ch. 5, 'The King's War', pp. 108ff.

of the Father in heaven from the heart that ensures entrance into the kingdom.[8] The most eloquent Spirit-induced witnessing and the most powerful miracles cannot ensure entrance into the kingdom.

In the Gospel of John, the renewal of the heart is strongly linked to the work of the Spirit that flows from what Jesus achieved through his death and resurrection. The new birth, which Jesus tells Nicodemus is necessary for entrance into the kingdom of God, is a work of the Spirit inextricably linked to faith in his sacrificial death (John 3:3–16).[9] Later, when he was teaching in the temple court at the time of the Feast of Tabernacles, Jesus 'said in a loud voice, "If anyone is thirsty, let him come to me and drink. Whoever believes in me, as the Scripture has said, streams of living water will flow from within him."' Looking back, John says that 'by this he meant the Spirit, whom those who believed in him were later to receive. Up to that time the Spirit had not been given, since Jesus had not yet been glorified' (John 7:37, 39).

It is inconceivable that the streams of living water flowing from people renewed in their hearts by the Holy Spirit means good words and miraculous actions only. Everything John records of the teaching of Jesus supports that what is meant here are the whole range of genuine acts of love and compassion that flow from the hearts of the disciples. That will mean sharing the good news and doing miraculous deeds, but the obedient heart from which those flow is crucial. It is for this profound heart renewal that Jesus went through the horrors of his final humiliation on the cross on his way to glorification. And it is in the outflow of this sincere inward goodness born of God that the deepest work of the Spirit is seen.[10]

The emphasis on word evangelism or signs and wonders may have obscured it, but this deeper work of the Holy Spirit can clearly be seen even in Acts. It is seen, for example, in the type of community born as a result of proclaiming that Jesus is the Messiah. It is said, 'All the believers were one in heart

---

8. Cf. Hacking, *Signs and Wonders*, pp. 101, 125, 204.
9. John 3:3 has one of the few references in John to the kingdom of God. His preferred term for the same reality is 'eternal life'. In John 3:14–15, faith in the crucified Son of God is said to be the way to eternal life. So new birth by the Spirit and faith in the crucified Son of Man must be aspects of the same reality.
10. The record of the conversation between Jesus and the Samaritan woman at the well of Sychar prepares the way for this dramatic declaration. John teaches on the Spirit as Paraclete in chapters 14–16, and what is said in those passages about the Spirit, truth and conviction of sin is consistent with what has already been said in John 3 and 7.

and mind' (Acts 4:32). At the deepest level of their being they believed that they belonged to each other. Because they belonged to each other they loved each other, and this was manifested in the way in which they shared with each other. 'No-one claimed that any of his possessions was his own, but they shared everything they had' (v. 32b). Oriented in their hearts towards God and his kingdom through their faith in Jesus born of the Spirit, they became indifferent to seeking their security in possessions. Love for God and others became the passion of their hearts, so they were free to share. Our Western and majority-world materialistic Christianity often implies they were a bit crazy and that their 'communist' experiment was doomed to failure. But they were clearly more consistent with the teaching of Jesus than we often are in all our pretended wisdom. Surely love cannot characterize a Christian community where some starve while others live in the lap of luxury? That is what the infant church understood only too well. To belong to Jesus, to be reborn by the Spirit, is incompatible with enjoying an excess of this world's goods while brothers and sisters starve. So, with simple and sincere hearts, the early church just shared what they had.

The close link between the work of the Spirit and the creation of a sharing community is powerfully illustrated in the tragic story of Ananias and Sapphira. They saw the honour in which the community held those who were prepared to sell property in order to share the proceeds with their poor brothers and sisters in the Christian community. So they decided to sell some property; but, rather than give all the proceeds of the sale to the apostles to share among the poor, they kept a portion for themselves while giving the impression that they were sharing it all. Their deception was miraculously discerned by Peter, who charged Ananias with lying to the Holy Spirit and Sapphira with testing the Holy Spirit (Acts 5:3, 9). With the church in its infancy it was vital that the community of love and trust the Holy Spirit was creating should not be violated by hypocrisy and lies. Like Achan, early in the story of the conquest of Canaan, Ananias and Sapphira paid dearly for their breach of fellowship.

Also significant is that as the community expanded and became international, the Spirit prompted care for the poor internationally. When some prophets from the Jerusalem church visited the growing church in Syrian Antioch, one named Agabus 'stood up and through the Spirit predicted that a severe famine would spread over the entire Roman world' (Acts 11:28).[11]

---

11. This is a fascinating example of Spirit-led disaster mitigation, which reminds us of Joseph's divine wisdom in saving Egypt and the surrounding peoples from the worst effects of famine.

Interestingly the response of the Christian community in Antioch was to make a collection for their brothers and sisters in Jerusalem that was delivered by Barnabas and Saul/Paul. Overcoming poverty was clearly on the Spirit's agenda for the early church.

The sanctifying work of the Spirit

This is where we come at last to the theological root of overcoming poverty. It is neither irreverent nor an exaggeration to say that God's biggest challenge has been to undo the rebellion against him in human hearts, from which flow all manner of evils, including poverty. Everything that has been said thus far about the history of redemption ultimately focuses on whether human beings can be changed from within. Everything God has revealed about just governance and just law avails nothing if people continue to be bad. Even those who have known nothing of God's revelation have been able at times to devise good systems of government and good laws, but these have also failed because it takes good people to make good principles of governance and good laws a reality.

In the case of Israel, even God's amazing act of rescue from slavery in Egypt and the miraculous preservation of the people in the wilderness did not prove enough of a moral incentive to obey God's just law. Even some of those who had been freed from Egyptian slavery rebelled against God and the just government he was establishing through Moses. So it is not at all surprising that subsequent generations who were encouraged to obey God by remembering how the nation was rescued from slavery took no notice and rejected God's way. In the end, Israel and Judah lost the land God had given them, because they were behaving just like other nations who had known nothing of God's redemption and rule. It was precisely when this was happening that the prophets spoke about a new covenant that would mean heart renewal, and a Suffering Servant Messiah who would die for the iniquities of his people.

As we have already seen, the atoning death of Jesus dealt with the sin that was an impossible barrier to our being indwelt by God. That Jesus has borne our punishment and fully assuaged the wrath of God makes it possible for those who are 'in Christ' to be indwelt by the Holy Spirit. In the context of historical theology, especially in the Protestant tradition, the last sentence has touched upon the doctrines of 'justification' and 'sanctification'. In the Protestant tradition, justification is the act of God in declaring a sinner justified and forgiven through faith in the merits of Jesus' atoning death. Sanctification is the process of making the justified sinner more and more like Jesus. In bringing the sinner to the point of justifying faith, and in the process of sanctification, the Holy Spirit is believed to be the critical divine agent who makes both the act and the process possible.

It is important to emphasize the role of the Spirit in both justification and sanctification, because there are dangers in distinguishing too radically or in merging these two aspects of salvation. On one hand, it was the genius of the Protestant Reformation to rediscover the wonder of a salvation that is a free gift of God's grace through Jesus Christ. But even Paul had to deal with the question of whether those who believe can continue to sin with impunity, because their salvation does not depend on anything they do (Rom. 6:1–23).The danger here is antinomianism or libertinism. On the other hand, not to make a distinction creates the danger of making salvation a matter of what we do. The danger here is legalism.

Unfortunately it is not enough to give the Holy Spirit a key role in the life of faith to avoid these dangers. For example, many enthusiastic groups have equated the presence of the Holy Spirit with a whole range of subjective experiences, but that has not preserved them from slipping into an arid legalism. Different groups have focused on the presence of the Spirit when Christians make prophetic utterances, fall over, speak in tongues and so on. Tragically for such groups, when the spectacular manifestations cease, as they inevitably seem to do, these people are left with a range of external practices they adopted when enthusiasm was at its height. Ironically many groups who have begun by extolling freedom in the Spirit have ended up in deep legalism, being preoccupied with what can and cannot be eaten or drunk, dress code, the structure of meetings and what can or cannot be done on certain days.

For those who focus on justification, libertinism is an ever-present danger. Where the focus is heavily on converting the lost, there is always a danger of neglecting or demoting what happens after conversion. This must at least be a part of the explanation why many so-called evangelicals live as if their faith has little to do with the way they live day to day, and is probably a key reason why rich evangelicals are able to enjoy more and more of this world's goods, while millions of their brothers and sisters in Christ are suffering the most abject poverty. The antidote to both tendencies is a biblical understanding of what the Holy Spirit does in the life of a believer.

In his first letter to the Thessalonian church, Paul reminds them that his gospel came to them 'not simply with words, but also with power, with the Holy Spirit and with deep conviction' (1 Thess. 1:5). When Paul spoke about Jesus, some Thessalonians were convinced that what he was saying about him, his sacrificial death on a cross and his resurrection were the truth and that the appropriate response was to believe and commit their lives to Jesus. That this happened was evidence of the work of the Holy Spirit. In 1 Corinthians, Paul is really making the same point when he says that 'no-one can say "Jesus is Lord," except by the Holy Spirit' (1 Cor. 12:3). What is in view here is the inward renewal and cleansing of the new covenant through the agency of God's Spirit prophesied by Ezekiel and affirmed by Jesus in his message to Nicodemus about the new birth (Ezek. 36:25–27).[12] This is clearly a subjective experience signalling a move from what was once described as a 'historic' faith to a 'saving' faith. Jesus and his historic actions are no longer known simply as historic facts but as events that mean forgiveness and cleansing. The strange warming of John Wesley's heart as he realized that Jesus had died for him will be the common experience of the myriad that will one day surround the throne of the Lamb. As Oliver O'Donovan states, 'first, the Spirit makes the reality of redemption, distant from us in time, both *present* and *authoritative*'.[13] It may be right to insist that justification is a forensic declaration of freedom from guilt that is totally independent of anything we can do, but it can be efficacious for me as a sinner only when I experience it as a reality in my own life through the power of the Holy Spirit. Added to this, what Jesus has done cannot be divorced from who he is. As his redemptive acts become a present reality to us, he becomes our Lord and Master. But, as already stated, to acknowledge Jesus as Lord is evidence of the presence of the Holy Spirit.

Not only is the Spirit active in our incorporation into the new covenant, but, as O'Donovan states, he also, secondly, 'evokes our *free* response to this reality as moral agents'.[14] Not only are we reborn by the Spirit, but we also live by the Spirit. Our initial cleansing and acceptance of the lordship of Jesus is the beginning of a lifelong process of cleansing and living under his lordship. The removal of guilt is the entrance into a life of diminishing the power of sin in us.[15] In Pauline terms, although we have been raised with Christ into newness of life, we are still in 'the flesh' and in 'the world' that is under the domination

---

12. I am convinced by D. A. Carson that this passage in Ezekiel and the following chapter's vision of the valley of dry bones is the most likely background to what Jesus says to Nicodemus; see *The Gospel according to John* (Leicester: IVP, 1991), pp. 191–198.
13. Oliver O'Donovan, *Resurrection and Moral Order: An Outline for Evangelical Ethics*, 2nd ed. (Leicester: Apollos, 1994), p. 102.
14. Ibid.; his italics.
15. This is beautifully expressed in couplets from Havergal's hymn 'Rock of Ages' ('Be of sin the double cure; / Cleanse me from its guilt and power') and Wesley's hymn 'O for a Thousand Tongues' ('He breaks the power of cancelled sin, / He sets the prisoner free').

of its evil prince. The wonder of the Spirit-induced appropriation of the fruit of redemption is that the indwelling Spirit enables us to choose freely the good and reject the acts of the flesh, the world and the devil. By faith we have been freed to love through the power of the Spirit at work within us (Gal. 5:6).

In both Galatians and Romans, where he speaks of living a life of love, Paul reminds us that to love our neighbour as ourselves is the essence of the moral law (Gal. 5:13–14; Rom. 13:8–10). We have seen something of what it might mean to do this in considering the teaching of the Sermon on the Mount. The significance of having the Holy Spirit indwell us is that living this life of love can become a reality. We can bear the fruit of the Spirit in our lives and become loving, peacemaking, patient, kind, good, faithful, gentle and self-controlled people. Here we are at the fountainhead of Christian care for the poor. It is inconceivable that anyone indwelt by the Spirit can be indifferent to the suffering poor. Living by the Spirit is the most powerful engine for overcoming poverty.

To tear apart the act of justification and the process of sanctification results from a neglect of the doctrine of the Holy Spirit. Accepting the love of God in the sacrificial death of Jesus the Messiah and living a life of love in grateful response are works of the one Holy Spirit. As O'Donovan states, 'The work of the Spirit as "witness" to the objective deed of God in Christ, and his work as "life-giver" who restores freedom and power to mankind enthralled, are not two distinct works but one. For man's thrall is precisely that he has lost touch with reality.'[16]

This work of the Holy Spirit must also be seen in the context of the overall mission of the triune God in his creation that has been so drastically marred by human rebellion. The final aim is a new humanity recreated in the image of Jesus Christ. As Paul says in 2 Corinthians:

> Now the Lord is the Spirit, and where the Spirit of the Lord is, there is freedom. And we, who with unveiled faces all reflect the Lord's glory, are being transformed into his likeness with ever-increasing glory, which comes from the Lord, who is the Spirit. (2 Cor. 3:17–18)

Ralph Martin comments that Paul's discussion in this passage

> reaches it's peak with . . . [the] asseveration that believers in Christ live in a new age where 'glory' is seen in the Father's Son and shared among those who participate in

---

16. O'Donovan, *Resurrection and Moral Order*, p. 109.

> that eon. It is the Spirit's work to effect this change, transforming believers into the likeness of him who is the groundplan of the new humanity, the new Adam, until they attain their promised destiny as 'made like to his Son' (Rom 8:29) and enjoy the full freedom that is their birthright under the terms of the new covenant.[17]

Our striving for holiness by the Spirit is not just an individual struggle, but an expression of the groaning of the whole creation reaching out towards the perfection that will be realized when Jesus will be revealed in all his glory at the second advent (Rom. 8:19–23). As Paul says, God has 'put his Spirit in our hearts as a deposit, guaranteeing what is to come' so that 'by faith we eagerly await through the Spirit the righteousness/justice for which we hope' (2 Cor. 1:22; Gal. 5:5). This brings us to the final section in our consideration of how we understand the process of overcoming poverty in the light of Jesus.

---

17. Comment on 2 Cor. 3:18, in Ralph P. Martin, *2 Corinthians*, Word Biblical Commentary on CD-ROM, vol. 40 (Dallas, Tex.: Word, 1998).

12. WHAT JESUS IS GOING TO DO: THE FINAL JUDGMENT

What is in view here is the role of Jesus in the end towards which our earth and its people are moving. Our triune 'God's plan for the universe is to bring about, through Jesus Christ, a transformed creation wholly governed by God, from which all evil and suffering will be banished and in which God will live with redeemed humanity for ever.'[1] The question is how this eschatological hope that includes the end of poverty influences the way in which we approach poverty now.

The Christian hope

The hope of a transformed creation is a living hope, because, as we have seen in the previous section, it can be experienced as a present reality as Jesus and his achievements become a living reality in our lives through the indwelling of the Holy Spirit. This explains why it is so often described in the NT as something radically 'new'. It is new wine that cannot possibly be contained in old

---

1. This statement comes from the Statement of Faith of Tearfund, a UK Christian relief and development organization. See <http://www.tearfund.org/Admin/Statement+Of+Faith.htm>, accessed 31 Mar. 2008.

wineskins, a new covenant in the blood of Jesus, a new commandment to love one another as we have been loved, a new life and a 'new way of the Spirit' as contrasted with the 'old way of the written code' (Mark 2:21–22; cf. Matt. 9:16–17; Luke 5:36–39; 22:20; 1 Cor. 11:25; 2 Cor. 3:6; Heb. 8:8, 13; 9:10, 15; 10:20; 12:24; John 13:34; Acts 5:20; Rom. 6:4; 7:6).

'If anyone is in Christ', says Paul, 'he is a new creation; the old has gone, the new has come!' (2 Cor. 5:17). There is a growing consensus that the phrase 'he is a new creation' should be translated 'there is a new creation'. The emphasis is not on the subjective experience of the new birth but on entering into the new age that has been inaugurated by Jesus.[2] The implication is that the old regime of the world, the flesh and the devil has been broken so that those who trust in Jesus participate in this new situation that is so radically new that it can be described as a new creation. But if this is in some ways a present reality in the believer's experience of life, it remains primarily an eschatological hope. As Hebrews says, 'In putting everything under [Jesus], God left nothing that is not subject to him. *Yet at present we do not see everything subject to him*' (Heb. 2:8bc; my italics). In fact, the more we think about the world in which we live, and not least about the billion people who live in terrible poverty, the more true it is that everything is not subject to him. The more we think about the suffering and injustice in our world, the more our hearts echo the cry of the penultimate sentence of the Bible to put an end to this terrible injustice and pain: 'Amen, come Lord Jesus' (Rev. 22:20b).

---

2. Martin comments on 2 Cor. 5:17, '*en Christō, kainē ktisis* in this context relates to the new eschatological situation that has emerged from Christ's advent.

'Tannehill (*Dying and Rising*, pp. 68–69) has correctly noted that this eschatological change must not be transformed into a subjective one, as if it were merely the individual's viewpoint that had changed. "If Paul were only able to assert that 'for me' or 'in my view' the old world has passed away, he would not be able to argue as he does that others may no longer judge him according to the flesh, for they would be as entitled to their viewpoint as he is to his. Paul's own argument in these verses depends upon the reality of the presence of the new aeon."

'*ta archaia*, "the old order" means the old world of sin and death, but also the realm of the *sarx*, "flesh." It has "gone" in the sense that its regime is broken, though its power remains (Gal 5:16–21, 24) to be neutralized in Christ' (Ralph P. Martin, *2 Corinthians*, Word Biblical Commentary on CD-ROM, vol. 40 (Dallas, Tex.: Word, 1998).

The 'general eschatology' branch of systematic theology deals with the events anticipated at the end of the world before it becomes apparent to everyone who has ever lived that Jesus is indeed Lord of all. The order of events and the precise nature of some of them have been hotly disputed, and some emphases do have implications for the way poverty is approached before the end. So it may be impossible in this context to ignore entirely the differences between Christians, and evangelicals in particular. But we shall focus on what commands general agreement.

First Jesus will be revealed in all his glory. Secondly there will be a general resurrection. All human beings will be raised bodily from the dead. Thirdly there will be a general judgment of all, with Jesus as judge. Fourthly those who are considered worthy will be welcomed into eternal life, while those who are unworthy will be consigned to eternal punishment. Finally the worthy will live for ever with God in a transformed heaven and earth, where righteousness/justice will reign.[3]

Although the Christian tradition has expressed belief in a general resurrection at the consummation throughout its history, because of the influence of Greek philosophy, especially Plato and Platonism, the eschatological focus has often been on the personal immortality of the soul rather than on the resurrection. For example, it is striking how brief or even silent many of the key Protestant creeds are on the resurrection. A renewed interest in the general resurrection among evangelicals, particularly since the 1950s or so, is to be welcomed. Theologians have been right to emphasize that the Christian hope is not the immortality of a disembodied soul but of embodied persons living eternally in the presence of God in a transformed earth. This new appreciation of the resurrection hope is consistent with a greater appreciation of our embodied existence in our present fallen world.

For example, although John Stott does not make a direct link between what he believes to be the true biblical view of human beings and the belief that our glorified state is going to be embodied, his definition of a human being as 'a body-soul-in-a-community' displays a marked increase in appreciation of embodiment.[4] There is no need to prove influence here. Both the rediscovery

---

3. The following passages represent something of the biblical foundations for these beliefs: Matt. 16:27; 19:28; 24:30; 25:31–33; Phil. 2:10; John 5:19; 1 Cor. 15; Rom. 8:23; 1 Cor. 6:13; Acts 24:15; 10:42; 17:31; John 6:39–40; Matt. 8:12; 9:47; 22:1–14; Luke 16:23; 2 Thess. 1:5–10; Heb. 12:26–28; Isa. 65:17–25; 2 Pet. 3:13; Rev. 21:1 – 22:5.

4. John Stott, *Issues Facing Christians Today*, rev. ed. (London: Marshall Pickering, 1990), p. 19.

of the wonder of the resurrection hope and the emphasis on embodiment as essential to our human being belong to the rediscovery of a more biblical doctrine of humankind. If even in glory people cannot be divided into body and soul on the basis of a presumption that the soul is superior, then, surely, it is unbiblical to divide people in this way in our present fallen world. Stott's conclusion from this biblical view of what we are as human beings still stands:

> Therefore if we truly love our neighbours . . . we will be concerned for their total welfare, the well-being of their soul, their body and their community. And our concern will lead to practical programmes of evangelism, relief and development. We shall not prattle and plan and pray, like that country vicar to whom a homeless woman turned for help . . . She later wrote this poem:
>
> I was hungry
> and you formed a humanities group to discuss my hunger.
> I was imprisoned
> and you crept off quietly to your chapel and prayed for my release.
> I was naked
> and in your mind you debated the morality of my appearance.
> I was sick
> and you knelt and thanked God for your health.
> I was homeless
> and you preached to me of the spiritual shelter of the love of God.
> I was lonely
> and you left me alone to pray for me.
> You seem so holy, so close to God
> but I am still very hungry – and lonely – and cold.[5]

Continuity between the present and the eschatological future?

Some theologians have gone further than seeing an affirmation of the value of physical existence in our fallen world, because the final state will be an embodied state. They have argued that the good done now in this world will be preserved in the post-resurrection state, and that believing this is an important motivation for social action. Commenting on Revelation 21:24, which he describes as a 'neglected scripture', Peter Kuzmic states that

5. Ibid.

> there is some continuity between the present and the future age. While not underestimating the biblical emphasis on discontinuity between this age and the next, we must at the same time point out the biblical teaching that there is some continuity as well. We are to work for a better world here and now, knowing that everything that is noble, beautiful, true and righteous in this world will somehow be preserved and perfected in the new world to come. In this sense, indifference to culture and social involvement, the fatalistic attitude that washes its hands of the world letting it go to further and expected corruption is irresponsible, and a betrayal of entrusted stewardship. This . . . is often true of much popular evangelical eschatology.[6]

This illuminating passage from Kuzmic comes from the published version of a paper he presented at the very significant Consultation on the Relationship between Evangelism and Social Responsibility (CRESR) held in Grand Rapids in June 1982 and jointly sponsored by the Lausanne Committee for World Evangelization and the World Evangelical Fellowship.[7] This view found its way into the official report of the consultation, but the way the author presents it suggests it was the view of only a minority of the participants at the conference. However, it was recognized that 'those who have the assurance of this continuity find it a strong incentive to social and cultural involvement'.[8]

---

6. Peter Kuzmic, 'History and Eschatology: Evangelical Views', in Bruce J. Nicholls, *In Word and Deed: Evangelism and Social Responsibility* (Lausanne Committee for World Evangelisation / World Evangelical Fellowship, 1985), p. 151.
7. Now known as the World Evangelical Alliance.
8. *Lausanne Occasional Papers, No. 21, Grand Rapids Report – Evangelism and Social Responsibility, An Evangelical Commitment* (Lausanne Committee for World Evangelisation / World Evangelical Fellowship, 1982), pp. 40–42. Tim Chester, in a chapter entitled 'Eschatology and the Transformation of the World: Contradiction, Continuity, Conflation and the Endurance of Hope', to be published in a book of papers arising mainly from the Tyndale Fellowship triennial conference in July 2006, refers to a number of evangelical authors who have advocated this view: A. A. Hoekema, *The Bible and the Future* (Exeter: Paternoster, 1978), pp. 39–40; see also p. 287; Kuzmic, 'History and Eschatology', p. 152; Vinay Samuel and Chris Sugden, 'Evangelism and Social Responsibility – A Biblical Study on Priorities', in Nicholls, *In Word and Deed*, p. 208; Vinay Samuel and Chris Sugden, 'God's Intention for the World', in Vinay Samuel and Chris Sugden (eds.), *The Church in Response to Human Need* (Oxford: Regnum, 1987), p. 146; Maurice Sinclair, 'Development and Eschatology', in Samuel and Sugden, *Church in Response*

The implication of what Kuzmic and others have claimed, in the context of this book, is that to believe that the fruit of our social actions on behalf of the poor will survive the general resurrection is a great incentive to action on behalf of the poor now. But this belief has been questioned on two fronts.[9] In the first place, questions have been asked about what precisely of what we do in this world is preserved in the world to come that can act as an incentive. This is a question of the nature of the continuity, if it exists, between this world and the next. For example, if someone gives their life in obedience to Jesus Christ to a successful political campaign on behalf of poor people who are being unjustly treated, will anything of that campaign and its consequences be preserved after the resurrection? In a state of perfection, where poverty will be inconceivable and justice will be totally ascendant, it is difficult to conceive that even the memory of a particular attempt to overcome poverty and establish justice could be that significant. It would be hard to hang on to a memory of a struggle for justice in a totally just situation that has no prospect whatsoever of being lost. This hardly seems that significant an incentive for action on behalf of the poor.

In the second place, even if a number of recent authors have testified to the significance of the belief in continuity for their commitment to social action, it is questionable whether this has been a particularly significant motivation historically. Motivation is a very complex topic and key motivations for social action may sometimes be inexplicit; but on the explicit level, eschatological continuity seems to be insignificant historically. William Wilberforce and his evangelical associates were explicitly motivated by the doctrinal conviction that all human beings are created in the image of God, by compassion towards the slaves in their unjust suffering, by guilt because the British state was complicit in the slave trade, and not by the belief that their actions would be significant in their post-resurrection lives. The testimony of the founders of what have become significant evangelical aid and development organizations such as World Vision in the US and the Tearfund family of agencies that originated

---

to Human Need, p. 171; Miroslav Volf, *Work in the Spirit* (New York: Oxford University Press, 1991), pp. 89–102.

9. For fuller critiques of this view, see Tim Chester, *Mission and the Coming of God: Eschatology, the Trinity and Mission in the Theology of Jürgen Moltmann*, Paternoster Theological Monographs (Carlisle: Paternoster, 2006). The main critic of this continuist view is Stephen N. Williams, *The Limits of Hope and the Logic of Love: Essays on Eschatology and Social Action* (Vancouver: Regent College Publishing, 2006).

in the UK witness to the lack of this eschatological motivation. Dr Bob Pierce, the founder of World Vision, seems to have been motivated by simple compassion after the pattern of Jesus generated by personal contact with children in need. The same was true for George Hoffman, Tearfund's first director. In a report of Tearfund's first four years, he said:

> After travelling across the Bengal plain to the border river, we returned to Calcutta physically and emotionally exhausted. Turning to my Bible, I continued from where I left off the day before, in the fourteenth chapter of St Matthew's Gospel: 'When Jesus came ashore he saw a great crowd; his heart went out to them, and when he realised how hungry they were he turned to the disciples and said, "Give them something to eat yourselves."' I realised afresh that the compassion of Christ and the command of Christ have not changed. His heart still goes out and His disciples must still obey His command to feed the hungry and care for the needy.[10]

Eternal rewards

To doubt whether belief in the preservation in the world to come of what we do for the poor in this world as a motivation for social action is not to say that eschatological hope is irrelevant to our actions in this world. Biblically the continuity between this life and the next is probably best expressed through the clear teaching on rewards. It seems obvious that what we do now is going to be recognized and rewarded.

We are assured in the NT that God is pleased with our deeds of love and kindness to the poor. Paul, when thanking the Philippian Christians for the gifts they had sent him, says that they were 'a fragrant offering, an acceptable sacrifice, pleasing to God' and that they would be credited to their account (Phil. 4:17–18; cf. Acts 10:4; Heb. 13:16; 1 Pet. 2:5). This concept of an account with God originates with the Lord Jesus himself, as seen in his teaching about heavenly as opposed to earthly treasure. As we have already considered in the Sermon on the Mount, this teaching about building heavenly capital is closely linked to showing generosity towards the poor. It is the generous eye that can resist the temptation to horde treasure in this world and thus build an incorruptible treasure with God.

This teaching is expanded in the application of the parable of the shrewd manager in Luke 16. Here the foresight of an unprincipled manager in

---

10. Cited in Mike Hollow, *A Future and a Hope* (Oxford: Monarch, 2008), p. 29.

preparing for his future comfort in this world is used as an illustration to encourage the followers of Jesus to exercise foresight in preparing for the next. There is a clear suggestion of doing things in this world that have a clear bearing on what will happen in the next. If we use the wealth at our disposal to bless the poor, then, when we die and wealth loses all meaning, there will be those who will welcome us with gratitude into our eternal dwelling. The reverse of this process is forcefully underlined in the parable of the rich man and Lazarus that follows on the heels of this parable.

What is taught in these parables is not that heaven is a reward for righteous acts, but that righteous acts are a response to the coming of the rule of God in Jesus the Messiah. It is Jesus who neutralizes the power of worldly security and the lust for power and recognition that is deeply embedded in our hearts. Making good use of the resources he gives follows our recognition of *who* he is. This is what enables us to see money as relatively unimportant in the total scheme of things, although the way we handle this 'little' thing is what proves whether we are worthy of the reward of really significant things that will last for ever (Luke 16:10–12).

That it is our attitude to Jesus which is the key to our heavenly reward is crucial to a correct understanding of the parable of the talents and the section on the sheep and the goats in Matthew 25. The servant who failed to make anything of the talent the master had given him failed because of his low opinion of the master. '"Master," he said, "I knew that you are a hard man, harvesting where you have not sown and gathering where you have not scattered seed. So I was afraid and went and hid your talent in the ground"' (Matt. 25:24–25). By contrast, the other servants had every confidence in the master and were happy to do everything in their power to make the most of what he had entrusted to them. They probably got a reward that was way beyond their expectation, but they would have been content with 'Well done, good and faithful servant!' (Matt. 25:21, 23). In the dramatic picture of the judgment in Matthew 25, which uses the homely image of a shepherd dividing the sheep from the goats, Jesus welcomes the 'sheep' into eternal life because of their kindness to him as embodied in his despised and often persecuted followers. The common understanding that this account of the judgment teaches that kindness to the poor in general is the condition of our entrance into eternal life is clearly erroneous. 'The least of these brothers of mine' (Matt. 25:40) can mean only the followers of Jesus. It is self-sacrificial identification with the least of Jesus' disciples, with whom he identifies himself totally, that is proof of a desire to be with Jesus eternally.

The most extended discussion of the hope of bodily resurrection is found in 1 Corinthians 15. What prompted Paul's discussion was a report that some in the church in Corinth were denying the general resurrection of the dead (1 Cor. 15:12). He counters this belief by arguing that to dismiss bodily resurrection as the Christian hope means dismissing the significance of Jesus' resurrection as well. For Paul, the resurrection of Jesus is the foundation of the believer's hope in an afterlife. The resurrection of Jesus is the proof of our resurrection. So Jesus is the first fruit of the age of the fully renewed humanity that will be revealed in the last day (1 Cor. 15:20, 23).[11] In that day, 'just as we have borne the likeness of the earthly man, so shall we bear the likeness of the man from heaven' (1 Cor. 15:49). Not only do we not see everything subjected to Jesus in the present age, but we are also continually faced with the reality of death. Our lives and everything we do are overshadowed by death. But the resurrection of Jesus is the guarantee that death has been conquered and that we shall one day share in his victory:

> For the trumpet will sound, the dead will be raised imperishable, and we will be changed. For the perishable must clothe itself with the imperishable, and the mortal with immortality. When the perishable has been clothed with the imperishable, and the mortal with immortality, then the saying that is written will come true: 'Death has been swallowed up in victory.'
>
> 'Where, O death, is your victory?
> Where, O death, is your sting?'
>
> The sting of death is sin, and the power of sin is the law. But thanks be to God! He gives us the victory through our Lord Jesus Christ. (1 Cor. 15:52–57)

Paul then concludes with an admonition that this glorious vision of the conquest of death in our resurrection as believers should motivate us into action now in this present age: 'Therefore, my dear brothers . . . always give yourselves fully to the work of the Lord, because you know that your labour in the Lord is not in vain' (1 Cor. 15: 58).

The crucial phrases in this exhortation are 'of the Lord' and 'in the Lord'. If by the Spirit's strength we do those things that are the Lord's will, and if we exert ourselves to serve God and neighbour, because of our relationship with the Lord we shall become more and more like him – and this will make our lives full of purpose, because in the resurrection we shall be completely transformed into his imperishable likeness.

---

11. The same concept is expressed by the use of 'firstborn' in other places (see Col. 1:18; cf. Rom. 8:28; Rev. 1:5).

The reward in 1 Corinthians 15 is the resurrection life itself. Earlier in the letter Paul had spoken of a reward following faithful service. In Jesus Christ, God provides a wonderful foundation for our lives as believers upon which we have a responsibility to build. The best building materials we can use, which are compared to gold, silver and costly stones, are materials that will survive the fire of God's judgment. Writing about the individual believer, Paul says, 'If what he has built survives, he will receive his reward. If it is burned up, he will suffer loss; he himself will be saved, but only as one escaping through the flames' (1 Cor. 3:14–15). But what is this reward that good builders on the foundation of Jesus Christ are to receive? We are not told. Even in this, Paul follows the example of the Lord himself. Jesus says that the reward in heaven of those who are persecuted is great; that those who do their acts of righteousness/justice simply for God's glory will be rewarded: 'Anyone who receives a prophet because he is a prophet will receive a prophet's reward' (Matt. 10:41). But we are never told precisely what the reward is (Matt. 5:12; 6:1, 4, 6, 18; cf. Mark 9:41; Luke 6:35).

The parable of the talents in Matthew 25 suggests that there is a gradation in rewards that is linked to the original endowment of the disciple. Both the five-talent and two-talent servant achieved a 100% increase in their original endowment. In Paul's terms, they both built with good materials and were both given much greater responsibility, having been faithful in relatively few things. But their greater responsibility was determined by what they did with what they had been given in the first place, and not by the effort employed in managing their master's property.[12] Those who have made little – or have had little opportunity to make something – of the endowment of saving grace will inherit eternal life. They will share in the perfectly ordered transformed earth where there will be no death, mourning, crying or pain, because they will be living with God. For us who live in this present world of death, mourning, crying and pain to be allowed entrance to a world without everything that sours our life now seems like an incomparably glorious reward. But this glorious reward, it seems, is only the bottom rung of the heavenly ladder of rewards. My imagination, I confess, fails me at this point. But what is clear is that the

12. Cf. Luke 12:48b, where Jesus teaches that there will be grades of punishment, depending on knowledge of a master's will – or the lack of it. The punishment of the servant who knows the master's will but does not do it will be heavier than that of the servant who does not know, because 'from everyone who has been given much, much will be demanded; and from the one who has been entrusted with much, much more will be asked'.

quality of eternal bliss is going to be affected by what we do with the grace we have received.

During the period of the Great Awakening in Wales, 'adorning our profession' was a popular way of describing what was expected of those who come to faith in Jesus. Like an undecorated Christmas tree, our salvation is complete in Jesus but we can decorate the tree with our own works of service. To keep the tree analogy, and to be more biblical, when we believe, we are like a new branch that has sprouted from the trunk of a vine. As long as that branch remains in the vine it will come to be adorned with leaves and fruit.

A great deal has been written already about this fruit of the Spirit or the works Jesus expects his followers to produce in obedience to his Father's will. These works of love towards fellow human beings are characterized by downward mobility. Our own well-being is not their motivational centre, but the well-being of others in need around us. The reason for expressing it in this way is in order to emphasize that the poor themselves can and do show love. From my experience, the godly poor always think of those who are in need around them although they may be in great need themselves. They are never just objects of charity. Since they are not focused on themselves, they can be simultaneously the receivers and dispensers of charity. So it is not those who are rich in resources only that can express love to the poor. The poor themselves can and do express love to the poor and often do so far more significantly than those who have abundant material resources. What grace expects is a loving response consistent with what we have been given by God. In Jesus' estimation, the poor widow who gave the tiny amount that was all she had gave more than those who gave much but had plenty left in their coffers (Luke 21:1–4). Unimaginable enhanced bliss awaits those who invest their material resources in love, joy, peace, patience, kindness, goodness, faithfulness, gentleness and self-control. This could be a powerful motivation for overcoming poverty, but maybe the greatest eschatological motivation of all is the prospect of hearing the Master saying to us on Judgment Day, 'Well done, good and faithful servant! You have been faithful with a few things; I will put you in charge of many things. Come and share your master's happiness!' (Matt. 25:21, 23).

The judgment of the unrighteous/unjust

Thus far the focus has been on the eschatological judgment of the righteous, but what about the judgment of the unrighteous? Jesus leaves us in no doubt that there will be those who will be excluded from the joy of the new heaven and earth as a result of his judgment. They are represented in the teaching of Jesus in Matthew's Gospel by (1) the foolish virgins whom the bridegroom says he never knew (Matt. 25:12), (2) the wicked, worthless servant who is thrown outside 'into the darkness, where there will be weeping and gnashing of teeth' (v. 30), and (3) the 'goats' on his left who as the cursed are sent away 'into the eternal fire prepared for the devil and his angels' (v. 41).

The emphasis in these passages is that exclusion from the glorious kingdom of God is dependent on how people regard Jesus. For the foolish virgins, the coming of the bridegroom did not have enough of a priority in their lives, so that they were fully prepared for it; the wicked servant did nothing with the master's property, because he had a low opinion of him; the 'goats' showed their low regard of the Son of man by ignoring and neglecting his followers. What we make of Jesus has become the standard that will be applied in the final judgment. As Paul said to the Athenians, God 'has set a day when he will judge the world with justice by the man he has appointed [and] has given proof of this to all men by raising him from the dead' (Acts 17:31). This is why there is relatively little talk of the judgment and wrath of God in the Gospels. There the emphasis is on Jesus as good news.

This is powerfully illustrated by the fact that when Jesus applied Isaiah 61:1–2 to himself in the synagogue in Nazareth, he ended his reading with 'to proclaim the year of the Lord's favour' (Luke 4:19), leaving out the next phrase in Isaiah, which is 'and the day of vengeance of our God'. We continue to live in the day of grace inaugurated by Jesus, and the door is still open to anyone to find forgiveness and a new life in the Spirit in him, but the Gospels and the rest of the NT make it very clear that one day this glorious door of mercy will be closed and everyone will have to face Jesus as judge.

Those who have not availed themselves of the mercy of God in Jesus will be punished by being excluded from the kingdom of God for the evil they have done. These evil deeds are described in various places in the NT and seem to be a characteristic of the very earliest Christian writings (see especially Mark 7:21–22; Rom. 13:13; 1 Cor. 5:10–11; 6:9–10; 2 Cor. 12:20; Gal. 5:19–21; Col. 3:5, 8; 1 Tim. 1:9–10; 2 Tim. 3:2–5; Titus 3:3; 1 Pet. 4:3; Rev. 22:15). These lists contain reference to a number of vices that are unquestionably the causes of poverty. In Romans 1, the consequence of rejecting the authority of the Creator, even before the final judgment, is that the wrath of God can be seen in the fact that such rebellious people's lives are filled with 'every kind of wickedness, evil, greed and depravity' and so on (Rom. 1:29). 'Wickedness' in the NIV translates *adikia*, which is one of the main generic terms for 'sin' in the NT. Often translated 'unrighteousness', *adikia* 'describes more forcibly the outwardly visible characteristics of that which stands under the power of sin'.[13] 'Wickedness' is therefore a valid translation because the emphasis is on evil human actions that can be seen in the way human beings deal with each other as a result of rejecting God.

The danger of greed

Greed (*pleonexia*) is listed as an example of *adikia* in Romans 1 and features in most of the other lists of sins/wickednesses in the NT. Jesus lists it among those evil things that come out of the heart of people which defiles them (Mark 7:22; cf. Matt. 20:15).

> In the catalogue of vices *pleonexia* is a mark of a life which lacks knowledge of God (Rom 1:29; 1 Cor 6:10f) . . . Where the bond between creature and creator is severed, human society falls into disorder. The man who no longer has his goal and fulfilment in God seeks fulfilment in himself, his possessions and acquisitiveness. Ultimately he makes himself into an idol that strives to subject everything to itself. For that reason Colossians 3:5 identifies covetousness with idolatry . . . In Matthew 6:24 and Luke 16:13 Mammon . . . , wealth itself is an idol which holds in its sway the man who seems to control it.[14]

It is unsurprising that Jesus strongly warns us about the danger of this wickedness.[15] When a man comes asking for mediation between him and his brother in a dispute over an inheritance, Jesus can see that the request does not flow from a heart desire for justice but for possessions. So he says to all who are within earshot, 'Watch out! Be on your guard against all kinds of greed [*pleonexia*]; a man's life does not consist in the abundance of his possessions' (Luke 12:15).He then goes on to underline his warning with the parable of the rich fool. In a simple story, Jesus captures the tragedy of a life possessed by possessions. The selfishness, anxiety, lost opportunities to bless God and neighbour are followed by utter futility, because the rich fool is called to account before he has the opportunity to enjoy his possessions, and, since he

---

13. Colin Brown (ed.), *The New International Dictionary of New Testament Theology* (Carlisle: Paternoster, 1971), vol. 3. pp. 575–576.
14. Ibid., vol. 1, p. 138.
15. Contrast this with the defense of greed by Ivan Boesky (later convicted of insider-trading charges) at the University of California at Berkeley's School of Business Administration on 18 May 1986, where he said, 'Greed is all right, by the way. I want you to know that. I think greed is healthy. You can be greedy and still feel good about yourself.' This speech was paraphrased in the film *Wall Street*.

has nothing invested with God, is banished from his presence. As Paul says, the greedy will not inherit the kingdom of heaven, and greed is one of the reasons why the wrath of God is coming (1 Cor. 6:9; Eph. 5:5; Col. 3:5).

However, the greedy, before they appear before God's judgment seat, are able to cause an enormous amount of damage to many people. Greed is one of the key causes of poverty in the world today, as it was in the times of the OT prophets. In condemning Jehoiakim for his greed, Jeremiah contrasts him with his righteous father, Josiah:

> 'Woe to him who builds his palace by unrighteousness,
> his upper rooms by injustice,
> making his countrymen work for nothing,
> not paying them for their labour.
> He says, "I will build myself a great palace
> with spacious upper rooms."
> So he makes large windows in it,
> panels it with cedar
> and decorates it in red.
>
> Does it make you a king
> to have more and more cedar?
> Did not your father [Josiah] have food and drink?
> He did what was right and just,
> so all went well with him.
> He defended the cause of the poor and needy,
> and so all went well.
> Is that not what it means to know me?'
> declares the LORD.
> 'But your eyes and your heart
> are set only on dishonest gain [Septuagint: *pleonexia*],
> on shedding innocent blood
> and on oppression and extortion.'
> (Jer. 22:13–17)[16]

Jehoiakim was typical of people throughout human history with power. Because his heart was dominated by greed, he used his power to satisfy his lust

---

16. Cf. Ezek. 22:27: 'Her officials within her are like wolves tearing their prey; they shed blood and kill people to make unjust gain [Septuagint: *hopōs pleonexia pleonektōsin*].'

for possessions even to the point of unjust exploitation and murder. Power in the hands of the greedy means poverty. In a world where 20% of its people own 80% of its wealth, it is difficult to avoid the conclusion that the 20% are greedy.

Tragically even rulers who have set out to do good for their people often end up using their power to increase their own wealth and the wealth of their family, and will stop at nothing, even murder, oppression and extortion, to enrich themselves. Sadly Africa seems to have been cursed with a surfeit of such rulers since independence from colonial rule. In the West, with its long tradition of democratic government, most rulers are unable to siphon off government funds to satisfy their personal greed, but rather become slaves of national greed. The US for example claims to be the most generous country on earth with its aid to poor countries. This claim is correct if the total amount given in aid is compared to that of other countries; but if the amount of aid as a proportion of the total wealth of the country is measured, then the US comes out as number 22 out of the 22 richest countries in the world.

Some time ago the rich countries promised to give 0.7% of their gross domestic product (GDP) in official government aid. By this standard the US comes out as the meanest country, with its proportion of 0.15% of GDP for aid in 2005. Yet in the same year, the US spent 4.06% of GDP on the military,[17] representing twenty-four times as much as that spent on aid.[18] The huge military spend is publicly justified more often than not in the name of national security and the defence and propagation of freedom and democracy around the world. Much less profile is given to national interests, but one suspects that it is the dominant factor.

It is not anti-US to enquire how the richest and most powerful nation in the history of the world uses its wealth in a world of massive poverty. One hundred years ago Britain would have been the subject of the enquiry, and one hundred years hence, if the Lord tarries, it will probably be China. As Jesus says, 'from the one who has been entrusted with much, much more will be asked' (Luke 12:48). Neither does the focus on the US here excuse those of us who belong to other rich nations and classes that are just as culpable before God.

No Western ruler could survive by reducing the living standards of the wealthy in their countries for the sake of the poor in other countries – or even

17. This represents $420.7 billion, which was 43% of the total spent on the military worldwide in 2005!

18. This is the most generous way of interpreting the figures. Some would argue that the US spends forty times more on the military than they do on aid.

in their own countries![19] Those who have many of this world's goods, and this includes individuals and large commercial interests, generally speaking expect more and more and look to the leaders elected with their support to deliver the increase. So the political leaders of the rich countries, even if they advocate a just sharing of goods, are beholden to those who want to preserve their own advantage and are not free to make their altruism a reality.

The reason for focusing on greed in people with power is not to divert attention from the danger of greed for every human being, but to highlight the fact that when the powerful are greedy, many people are oppressed, exploited and impoverished. But pandering to greed either by commission or omission is a dangerous activity, because greedy people have no place in the kingdom of God. In the judgment, the poor will be vindicated in the condemnation and eternal exclusion of the greedy from God's presence. Remembering this should be a comfort and strength to those who are striving for justice for the poor while waiting for the Lord's coming to judge. In so many situations, greedy people frustrate attempts to overcome poverty: corrupt rulers and officials who divert into Swiss Bank accounts money meant for the poor, businessmen who exploit desperate workers to maximize profits, moneylenders who enslave people with usurious interest rates, politicians who pander to powerful business interests rather than courageously cancelling poor-country debts or increasing the level of aid. As I write these words, the scandal of the President of the World Bank arranging for his girlfriend to receive a $200,000 annual salary is ongoing. In defence of his action, he said there were around a thousand employees in the World Bank receiving a similar salary. That is a total annual salary of $200 million for about 10% of the employees of a bank specifically set up to help the poor!

That the greedy are able to succeed with impunity can be deeply frustrating for those seeking justice for the poor. This frustration is expressed on a number of occasions in the OT. Habakkuk, for example, in proclaiming woes on Babylon says:

> Woe to him who piles up stolen goods
> and makes himself wealthy by extortion!
> How long must this go on?
> (Hab. 2:6; cf. Ps. 94:3ff.)

---

19. I was amazed to find the following statement in the World Fact Book on the official website of the US Central Intelligence Agency (CIA): 'Since 1975, practically all the gains in household income [in the US] have gone to the top 20% of households.'

Palm 10 is full of frustration with the fact that greedy oppressors not only seem to get away with their evil deeds, but prosper in them:

> In his arrogance the wicked man hunts down the weak,
> who are caught in the schemes he devises.
> He boasts of the cravings of his heart;
> he blesses the greedy and reviles the LORD . . .
> His ways are always prosperous;
> he is haughty and your laws are far from him;
> he sneers at all his enemies.
> He says to himself, 'Nothing will shake me;
> I'll always be happy and never have trouble' . . .
> His victims are crushed, they collapse;
> they fall under his strength.
> He says to himself, 'God has forgotten;
> he covers his face and never sees.'
> (Ps. 10:2–11)

The psalmist calls on God to arise, to remember the helpless and bring the wicked to account. He then ends the psalm by expressing his faith in the Lord as a king who defends

> the fatherless and the oppressed,
> in order that man, who is of the earth, may terrify no more.
> (v. 18)

There is only the barest hint of hope for an eschatological judgment as the psalm ends. For the psalmist, it is really a case of hoping against hope that the wicked will not escape the consequences of their evil actions. In Psalm 73, a belief in the certainty of judgment is stronger. Here again the success and prosperity of the wicked brings the psalmist to the edge of unbelief. He says:

> my feet had almost slipped;
> I had nearly lost my foothold.
> For I envied the arrogant
> when I saw the prosperity of the wicked . . .
> This is what the wicked are like –
> always carefree, they increase in wealth.
> Surely in vain have I kept my heart pure . . .
> (Ps. 73:2–3, 12–13)

How graphically these sentiments express the frustrations of those who strive to overcome poverty. All the effort seems so futile at times. The greedy rich proceed unhindered in their unjust amassing of wealth at the expense of the poor, and then seem to enjoy their luxurious lives without any pangs of conscience.[20] Hope comes to the psalmist when he enters the sanctuary of God, because it is then that he understands the 'final destiny' of the wicked (v. 17). In the presence of God, he sees that their boasted material security can be quickly lost. But even if it is not, he will remain in the presence of God for ever, while the wicked will finally come into judgment and all their vaunted arrogance and success will perish:

My flesh and my heart may fail,
but God is the strength of my heart
and my portion for ever.

Those who are far from you will perish;
you destroy all who are unfaithful to you.
(Ps. 73:26–27)

With the resurrection of Jesus, the hope of an eschatological judgment of the wicked only unclearly perceived in the OT comes into full focus. In the light of his resurrection, the following words of Jesus speak powerfully to the hearts of those struggling to overcome poverty against what often seem to be impossible odds posed by the greedy powers of this world: 'Do not be amazed at this, for a time is coming when all who are in their graves will hear his voice and come out – those who have done good will rise to live, and those who have done evil will rise to be condemned' (John 5:28–29).

Freedom from fear

The scriptural belief that justice will prevail in the end is a great encouragement to Christians for whom seeing the kingdom or rule of God come on earth as it is in heaven is their first priority in life. In the first place, it helps to free them from fear. To declare Jesus as Lord is always a threat to the powers of this world. On the global scale, the greatest worldly power at the moment is the Western consumerist 'empire', with its heart in the US. The core message of this great power is that the highest good is the freedom

20. The party scenes in the film *The Last King of Scotland* powerfully illustrate this point. One feels the injustice of the enjoyment of the rich who surrounded Idi Amin while his regime perpetrated the most brutal oppression imaginable.

to consume.[21] The contrast with the Christian core vision of faith in Jesus the Messiah expressing itself through love is startling. Paul expresses this clearly, using himself as an example, in his final words to the Ephesian elders:

> I have not coveted anyone's silver or gold or clothing. You yourselves know that these hands of mine have supplied my own needs and the needs of my companions. In everything I did, I showed you that by this kind of hard work we must help the weak, remembering the words the Lord Jesus himself said: 'It is more blessed to give than to receive.' (Acts 20:33–35)[22]

The tragedy of Western Christianity is that it is not challenging globalizing consumerism, but *conforming* to it.

If by the power of the Spirit we found strength to work hard in order to help the weak/poor and to become known for our giving rather than receiving, there is no doubt that we would suffer persecution. In many countries in the majority world, seeking to live under the lordship of Jesus Christ does mean persecution by the ruling powers. Zimbabwe, India, Sri Lanka, Indonesia and Vietnam provide examples of a range of different ideologies and religious powers that feel threatened by the lordship of Jesus to the point of aggression towards his disciples. One major challenge for Christians in such situations is to make sure that the hatred they suffer is a reaction to their genuine Christian love and not to their perceived advocacy of the Western consumerist dream. But to know that the enemies of Jesus will face judgment for their persecution of his followers, and that they can ultimately do nothing to endanger their eternal salvation, should free faithful disciples from fear and give them boldness as advocates of the just and loving rule of their Lord.

Freedom to love

In the second place, it frees us to love. Anger is a perfectly understandable reaction to the evil actions of the powerful men and women of this world.

---

21. This is strikingly confirmed by George Bush's first words on 9/11 from the Oval Office: 'America is open for business.'

22. My point here focuses on the motivation for working. F. F. Bruce's comment on v. 35 is also interesting in the context of my discussion: 'The emphasis on the Christian duty of working was perhaps necessitated by exaggerated eschatological expectations, such as Paul corrects in 2 Thes. 2:1ff. Cf. 1 Thes. 4:11; 5:12ff.; 2 Thes. 3:7–12; 1 Cor. 4:12; Eph. 4:28' (*The Acts of the Apostles: The Greek Text with Introduction and Commentary* [London: Tyndale, 1951], p. 383).

Consider the consequences of the Iraq War. Thousands of ordinary Iraqi men and women have been slaughtered in internecine strife between the Sunni and Shia communities, as everyone with a modicum of understanding of Islam and Middle Eastern history predicted; the church in Iraq has seen a marked increase in persecution and is being decimated through migration out of Iraq. And this to satisfy the hubris of the US military establishment in particular, who under the leadership of George Bush supported by Tony Blair initiated a terribly destructive war on the basis of lies.

Then consider what the International Monetary Fund (IMF) and World Bank have done in Africa by imposing structural adjustment programmes on African countries before they give any credit. Ghana is a good example. This country had a thriving canned tomato and rice industry, with farmers being supported with small subsidies. The tomato industry was particularly important to northern Ghana, which is by far the poorest part of the country. The IMF and World Bank insisted that in order to get any more credit Ghana had to free their agricultural market and cut all subsidies to tomato and rice farmers. Having no option but to agree, the Ghanaian rice and tomato industry was quickly destroyed and many people were pushed into absolute poverty, because the market was flooded with subsidized rice from the USA and subsidized canned tomatoes from Italy! I must confess that my blood boiled as I walked around Ghanaian markets and shops and saw 'California' (the richest region of the richest country on earth) stamped on all the sacks of rice and 'Italy' on all the cans of tomatoes. The callousness of the executives of the IMF and World Bank and their political masters in the rich countries of the world seems beyond belief.

These are just two situations where the actions of the powerful have led to suffering and poverty and generated anger in me towards the perpetrators. But there are probably as many possible objects of anger as there are Christians involved in the struggle against poverty. However, although Paul concedes that it is possible for a disciple to be angry and not sin (Eph. 4:26),[23] generally speaking, as James says, 'man's anger does not bring about the righteous life that God desires' (Jas 1:20). Far better to hand over our anger to God and let him deal with those who cause the suffering of the poor, which he undoubtedly will on Judgment Day. Then, because we can hand over our anger to God, we shall be free to love – even our enemies. As Paul says:

---

23. One of the conditions for such anger is that it be short-lived: not an anger to sleep on!

> Do not take revenge, my friends, but leave room for God's wrath, for it is written: 'It is mine to avenge; I will repay,' says the Lord. On the contrary:
>
> 'If your enemy is hungry, feed him;
> if he is thirsty, give him something to drink.
> In doing this, you will heap burning coals on his head.'
>
> Do not be overcome by evil, but overcome evil with good. (Rom. 12:19–20)[24]

---

24. In his grace, God not only takes on the burden of anger on our behalf but also the burden of glory (Eph. 1:6, 12, 14).

PART THREE: GOD'S GOVERNED SOCIETY – THE CHURCH

In the OT, the method of divine government was revealed through God's election of representative individuals, who through their characters and words put God's stamp on his covenant people. Abraham, Moses and David, as we have seen, were outstanding examples of godly rulers called and equipped by God to serve his purpose of making Abraham's posterity into a great nation through whom all the nations would be blessed. They were inspired individuals, but their role was to shape God's nation in God's land for the benefit of all nations. From its beginning in the promise to Abraham, God's redemptive purpose had a special type of community in view. Even as the old-covenant people faced exile and the loss of their land, God was promising another individual who would fulfil the Abrahamic promise and become the ruler of the new-covenant people who would be called together from every nation. Since the fall, God's purpose has been to form an ordered society under divine rule in an ordered earth. In view of the clear OT evidence, it is surprising that some NT scholars have doubted whether Jesus intended to establish a society that would look to him as Lord. From its beginning in the promise to Abraham, God's redemptive purpose envisaged a people who would be blessed and a be blessing to others. This scepticism about Jesus' intention may have been influenced by what the institutional church has been in many places at different times, but that should not be allowed to obscure the biblical evidence for God's intention to have a people called by his name. That Jesus was conscious of having come to fulfil God's purpose as revealed in the OT would necessarily mean a new and identifiable human society. We have already considered some of the characteristics of the members of this new society in the chapters on the acts and teaching of Jesus. In this section, we shall consider the corporate significance for our present broken world of the ordered society that recognizes the lordship of Jesus the Messiah.

13. THE ORDERED SOCIETY OF THE SUPREME RULER

We finished the previous chapter with God's judgment of the wicked and begin this chapter on the present role of the Messianic community with the vision of its post-judgment consummation. What we have in Revelation 21 – 22 is a highly symbolic picture of what the society that has come under the authority of Jesus the Messiah in this present age will be in the age to come. There are big differences between now and then, but they are circumstantial differences; the essence of the messianic community is the same in both ages. So the picture of what the church will be then tells us something about what it is now.

John saw a new heaven and earth without chaos or disorder, as symbolized by the absence of any sea. He then saw

> the Holy City, the new Jerusalem, coming down out of heaven from God, prepared as a bride beautifully dressed for her husband. And I heard a loud voice from the throne saying, 'Now the dwelling of God is with men, and he will live with them. They will be his people, and God himself will be with them and be their God. He will wipe every tear from their eyes. There will be no more death or mourning or crying or pain, for the old order of things has passed away.' (Rev. 21:2–4)

Later 'One of the seven angels who had the seven bowls full of the seven last plagues' came and said to John, 'Come, I will show you the bride, the wife of the Lamb.' What he sees again is 'the Holy City, Jerusalem, coming down out of heaven' in all its glory (21:9–10).

This imagery of the people of God and the suffering Messiah, symbolized by the Lamb as 'city' and 'bride', is deeply rooted in OT prophecy. Jerusalem/Zion, built on Mount Moriah where God provided a substitutionary sacrifice for Isaac, was the place where the tabernacle or tent of meeting between God and his people became the permanent temple built by Solomon to David's design. Sanctified by the presence of God, Jerusalem became the archetypal just society with God at its heart that would be a witness and blessing to the nations. Tragically even before the end of its builder's reign, signs of declension were already in evidence so that eventually Israel and then Judah were berated by the prophets for being an unfaithful wife. The evidence of unfaithfulness was consistently idolatry and social injustice. But as the temple and city were destroyed and its people taken into exile, God promised a time when a New Jerusalem would be built and its people would become God's faithful bride. This was a prophecy of an ordered society without idolatry and social injustice.

By fulfilling the meaning of the temple as the place where people find forgiveness through substitutionary death, Jesus became the heart of the New Jerusalem. So John saw no temple in his vision of the New Jerusalem, 'because the Lord God Almighty and the Lamb are its temple' (21:22). What he saw was an ordered society, a city, completely happy and at peace and completely subjected to the authority of God (22:3). Unlike earthly cities, this city was completely secure. Its walls were massively long and high, but the gates were never shut, because there was no night. This is a wonderful picture of total security that contrasts starkly with the image of shopkeepers in cities of this world bringing down their barriers as they close their businesses for the night, or the high walls and security guards and fierce dogs needed to protect the homes of the rich – especially at night. The security of the city is the security of bright unceasing light. The impurities of the darkness dare not approach its gates for fear of complete exposure, but there is room and a welcome for people from all nations who 'walk by its light, and the kings of the earth will bring their splendour into it' (21:24). The city of the vision was also a new Eden, a garden city, with the 'river of the water of life, as clear as crystal, flowing from the throne of God and of the Lamb down the middle of the great street of the city. On each side of the river stood the tree of life' bearing abundant fruit and leaves that would bring healing to the nations from the curse of war (22:1–3).[1]

---

1. Aune's conclusion in his comment on 'No longer will there be any curse' is that 'it appears that *katathema* is the author's way of interpreting *ḥērem*. Thus the word

It is a picture of a society enjoying the fruits of human ingenuity and creativity within the framework of a perfect government without destroying the purity and glory of the created order. A holy city indeed!

Returning to the massive walls that signified complete security, we find they 'had twelve foundations, and on them were the names of the twelve apostles of the Lamb' (21:13). When Peter confessed to Jesus that he was 'the Christ/Messiah, the Son of the living God', Jesus said that he was the foundation on which he would build his church (Matt. 16:16–18). This became a reality on the day of Pentecost when Peter's preaching, which resulted in three thousand converts, marked the public launch of the gathered community of Jesus Christ. He was soon joined by the other 'apostles' and by many prophets who, according to Paul, provided the foundation on which the reconciled community of the church was built. The context of Paul's statement is his argument that God's mercy shown in the death of Jesus Christ has made possible not only the reconciliation of Gentiles (non-Jews) with God but consequently also the reconciliation of Jews and Gentiles. For Paul, because the religious barrier between Jews and Gentiles represented the biggest barrier to reconciliation between people, its breaking down in Christ represents the possibility that is now there of reconciliation between any and all enemies. So writing to Christians in Ephesus, and probably other churches in the surrounding area, he could say that 'you are no longer foreigners and aliens, but fellow-citizens with God's people and members of God's household, built on the foundation of the apostles and prophets, with Christ Jesus himself as the chief cornerstone' (Eph. 2:19–20). What Paul claims for the church now is at least something of what John saw in all its glory in his vision of the holy city. As Paul says in his conclusion to the section on the unity of Jews and Gentiles in Christ, 'you too are being built together to become a dwelling in which God lives by his Spirit' (Eph. 2:22).

In the New Jerusalem, God's unifying presence will be totally dominant; but his presence by his Spirit in the church is a real presence, too, even if manifested amidst the imperfections of this present age that is passing away. This being so, church gives us a genuine foretaste of the glory to come. Church is a foretaste of heaven and Revelation is absolutely clear that there will be no poor people in heaven.

---

refers not generally to curses, accursed things, or persons but specifically to the promise that "the curse of war" will no longer exist' (David Aune, *Revelation 1–5*, Word Biblical Commentary on CD-ROM, vol. 52a [Dallas, Tex.: Word, 1998]).

What is it about the church now that foreshadows the complete subversion of poverty in the age to come? In attempting to answer this question, we are really answering the more fundamental question What is church? The framework for the answer in what follows is provided by Oliver O'Donovan's idea that the shape of the church is a recapitulation of the Christ-event:

> The shape of the pre-structured church . . . is the shape of the Christ-event become the dynamics of a social identity. In describing that shape, we may follow the heuristic guide we have deployed in speaking of the Christ-event itself: the four moments of Advent, Passion, Restoration and Exaltation shape a society which continually gathers, suffers, rejoices and speaks.[2]

We shall consider the church as a gathering and suffering community in this chapter, and then devote the following two chapters to the church as a rejoicing and speaking community.

The church is a gathering community

The word 'church' in the English NT translates the Greek *ekklēsia.* Reflecting its meaning in its Greek context, the basic meaning of *ekklēsia* is the assembly or gathering of disciples of Jesus Christ. Fundamentally *ekklēsia* is a dynamic term meaning an event or a happening, and this is its meaning in the overwhelming majority of the cases of its use in the NT. There are two main types of gathering:

- A *local assembly* or gathering of Jesus' disciples at any time and in any place. This is by far the most common sense of the word in the New Testament (e.g. 1 Cor. 14:19, 23, 28, 35; Phil. 4:15).
- *All the disciples everywhere and throughout history*, conceived as one congregation focused on Jesus as Lord. This is the one great gathering around the throne of Messiah Jesus that will be revealed in all its glory at the second coming (e.g. Col. 1:18, 24; Eph. 1:22; 3:10; Heb. 12:23).[3]

---

2. Oliver O'Donovan, *The Desire of the Nations: Rediscovering the Roots of Political Theology* (Cambridge: Cambridge University Press, 1996), p. 171.
3. But, as with so many others, the term *ekklēsia* also develops with the growth of the Christian movement, and this is reflected in the NT itself: (1) *A house church.* This was the gathering of believers who met in a house. Until the third century, Jesus'

But, in trying to get to the heart of the NT meaning of 'church', it would be a mistake to focus too much on the term *ekklēsia.* It is interesting that Luke, who wrote the Gospel bearing his name as well as Acts, does not use the word *ekklēsia* until Acts 5:11. By that point the sort of loving community of disciples of Jesus that resulted from the outpouring of the Holy Spirit had become highly visible (Acts 2:42–47; 4:32–35). What is important is the focus on Jesus as Lord and the quality of communal life that arises from that focus. This is seen, for example, in the description of the disciples as those 'called to be saints/holy/to belong to Jesus Christ' or, as Peter describes them, 'a chosen people . . . a holy nation, a people belonging to God' (Rom. 1:6, 7; 1 Cor. 1:2; 1 Pet. 2:9). For Peter, who interestingly does not use the term *ekklēsia* at all in his letters, the disciples as the NT people of God are urged as aliens and strangers in the world, 'Live such good lives among the pagans that, though they accuse you of doing wrong, they may see your good deeds and glorify God on the day he visits us' (1 Pet. 2:12).

The church is the gathering of believers or disciples around the throne of the One described in previous chapters as he who

- is superior in every way, as the incarnate Son of God, to any bearer of God's revelation before or after him
- touched the untouchable, cast out demons and died and rose again for our justification
- showed us by his teaching and example that it is possible to live in this world in a way that reflects what it will be like to live in the world to come
- enables us by his Holy Spirit to grasp by faith the significance of his death and resurrection, and propels us into the world to live his life of self-sacrificing service
- will one day judge both the living and the dead, and reign eternally over his renewed humanity in a new heaven and earth.

---

disciples had no special buildings of their own to meet in, so most met in private homes (see e.g. Phlm. 2). (2) *All the disciples in a particular locality*. Here *ekklēsia* refers to the people who belong to the congregation of disciples, even when they are not gathered (see e.g. Acts 9:31; 1 Cor. 1:2). (3) *The disciples in a particular locality who are under the care of a group of elders*. This suggests that the gathering of believers took on very early at least some of the characteristics of an institution (see e.g. Acts 20:17, 28; Jas 5:14).

This Jesus has already been given a name above every name, and it is certain that one day everyone throughout history will bow the knee and confess that he is Lord – the ultimate embodiment of just government. The local gatherings all over the world today called 'church' are simply gatherings of those who have already bowed the knee to Jesus and look to him as Ruler.

That Jesus is the unifying focus is made clear in many of the pictures of the church we have in the NT. We have already seen that in the picture of the church as a holy building, Jesus is the cornerstone on which the whole structure depends. The same is true of some other pictures: he is the shepherd who leads and protects the flock; he is the vine from which the branches derive their life so that they can produce fruit; he is the head that controls the diverse members of his body. There can be no doubt as to who holds the reins of government in the church.

The pictures of the church also tell us about the nature of Jesus' government. In the case of the shepherd and his flock, the emphasis is on the intense love of the shepherd who voluntarily gave his life for them. The picture of the vine is a picture of such intimacy between the Ruler/Lord and his followers that he goes on to call them friends taken into his confidence. Then again, although there are many members in the body, and some are hidden away because to show them would be dishonourable, every one is vital to the efficient functioning of the body. Without the head they would be nothing, but joined to him every member is vitally important. There is no hierarchy of value in the community Jesus rules. This amazing fact is also underlined in Jesus' picture of his church as a *family* or *household*. In a previous book, I wrote about this as follows:

> When Jesus says that his followers are brothers he implies that they are members of the same family. Fairly early on in his ministry, when people were very keen to hear him, his family came to the conclusion that he was out of his mind. They went together to take him home but were unable to get into the house where he was teaching because of the crowd. They managed to get a message to him to say that they were waiting to speak to him outside the house. When he heard their message Jesus said, 'Who is my mother, and who are my brothers?' Pointing to his disciples, he said, 'Here are my mother and my brothers. For whoever does the will of my Father in heaven is my brother and sister and mother' (Matt. 12:48–50).
>
> The phrase 'my Father in heaven' is unique to Matthew. What is interesting about the reference is that 'father' is absent from the list of those who belong to the Father's household. Mothers, brothers and sisters are included, but not fathers. Is it possible that Jesus is making a statement about the nature of authority in his family by omitting 'father' from the list? It is certainly true that household government in

> the time of Jesus was patriarchal. The father was the authority in the home, and all the members of the household were in different degrees of subservience to him. But in the household of Jesus, the father is his Father in heaven and all other members are on the same level as mothers, brothers and sisters. This could also be the reason why Jesus forbids his followers to call anyone 'Father' in the discourse in Matthew 23 (Matt. 23:9).[4]

It is good to be reminded by this teaching of Jesus that the ultimate shape of the relationship between God and his people involves the Father and the Son.[5] The appropriateness of the Son being the Lord/Ruler is because he is, as Son of Man, one of us. Even though he is our King, because he has experienced, apart from sin, everything we can experience, including death, he can be very close to us. The clear implication of what he says about the family of the Father in heaven is that he is a brother among brothers, sisters and mothers. As Hebrews puts it, 'Both the one who makes men holy and those who are made holy are of the same family. So Jesus is not ashamed to call them brothers' (Heb. 2:11).[6]

Because Jesus' authority is expressed through self-sacrificing service, it is an intimate and equalizing authority. Not only does the type of love shown by Jesus make friends of all who experience it, but it also declares that they are of equal value. Accepting his intimate lordship dissolves all detrimental distinctions between people. Some of the implications of this type of lordship will be developed later. What is emphasized here is that this is the Lord who is the focus of church, which is the gathering of people who recognize him for who he is.

On the morning of the day of Pentecost, the small group of disciples gathered, as they probably had done every day since Jesus told them just over a week before to stay in Jerusalem, to wait for the coming of the Holy Spirit in power. We are not told exactly where they gathered or what they did together, except that they were sitting. When the Spirit came, this sedentary group was immediately propelled into the public square to declare the wonders of God in a way that appeared to onlookers akin to drunken revelry! Then Peter stood up to explain what was happening, and in a careful argument firmly rooted in the OT declared that Jesus had been made by God 'both Lord and

---

4. Quote from D. Hughes with M. Bennett, *God of the Poor: A Biblical Vision of God's Present Rule* (Milton Keynes: Authentic 2006), p. 79.
5. In the vision of the glorified church, the throne of God and the Lamb is at the heart of the city (see Rev. 22:1, 3).
6. The whole passage from Heb. 2:5–18 focuses on this theme (cf. also Heb. 4:14–16).

Christ/Messiah' (Acts 2:36). The result of the 'sermon' was that three thousand people repented, believed in Jesus as Lord, were baptized and added to the gathering of disciples. This set the pattern for the future of the church. Those who have gathered to Jesus as Lord seek to gather others to the same confession. To taste the rule of Jesus in his governed community inevitably creates a desire to see his rule extended over the lives of those who do not recognize his lordship.

In all the disputes about the precise relationship between 'evangelism' and 'social' action' in the evangelical community since the publication of Carl Henry's *The Uneasy Conscience of Modern Fundamentalism* in 1947, no one has disputed that it is an absolutely fundamental function of church in the power of the Spirit to gather unbelievers into the fold of those who bow the knee to Jesus as Lord. There has never been any dispute about the need to proclaim the good news of Jesus but about the content of the good news, the method of proclamation and the impact of the good news on the lives of those who embrace it. Fundamental for those who believe that evangelism and social action are inseparable is the conviction that the purpose of evangelism is to gather people into the community of those who desire to live together under the lordship of Jesus the Messiah. If this is the case, evangelism is a profoundly political activity because politics has to do with government, and here we are thinking about a people who voluntarily come under the government of Jesus Christ. Standard evangelical phrases like 'coming to know Jesus as personal Saviour' or 'believing in Jesus for the forgiveness of sin' must be placed in a wider context if they are to describe adequately what happens when someone becomes a Christian. It is when these phrases are set in the context of the many biblical images of the relationship between Jesus and his followers as that of shepherd/flock, brother/family-household, vine/branch, head/body, foundation/building that we get the fuller picture of what it means to be saved. The biblical imagery points incontrovertibly to the fact that at the heart of the good news of the gospel is an ordered society under the government of Jesus. It is our privilege as Christians to proclaim to those who will come to Jesus as Saviour an alternative form of government to the one we experience in the world. What this means should become clear in the remainder of this attempt to describe church as a foretaste of heaven, where poverty will be impossible.

The church is a suffering community

Why was Jesus killed? This is Peter's answer in the first Christian sermon recorded in Acts 2:

> Men of Israel, listen to this: Jesus of Nazareth was a man accredited by God to you by miracles, wonders and signs, which God did among you through him, as you yourselves know. This man was handed over to you by God's set purpose and foreknowledge; and you, with the help of wicked men, put him to death by nailing him to the cross. (Acts 2:22–23)

The fact that Jesus was able to do the amazing things he did was evidence of his Father God's approval, so that the claims he made for himself were not empty boasts. In one of his many disputes with the Jewish religious authorities recorded in John's Gospel, he says:

> Why then do you accuse me of blasphemy because I said, 'I am God's Son'? Do not believe me unless I do what my Father does. But if I do it, even though you do not believe me, believe the miracles, that you may know and understand that the Father is in me, and I in the Father. (John 10:36b–38)

In the Synoptic Gospels, the miracles are seen as evidence of the coming of the kingdom or rule of God. His mighty works are clear evidence that the disorder in the world, ultimately caused by sin, is being pushed back so that the light of God is penetrating the darkness of this world: 'But if I drive out demons by the finger of God,' Jesus claims, 'then the kingdom/rule of God has come to you' (Luke 11:20).

Yet, despite the incontrovertible evidence that he was accredited by God, he was handed over by the Jewish religious authorities and their supporters to the Roman authorities to be executed by crucifixion. We have focused on 'God's set purpose and foreknowledge' (Acts 2:23) in the section on the sacrificial death of Jesus in chapter 6. Here we shall focus on the part the Jewish religious authorities played in collusion with the Roman imperial authority. In this context, we see the political motivation behind the plot to kill Jesus. This implies that Jesus was seen as a political threat. He was perceived as someone who was setting up an alternative form of government that threatened the status quo. Jesus' claim to absolute authority over the individual and communal lives of his disciples as well as over the institutions his enemies controlled indicates that they were right to feel threatened.

As we have seen, under the OT covenant the government of God's people was delivered through judges, priests, prophets and kings. In the time of Jesus, the national security function of king was in the hands of the Roman Empire represented by Pilate. However, the Pharisees and teachers of the law had considerable authority over the everyday lives of

Jews.[7] The Romans allowed for much of Jewish life to be controlled by the Pharisaic understanding and application of OT law (Torah), but by way of moral persuasion rather than legal coercion. They were denied the power of law courts with which to enforce their will. The priestly function was in the hands of the high priest, Annas, and his family, who controlled the temple cult in Jerusalem and had significant influence over the legal system through their control of the Sanhedrin, the Jewish high court. This powerful priestly group in Jerusalem seems to have been close to the Sadducees, who were probably a school of OT interpretation opposed to the Pharisees.[8] The prophetic function, dormant until being revived in John the Baptist, became a distinguishing characteristic of the age of the Spirit.

That it was the unlikely united hatred of the Jerusalem priesthood, their Sadducean allies and Pharisees that took Jesus to the cross indicates it was the power of these three political groups that he challenged. The Pharisees represent the power of opinion formers and professionals. They believed theirs was the correct understanding of the implications of the law of God for their generation, and being diffused among the population did everything in their power to see to it that others observed the law in the way they prescribed. Their influence was felt among Jews in Judah, Galilee and the diaspora. Some of their number were acknowledged experts on the law and were suspicious of those who taught the law if they had not been trained by their experts. They were generally not from the Jewish landed aristocracy, but it would not be at all surprising that some from this class would be attracted to them. The presence of the Pharisees Nicodemus and Gamaliel in the ruling council or Sanhedrin testifies to their presence at the heart of the Jewish power structure but they were clearly not the dominant force there (John 7:50; Acts 5:34). That both these Pharisees attempted to temper the hatred of the Sanhedrin towards Jesus and his followers is also significant, although the majority colluded in the scheme to get rid of Jesus. Their motivation for this was the radically different

---

7. There is no scholarly consensus about the origins or influence of the Pharisees. They may have been one of a number of groups vying for popular influence in the time of Jesus. But whatever their overall significance, they clearly attempted to guide the behaviour of their fellow Jews and their approach clashed with that of Jesus.

8. I am conscious of the ongoing historical debate about the definition of the various power groups in NT Palestine and the relationships between them. Even accepting as I do the historical reliability of the NT evidence, the picture remains somewhat complex.

interpretation of the law offered by Jesus that completely undermined their authority. Opinion formers do not like to see the people they are influencing departing in droves to someone else for guidance, who flatly contradict some of their cherished beliefs and practices. It was also particularly galling that the One whom the people preferred was not properly trained. The clashes became increasingly acrimonious, to the point that cooperation with the despised high-priestly group and the Sadducees could be contemplated.

The high-priestly class supported by the Sadducees was a significant political power in Judah. Judah had lost the relative independence it enjoyed within the Roman Empire under Herod the Great when his successor Archelaus was deposed in AD 6 and replaced by a Roman prefect. Pilate, appointed in AD 26, was the fifth prefect and was probably elevated to procurator soon after his appointment. He controlled the army and had ultimate power over life and death, being able to change any capital sentence the Sanhedrin passed. The power to appoint the high priest was also in his gift. However, he would have been obliged to appoint someone from the high-priestly family, who, therefore, remained the dominant force among the Jewish aristocracy.

The economic basis of the high-priestly family's power came from their control of the temple cult in Jerusalem. With the Jewish population widely dispersed in the Roman Empire and beyond, Jerusalem became one of the most popular pilgrimage centres in the ancient world. With large numbers coming to Jerusalem every year for the three pilgrim festivals of Passover, Weeks and Tabernacles, income was generated for many in Jerusalem but particularly for the high priest's family. By selling the goods needed for offering sacrifices on the temple premises and charging for changing money into the temple currency in order to pay the temple tax, they maximized the opportunity offered by the cult to enrich themselves. Many in Jerusalem were economically dependent on the temple, and even if they were unhappy about the fact that the lion's share of the economic benefit went to the family of the high priest, would be opposed to any move to diminish the appeal of the temple and its cult. It is clear in the Synoptic Gospels that when Jesus came to be seen as undermining the lucrative temple business, the high priest joined with the Sadducees and Pharisees to get rid of the threat Jesus posed.

Jesus' triumphal entry into Jerusalem, his driving out of the money changers and sacrifice sellers and his teaching and healing in the temple courts were correctly perceived by the temple authorities as a bid to take over the temple. In fact, the strange incident of the withering of the fig tree and the parable of the tenants clearly indicate that control of the temple was being taken away from its present incumbents. It is highly significant in this context that the first recorded evidence against Jesus when he appeared before the Sanhedrin was that he had said, 'I will destroy this man-made temple and in three days will build another, not made by man' (Mark 14:58; cf. Matt. 26:60b).

Through the triumphal entry and the following events it seems Jesus was deliberately challenging the political power of the high priest and his family in order to precipitate the crisis that would lead to his death. But according to Mark's Gospel, the chief priests and teachers of the law were already 'looking for some sly way to arrest Jesus and kill him' (Mark 14:1) before these events. The account in John 11 of a plot to kill Jesus gives an insight into the nature of their plotting. Here we see the jealousy of the Pharisees and the fear of the high-priestly clan coalescing. Jesus was becoming very popular in Jerusalem and its environs as a result of his amazing miracles – including the raising of Lazarus, who had been dead for days, which is the immediate context of the plot. The impulse came from the Pharisees, but nothing official could be done without the chief priest's clan, because they controlled the Sanhedrin. Carson comments:

> The highest judicial authority in the land was the Sanhedrin, which under Roman authority controlled all Jewish internal affairs. It was simultaneously a judiciary, a legislative body, and, through the high priest, an executive. In Jesus' day the . . . members of the Sanhedrin were dominated by the chief priests, i.e. priests drawn from the extended family of the high priest, who presided over it . . .[9]

So Caiaphas, the presiding high priest, called a meeting of the Sanhedrin to discuss what should be done about Jesus. One can almost hear the fear of the priestly clan in particular in the account of the mood of the gathering: 'If we let him go on like this, everyone will believe in him, and then the Romans will come and take away both our place and our nation' (John 11:48). Notwithstanding the fact that the position of high priest was often very precarious under Roman rule, the self-centredness of this statement is breathtaking. It was 'our' place and nation they were afraid of losing! Scholars are of the opinion that the 'place' in mind here is the temple, and that what was being feared was the loss of personal wealth, power and influence that would follow any major disruption Jesus caused. Caiaphas' proposition that Jesus should be killed for the sake of the nation really meant that he should be killed so that he, Caiaphas, could keep his wealth and power! This clearly illustrates what often drives the politics and rulers of this world, but it also leaves us in no doubt that, from the human perspective, Jesus was killed because he was

---

9. D. A. Carson, *The Gospel according to John* (Leicester: IVP, 1991), p. 420.

perceived to be a political threat. And the perception was and is correct, because Jesus does lay claim to government. The existence of a people under the rule of Jesus inevitably means a reduction in the power and authority of the governments of this world.

The governments of this world have always recognized this when churches become significant enough for them to take note of them. Jesus also warned his disciples on a number of occasions that this would be the case. He 'envisaged . . . . a witnessing and suffering church'.[10] In the Beatitudes, Jesus describes the character of a Christian community that is transparently good. What government would not want citizens who were passionate about justice, sincerity, mercy and peace? Yet the final beatitude assumes that such communities will be persecuted. Jesus then goes on to proclaim blessing on the disciples listening to him, because they would be persecuted. And just as Jesus is persecuted because of who he claims to be, his followers will be persecuted for accepting that Jesus is who he claims to be.[11] When he sends out his disciples to proclaim the nearness of the kingdom and to 'heal the sick, raise the dead, cleanse those who have leprosy, [and] drive out demons', he warns them that this sort of activity will lead to persecution (Matt. 10:17–20).[12] Here again Jesus is the crucial factor in the persecution. 'On my account', he says, 'you will be brought before governors and kings . . .' (Matt. 10:18).[13]

The development of the teaching of Jesus on himself as the Vine in John 15 underlines the certainty of suffering for the church. He has been describing a community that has been taken into the confidence of the Messiah as friends, whose life together is to be characterized by love. Immediately before going on to talk about the suffering and persecution that await them, he says, 'This

---

10. D. A. Carson on Matt. 10:16, in *The Expositor's Bible Commentary* on CD-ROM, vol. 21 (Nashville: Thomas Nelson, 2007).

11. Matt. 5:11: 'Blessed are you when people insult you, persecute you and falsely say all kinds of evil against you because of me.' Cf. 1 Pet. 4:14: 'If you are insulted because of the name of Christ, you are blessed, for the Spirit of glory and of God rests on you.'

12. I am conscious of the critical questions this passage raises. I see no problem in accepting that in the precise form in which we find it in Matthew's Gospel the material reflects the experience of the church at the time the Gospel was written. However, I do not believe that this precludes the possibility that the material reflects the genuine teaching of Jesus.

13. Cf. other passages in the Synoptic Gospels that deal with the inevitability of persecution for the church (Matt. 24:9–14; Mark 13:9; Luke 6:40; 12:11–12; 21:12).

is my command: Love each other' (v. 17). Then he warns them that their community of love will be hated by the world just as the world hated him. Here 'the world . . . , as commonly in John, refers to the created moral order in active rebellion against God'.[14] The governments of this world generally belong to this rebellious created moral order. That is why Satan was able to offer them to Jesus if he bowed down to worship him (Matt. 4:8–9).

However, this hatred that the world shows to Jesus and his followers is not the last word. The picture presented by Jesus is bleak, and in the context of the impending climax of the hatred of the Jewish government, understandably the darkness was intense. But in the midst of the darkness there is a sentence full of hope: 'If they obeyed my teaching, they will obey yours also' (John 15:20c). Some commentators feel that the passage is so bleak that it is inconceivable that Jesus should inject a ray of hope into it. So the New English Bible translates this phrase negatively as 'they will follow your teaching as little *as they have followed mine*' (my italics). But this contradicts the hope for the world offered in the gospel.[15] God has loved the world so much that whoever believes in Jesus will have eternal life. The implication here is that the possibility is there for those who are in the world to accept the authority of Jesus. Again, when Jesus says that 'the bread of God is he who comes down from heaven and gives life to the world' (John 6:33), he must mean that it is possible for those in the world to taste the bread of life, the Messiah (John 3:16–17; cf. 4:42; 6:51; 8:12; 9:5; 17:21). In fact, without the possibility of those in the world obeying the teaching of Jesus and his followers, there would have been no church in the first place. The glorious truth is that the church that follows its Master along the path of suffering continually witnesses to the possibility of change for the world – and that

14. Carson, *Gospel according to John*, p. 525.

15. Ibid. Beasley-Murray, commenting on John 15:20, argues that 'Such a deduction does injustice to the presentation of both world and Church in our Gospel. It appears to assume that in John the "world" is and can only be *always* irrevocably evil and hostile to Jesus, but this is not so, as may be seen in such passages as 6:33, 51; 8:12; 9:5, and notably 3:16–17; 4:42; 17:21. If the Jews are especially in mind as representatives of the world (as is the case), we should also recall instances wherein positive response among them to Jesus is recorded, e.g., 2:23 (however unsatisfactory!); 3:1–2; 8:31; 12:9, 11. Barrett's comment accordingly is justified: "The Mission of the Church will result in the same twofold response as the work of Jesus himself (cf. 12:44–50)" (480; similarly Bultmann, 549; Lindars, 494; Schnackenburg, 3:115; Bruce, 313)' (George R. Beasley-Murray, *John*, Word Biblical Commentary on CD-ROM, vol. 36 [Dallas, Tex.: Word, 1998]).

includes the world's governments and rulers. This means that martyrdom is not the only possibility as the church witnesses to the alternative government of Jesus. As O'Donovan states, 'The church does not philosophise about a future world; it demonstrates the working of the coming Kingdom within this one. Through the authorisation of the Holy Spirit it squares up to civil authority and confronts it. This may lead to martyrdom *or to mutual service*.'[16]

This means that it is possible for the church through its self-denying witness to influence the government to act justly. The church that serves the poor may influence the government to serve the poor. However, there is no guarantee. The only guarantee Jesus gives us is that living under his government and thus refusing total allegiance to any government in this world will lead to persecution. Without running the risk of persecution, and even martyrdom, we shall never know whether any government is prepared to join with us in the task of doing justice that leads to overcoming poverty.

---

16. O'Donovan, *Desire of the Nations*, p. 217; my italics.

14. THE CHURCH IS A JOYFUL COMMUNITY

The impact of the resurrection: a new humanity

The intense sorrow of Golgotha was followed by the glorious joy of the resurrection, although the joy did not become glorious until the disciples were filled with the Holy Spirit on the day of Pentecost.[1] We have already focused on the significance of the coming of the Holy Spirit for the individual believer's involvement in overcoming poverty; here we shall focus on its communal implications.

Before the resurrection of Jesus, everything in the created order was overshadowed by death. There are intimations in the OT that the living God who is always present would not leave his creation to futility. But it was the resurrection of Jesus that put this beyond doubt. On the Friday afternoon Jesus died, Joseph of Arimathea, Nicodemus and a number of women disciples placed his body in a newly created rock tomb. Early on Sunday morning women and then

1. I have wondered if all the disciples of Jesus were filled with the Spirit on the day of Pentecost, since it is unlikely they were all in Jerusalem to be part of the events recorded in Acts 2. I am thinking particularly of those who had responded in faith as a result of their encounter with Jesus, such as the Gerasene demoniac, the Samaritan leper and the woman he met at the well near Sychar.

some of the male disciples went into the tomb and saw that the body of Jesus was no longer where it had been placed on the Friday, although his grave clothes were still there. Then Mary Magdalene and some of the women saw him, and over a period of forty days he kept appearing at different times and in different places. He was unquestionably the Jesus they had known before his death, and he even bore evidence of his crucifixion in his resurrected body. And yet he was different. As Paul says, he was 'the firstfruits of those that have fallen asleep' (1 Cor. 15:20). He was the prototype of a new humanity freed from sin and death. This is why Jesus' disciples are a joyful people. The futility of death is not God's last word to his created order. As disciples we now wait for the redemption of our bodies, and 'in hope that the creation itself will be liberated from its bondage to decay and brought into the glorious freedom of the children of God' (Rom. 8:21). We groan, the whole creation groans and even God's Spirit within us groans (Rom. 8:22–26), yet it is not a groaning of despair but for a new creation sure to come now that Jesus has been raised from the dead.

Again Paul says that as 'the beginning and the firstborn from among the dead', the risen Lord Jesus is 'the head of the body, the church' (Col. 1:18). As prototype of renewed humanity, he is both the origin of and the supreme authority among those who will be gathered to share in his indestructible life. The relationship between Jesus Messiah and the communities of disciples gathered to him is so close that their identity is sometimes merged. It is this identification of Jesus with his *ekklēsia* that is the key to understanding the 'parable' of the sheep and the goats in Matthew 25:31–46. Those who enter the kingdom are those who have identified with the least of Jesus' brothers and sisters in their rejection and suffering. The superficial understanding of this passage as saying that the test of entry to the kingdom will be whether we have been kind to the poor is common. It is especially frustrating constantly to meet this understanding among evangelical Protestants whose tradition rightly emphasizes the overwhelming testimony of the Gospels that the test of entrance to the kingdom will be our response to its King, the Lord Jesus. That he identifies himself with his disciples/church to such an extent that what we do to them is identified with what we do to him is not only consistent with the thrust of the NT but is also a wonderful affirmation of the importance of the gatherings of disciples in the scheme of salvation (cf. Matt. 10:40–42). Other passages confirm this understanding. When the apostle Paul, as Saul the persecutor, was on his way to Damascus in pursuit of Christians, what the risen lord said to him was, 'Saul, Saul, why do you persecute *me*?' (Acts 9:4; my italics). In 1 Corinthians, Paul identifies the church as the body of Christ: 'The body is a unit, though it is made up of many parts; and though all its parts are many, they form one body. So it is with Christ' (1 Cor. 12:12). What is in view here is not an ontological or mystical union between Christ and his church, but that Christ is the unifying and ruling force (the head) of his body politic.[2] The emphasis in the passage, as in 1 Corinthians as a whole, is on unity with the focus on Christ as the uniting force in his ordered society.

The Greek concept of the body politic, with which church members in Corinth would have been very familiar, was hierarchical and stratified, with the lower echelons of society existing in order to see to the comforts of the higher. Already in I Corinthians 1:26ff., Paul has turned this concept on its head by emphasizing that in the body politic of Jesus the lowly people without any nobility or influence are dominant. In chapter 12, he stresses that the members we might think are less honourable are to be treated with special honour (1 Cor. 12:22–26). The sum of his argument is that all in the ordered society of Jesus are to be valued with those who in the world's eyes would be considered insignificant being given greater value. The more able, gifted, powerful and better-off members exist in order to serve the less able, gifted, powerful and well off. In the joyful community of Jesus, power is given away or seen as an opportunity for service.

The early church was a sharing community

The contours of this collective identity of our risen Lord can be seen clearly in the way his body, the *ekklēsia*, is described in the NT. The way in which the early church is described in Acts witnesses to the way those who had experienced the risen life of Jesus in the power of the Holy Spirit delighted in each other:

> All the believers were together and had everything in common. Selling their possessions and goods, they gave to anyone as he had need. Every day they continued to meet together in the temple courts. They broke bread in their homes and ate together with glad and sincere hearts, praising God and enjoying the favour of all the people.
>
> All the believers were one in heart and mind. No one claimed that any of his possessions was his own, but they shared everything they had. With great power the apostles continued to testify to the resurrection of the Lord Jesus, and much grace

2. For a full discussion of the history of interpreting this verse, see Anthony C. Thistleton, *The First Epistle to the Corinthians*, New International Greek Testament Commentary (Carlisle: Paternoster; Grand Rapids: Eerdmans, 2000), pp. 990ff. I agree with Thistleton's conclusions.

> was upon them all. There were no needy persons among them. For from time to time those who owned lands or houses sold them, brought the money from the sales and put it at the apostles' feet, and it was distributed to anyone as he had need. (Acts 2:44–47a; 4:32–35)

Practical Christian people consider the joyful exuberance of this newborn church as misguided and reckless. From within the Western framework of thought about earthly security they declare such behaviour unsustainable. It is unsurprising, they say, that Paul had to organize a collection to support Christians in Jerusalem some years later. It is true that the disposal of assets such as land in order to feed the poor is unsustainable, even if more and more people with assets to sell are added to the church. There must be wealth production as well as asset disposal if the poor are to be fed. In fact, the founders of the church realized that this was the case. Paul's two letters to the church of the Thessalonians are among the earliest documents in the NT canon. In both letters, Paul encourages the brothers – and sisters – to look to their own affairs and work with their hands to provide for themselves and their families. 'For even when we were with you,' Paul writes, 'we gave you this rule: "If a man will not work, he shall not eat"' (2 Thess. 3:10).[3] Around ten years later, in his letter to the Ephesians, Paul adds the motivation of being able to provide for those in need when exhorting converted thieves to engage in productive work: 'He who has been stealing must steal no longer, but must work, doing something useful with his own hands, that he may have something to share with those in need' (Eph. 4:28).

Some years later, in the first letter to Timothy, Christians in Ephesus, who were rich in this present world, were to be commanded 'to be generous and willing to share' their excess with those in need. Rich Christians who have to be commanded to share are not delighting in their neighbours in the way the first Christians delighted in theirs.

The need to command someone to be generous suggests a measure of reluctance and is a far cry from the exuberant and spontaneous generosity of the first generation. Sadly Western and Westernized Christians are in as much

3. This is part of an extended section of the letter (3:6–15) dealing with the importance of not being idle but working to earn one's bread. Cf. also 1 Thess. 4:11–12 and the comment in T. Adeyemo (ed.), *Africa Bible Commentary* (Nairobi: Word Alive; Grand Rapids: Zondervan, 2006), p. 1463: 'Everyone should be involved in productive work, for as a proverb says, "the one who does not plant peanuts will be holding out his hand at harvest time."'

need of this command to share as richer Ephesian Christians were in the first century. The winter of nominalism is never long in coming.[4]

That is why we need to return again and again to consider the quality of the communal life of the first disciples filled with the Holy Spirit. It is all too easy to fall short of delighting in fellow believers. What is most striking about the description of the community of believers in Jerusalem after Pentecost is the emphasis on the way they shared their material possessions. They met often to be taught by the apostles about their new faith and to pray. They clearly delighted in each other's company, but the climax of their delight was seen in sharing possessions and particularly as they shared their food. This sharing of food often happened during mealtimes, with those who had excess welcoming to their tables those who had need. It was all done with gladness, sincerity and praise to God, making people who were looking on from the outside well disposed towards them. Their joy was obvious and infectious. It is unsurprising that outsiders joined their community daily (Acts 2:42, 44–47).[5] As their community grew rapidly, the number of needy people joining the community probably grew as well and larger resources were needed to share with them. So it soon became common practice for richer members to sell assets so that what could not be said of the people of Israel at any time in their history could be said of the followers of Jesus: 'There were no needy persons among them' (Acts 4:34). There is a clear echo of Deuteronomy here, where God revealed that full obedience to his law would mean the disappearance of poverty:

> there should be no poor among you, for in the land the LORD your God is giving you to possess as your inheritance, he will richly bless you, if only you fully obey the LORD your God and are careful to follow all these commands I am giving you today. (Deut. 15:4–5)

That there were no needy persons among the earliest disciples and the spontaneous way in which they shared proves the existence of the new covenant characterized by the law being written on the heart.

---

4. Stephen Williams's comment on this section (in private correspondence) is worth sharing: 'This seems important. The early communal life (of the church), like Zacchaeus' promise of restitution, indicates the spontaneous effect of life in the Spirit. It is a sign of the Spirit when we need wisdom to restrain our zeal rather than [a] command to galvanise into action.'
5. I have not focused on the wonders and miracles mentioned in v. 43, but they also contributed to people thinking well of the community.

But it is unlikely the apostles had no part to play in guiding the Jerusalem community in this direction. We can only speculate about what the apostles taught precisely, but since the strong conviction that the messianic age had dawned with the resurrection of Jesus marked their teaching from the beginning, we can assume that the vision of the messianic age as an age of wholehearted devotion to God's will would include God's concern for the poor and needy.

It is also true that the church in Jerusalem was unique. Jews and proselytes from many nations came to Jerusalem for the three pilgrim feasts of Passover, Weeks (Pentecost) and Tabernacles. So the first Christian gathering was probably made up of a majority of temporary residents in the city. In all the excitement, they may have stayed rather longer than their budget allowed. An atmosphere of permanent festival could also be sustained among pilgrims who were really on holiday and had no need to attend to their normal employment. Some of the sharing, therefore, could have been more like enabling people to stay at a conference that was so good that no one wanted to leave and go home! But there would also have been included in the celebration converts from among the pilgrims and the residents of Jerusalem who were genuinely poor. The character of this first church may have made it easier to put everything individual members and families possessed at the disposal of all, but that should not cancel out the fact that they did it.[6]

There is evidence that the Jerusalem congregation, even though it was the original Christian congregation providing leadership to other Christian congregations for a generation, remained a congregation with a large proportion of members who needed physical support. That Jerusalem was not in the richest part of the empire and that the church was always primarily made up of pilgrims may have contributed to this reality. There is also some evidence that the Jerusalem church came to think of itself as 'the poor', so that when the Jerusalem-based apostles asked Paul to 'continue to remember the poor' (Gal. 2:10), they could have been asking him to remember that the church in Jerusalem was the mother church and continue to express solidarity with them in doctrine and material support. Paul was faithful in doing what the Jerusalem apostles requested.[7]

---

6. With some exceptions undoubtedly – Ananias and Sapphira being the most notable (Acts 5:1–11).
7. The most obvious example of Paul's faithfulness is the offering for the Jerusalem church, which he organized from the Gentile churches he had established (see Acts 24:17; 1 Cor. 16:1–4; 2 Cor. 8 – 9; Rom. 16:25–28).

The testimony of the epistles

Even if the original church in Jerusalem was unique, the type of community it exemplified was typical of congregations of disciples of Jesus formed in the apostolic age. At least what the apostles expected from gatherings of disciples in the NT letters would make them 'caring, inclusive and distinctive [communities] of reconciliation reaching out in love to the world'.[8] The evidence that they were to reach out in love to each other is overwhelming. Yet love is not only an abstract concept, but also a warm feeling with hands and feet. Sharing all we have with the poor is not a final proof of the existence of love, because even this can be done for selfish ends (1 Cor. 13:3). Even so, sharing with the poor in the context of the Christian community can be a strong indication of the existence of true love. A small sample of the apostolic evidence with special emphasis on care for the poor will suffice.

Galatians

Paul's letter to the Galatians is a strong contender for the earliest document in our NT. As with many of the letters, the one to the Galatian churches was written because they were in danger of not being the communities they were intended to be. Paul reminds them, 'The only thing that counts is faith expressing itself through love' (5:6). They needed a right understanding of what Jesus had achieved for them in his death and resurrection, but to be authentic that understanding had to express itself in a community characterized by love. Love meant being kind, good and faithful to each other and to everyone with whom they came into contact. 'As we have opportunity,' he says, 'let us do good to all people, especially to those who belong to the family of believers' (6:10). Doing good meant carrying each other's burdens. Poverty is unquestionably a heavy burden to carry.

2 Corinthians 8 – 9

While organizing a major collection for the church in Jerusalem, Paul had occasion to write at length to the church of God in Corinth about the principles of sharing with the poor (see 2 Cor. 8 – 9).[9] He was really forced to do this

8. *Tearfund: Mission, Beliefs, Values Strategy* (Teddington: Tearfund, n. d.).
9. What follows is based on these two chapters. As mentioned above, Jerusalem had a special place at the beginning of church history, so there were good theological reasons for the Gentile church needing to express solidarity with the original Jewish church. However, this does not mean that Paul's discussion of his collection is irrelevant to sharing with the poor in general.

because having been enthusiastic about the idea of making a collection, the Corinthians were slow to put their hands into their pockets. So he encourages them with a series of powerful arguments. First he draws attention to the good example of churches much poorer in material resources than they. Because he knew that the Macedonian churches were not that well off, Paul had not asked them for money for the collection. Hearing about it from other sources and despite their 'extreme poverty', they insisted on playing their part. They dedicated themselves to the Lord and then gave 'beyond their ability'. In a world where so much emphasis is laid on getting resources from the rich West in order to overcome poverty, Paul makes an important point here: the poor churches are the most generous churches. It is a fact that people who claim to be evangelical have become less and less generous as they have become richer and richer since the 1980s.[10] There is a need to stir the conscience of the Western and Westernized churches, but that must not be done at the expense of recognizing the crucial place of the generosity of the poor churches. There has been a tendency in areas with a lot of extreme poverty to think that nothing can be done without the input of Western money. Western aid agencies and missionaries must bear the major responsibility for creating this mindset, but they have also been joined by Westernized indigenous church leaders and professionals. This has become one of the greatest barriers to overcoming poverty, because churches of the poor have been disempowered and have been robbed of the opportunity by God's strength to give 'even beyond their ability'. Despite this, the churches of the poor probably continue to be the most generous, and potentially the most significant, force in the effort to overcome poverty.

Secondly Paul focuses on the grace of our Lord Jesus Christ and understands 'grace' in this context as the voluntary giving up of what legitimately belongs to Jesus in order to enrich those who are poor. In one sense, this argument is in parenthesis, but in fact it is the foundation of his first argument. The first nine verses of 2 Corinthians 8 are full of 'grace'. The Macedonian churches acted in the way they did because of the grace God had given them; they pleaded with Paul for the privilege 'of sharing in this service or expression of grace [*charis*], to the saints'.[11] Paul sent Titus, who had initiated collecting among the Corinthians,

10. Ronald J. Sider, *The Scandal of the Evangelical Conscience* (Grand Rapids: Baker, 2005), p. 21.

11. This phrase translates *tēn charin kai tēn koinōnian tēs diakonias tēs eis tous hagious*. It brings together the key terms in the NT used to express the sharing of goods in the community of the church: *charis* (grace), *koinōnia* (fellowship) and *diakonos* (service).

to complete the collection described as 'this grace'. He commended the Corinthian church for the excellence of their faith, speech, knowledge, earnestness and love, but he now wanted to see them, like the Macedonians, excelling 'in this grace of giving' also. It is only after linking 'grace' four times with sharing what they had with the poor that he makes the unanswerable point 'For you know the grace of our Lord Jesus Christ, that though he was rich, yet for your sakes he became poor, so that you through his poverty might become rich' (v. 9). Grace is about the voluntary glad abandonment of rights, privileges and comforts in order to bless those who are lacking, and in this passage there can be no doubt that it includes sharing material possessions with the poor.

Thirdly there is no need for the sharing to be disproportionate. It is true that the Macedonians excelled themselves and gave in a way Paul thought impossible, but from the practical perspective no one was being asked to give what they did not have. The fundamental issue is how we view what we have in the light of Jesus' immense generosity.

Fourthly a key guiding principle in judging the proportion of what we have to share should be equality. The principle is supported by reference to the way in which God provided the manna in the wilderness. Since it was provided on a daily basis and was impossible to preserve, the Israelites were forced to gather it according to their daily needs. So those who needed a large amount for a large family gathered a large amount, and those who needed a small amount for a small family gathered only a small amount. Each day everyone had enough to meet their needs. In an unequal world where some in the community of Jesus are able to gather far more than is required for their daily need, while others, despite their intense effort, gather too little, Paul encourages us to aim for equality. Inequality is in fact always an opportunity for showing grace by those who have more than enough, and as the fortunes of states change over time it is perfectly possible for recipients of grace in one generation to become the dispensers of grace in another. The crucial point for the family of God is that we should always be aiming for greater equality. This is an immense challenge for those of us who enjoy a Western standard of living. Many of us belong in the top 10% of the world's owners of wealth, where wealth is defined as 'the value of physical and financial assets minus debts'. To belong to this group meant owning average assets worth $61,000 in 2006. Those who belong to this group own three thousand times what is owned by the average member of the bottom 10%![12] Obviously in order to make a

12. See <http:// www.iariw.org/papers/2006/davies.pdf>, accessed 31 Mar. 2008. The information on the website comes from James B. Davies, Susanna Sandstrom,

proper comparison we need to take purchasing power parity into consideration, but even when that is done, the average member of the top 10% is many times wealthier than a member of the bottom 10%. Added to this, the gap between rich and poor has been getting bigger since the 1980s, and, tragically, as the wealth gap has widened, evangelical Christians in rich countries have become meaner! These statistics are an immense challenge to the Western and Westernized churches to take seriously what this principle teaches about what it means to be filled with resurrection joy.

Fifthly sharing needs to be done with transparent integrity. The way Paul achieved this was by getting the churches to choose a person who was known for his integrity to accompany Paul and his companions when they took the collection to Jerusalem. He would be able to report back if the money had been safely delivered and used for the purpose for which it was intended.

Sixthly giving for the poor should be warm-hearted and generous. Churches should be aware of the immense privilege that is theirs of belonging to the people of God as a result of God's indescribable gift of his Son. As they think of this wonderful family called into existence in different parts of the world, they should be generous in their attitude towards them and especially towards those who are suffering poverty among them. This should be particularly true in the case of the church of the Jews, because their salvation came from among God's ancient covenant people. So, like the farmer who sows generously, they should give generously and cheerfully to alleviate poverty, and God will honour their giving in every way. One of the most significant results will be thanksgiving and praise to God. If the contemporary church took heed of Paul's teaching here and began to share its huge resources generously with the poor, the evangelistic impact on the world could be unimaginably great. As Leo the Great says in one of his sermons:

> We must show more liberal bounty toward the poor and those who suffer from all kinds of affliction in order that many voices may give thanks to God . . . no other devotion of the faithful is more pleasing to the Lord than that which is directed toward the poor. Where he finds merciful concern he recognizes the reflection of his own kindness. Let the almsgiver feel happy and secure, for he will have the greatest gain if he has saved the smallest amount for himself; as the blessed apostle

---

Anthony Shorrocks and Edward N. Wolff, *The World Distribution of Household Wealth* (University of Western Ontario, Canada; WIDER-UNU, Finland; Levy Economics Institute of Bard College and New York University, World Institute for Development Economics, 2006).

Paul says: 'He who supplies seed to the sower both will supply bread for food and will multiply your seed and increase the harvest of your righteousness' in Christ Jesus our Lord.[13]

Romans 12

The final point from the passage in 2 Corinthians links with the encouragement for those referred to in Romans 12 who have the gift of 'contributing to the needs of others' to 'give generously', for 'those that care' to do so 'with zest' (v. 8),[14] and those with the gift of showing mercy to do so 'cheerfully'. Here it is absolutely clear that practical care of the poor is of the essence of what it means to be church, the one body of Christ in which 'each member belongs to all the others' (v. 5). The grace manifested in the giving of different gifts, including those referred to above, speaks loudly of church as a community in which great care was taken of its poor members. Paul underlines this by going on to say that the gathering of disciples should be 'devoted to one another in brotherly love', which among other things means sharing 'with God's people who are in need' (vv. 10, 13). Here again the language used comes from the context of the family, so that the delight the disciples of Jesus should have in one another across all the barriers of ethnicity, class, gender, distance and so on should be like the delight family members have in each other. And in Paul's context, as in many contexts today, the natural thing for family members to do is to look after one another when need arises.

Hebrews and James

Paul is not the only NT author to emphasize this type of care in the context of church. Hebrews encourages the community of disciples to offer through Jesus the twin sacrifices of praise and sharing with others in need, because God is pleased with such sacrifices (Heb. 13:15–16). James says that the sort of religion God approves is looking 'after orphans and widows in their distress' (Jas 1:27). The word translated 'religion' (*thrēskeia*) here is a rare word in the NT that refers to the outward manifestation of someone's inward religious convictions. James

---

13. Cited in 'Explanation' of 2 Cor. 9:6–15, in Ralph P. Martin, *2 Corinthians*, Word Biblical Commentary on CD-ROM, vol. 40 (Dallas, Tex.: Word, 1998).

14. I am convinced by Dunn's argument that the RSV translation of *ho proïstamenos en spoudē* as 'he who gives aid, with zeal' is to be preferred to the phrase translated 'if it is leadership, let him govern diligently' in the NIV. See his comment on Rom. 12:8, James D. G. Dunn, *Romans 8–16*, Word Biblical Commentary on CD-ROM, vol. 38 (Dallas, Tex.: Word, 1998).

is speaking about what people see of a person's devotion to God that provides evidence whether the devotion is true or not. What they see, if it is true devotion, is care for orphans and widows. The phrase 'orphans and widows' has a long history in the Bible. It is a constant refrain of the OT that God is the protector of the orphans and widows. They represent the weakest and most vulnerable members of society. Orphans have lost their fundamental means of support. The widow likewise has lost the one who was meant to care and provide for her. These two categories represent those who are unable to care and provide for themselves. Those who are really religious are seen to be the ones who care practically for the helpless ones in their community.

1 John

John in his first letter begins his discussion of the meaning of brotherly love in the Christian community by referring to a family situation in which the complete opposite was the case – the act of Cain in butchering his brother Abel. The world under the domination of the evil one is characterized by jealousy, suspicion and hatred, which are manifested in violence and murder. This way of death is contrasted by the way of life characterized by acceptance, affirmation and love, which are expressed in self-sacrificing service. This approach, which is the opposite of Cain's, is exemplified by Jesus: 'This is how we know what love is: Jesus Christ laid down his life for us. And we ought to lay down our lives for our brothers' (3:16). The heroic-sounding challenge to follow Jesus and lay our lives down for our brothers is exemplified by the somewhat mundane action of sharing our possessions with them when they are in need. John continues, 'If anyone has material possessions and sees his brother in need but has no pity on him, how can the love of God be in him?' (v. 17).[15] The equation here is simple: those who say they have the love of God in them but do not share the excess possessions they have with a brother or sister in need are liars.

The church in the world

The resurrection of Jesus and the coming of the Spirit marked a decisive step in the renewal of the created order as a whole, but the main focus of the NT is on the community of the resurrection, the gathered disciples of Jesus, the

---

15. One is tempted to say at this point that evangelicals have quoted John 3:16 *ad nauseam*, but have often forgotten about this other John 3:16.

church. We have focused so far on how overcoming poverty in the context of church is evidence of the reality of the new humanity in Jesus Christ. The new humanity is obviously a communal reality, but when that communal reality becomes manifest through the church, it witnesses to the reality of the eschatological community yet to come. Real church points to God's intention for the human community in general. The use of 'body' as an image of the church points to this. Commenting on the 'body' image in Romans 12:4–5, Dunn states:

> The fact that the imagery was well known to describe the body politic probably implied also that for Paul the Christian congregation's functioning as a body could itself serve as a model for the functioning of the wider (secular) society. And as the body of Christ the members could think of themselves so functioning as the principal medium of Christ's continued presence in human society. That this was to be no mere 'spiritual' presence within, far less a withdrawal from that wider society in a completely separate identity, was already implicit in the exhortation of [Rom. 12:1]: their functioning as one body in Christ included the daily embodiment of the life of the Spirit in the all-too-physical realities of human existence.[16]

At its simplest level, the wider impact of church is felt in its practical care for those who do not belong. The heavy emphasis in the NT on Christians caring for each other and sharing with the poor among them is there to highlight the fact that the church is an eschatological community. Jesus taught that his community was to be a visible source of good works, like a city set on a hill. Jesus also said that, although they were an alternative society that did not belong to this world, he was sending them into the world as the Father had sent him into the world (Matt. 5:14–16; John 17:15–18; 20:21). The sort of self-sacrificial love expected of the community of disciples would be impossible to confine within it. That the community was expected to love its enemies and do good to them, as Paul underlines in Romans 12:14–21 on the basis of the teaching of Jesus, is conclusive proof of this. As Dunn comments:

> Also significant is the extent to which Paul takes for granted actual contact of his listeners with the wider city community, and awareness of the moral standards prized by others: they must live at peace (v 18) and seek to have as positive relations with their unbelieving neighbors and associates as possible; they must be mindful of what

---

16. See 'Explanation' of Rom. 12:4–5, in James D. G. Dunn, *Romans 9–16*, Word Biblical Commentary on CD-ROM, vol. 38b (Dallas, Tex.: Word, 1998).

others value and hold in high regard and be sure not to let their ethical and aesthetic standards leave them open to the criticisms of Stoic or Cynic (v 17); they should be known for their wholehearted committal to oneness with the deprived (v 16), they should show hospitality to enemy as well as fellow believer (v 20), and their relationships within the wider community could result in persecution (vv 14, 17, 19–21). All in all Paul has no thought of the Roman Christians as compartmentalizing their lives (into spiritual and ordinary affairs) or of living their lives cut off from contact with the wider community. He takes it for granted that Christians will live out their daily lives and wider relationships motivated by the same love as in their relationships with fellow believers.[17]

The impact of the apostolic household codes

This overspill can be seen clearly in the way the principles of the communal life of the Christian community are applied to what have become known as the 'household codes' prevalent in the first century of the Christian era.[18] What is said about the wife–husband, child–parents, and servant–master relationships in Ephesians is a particularly good example of the way in which these creation orders are redefined by Christian community. Submission would have been the key word to define the appropriate attitude of the wife/child/servant in both Greek and Jewish society in the first century. Paul begins from this assumed starting point for the three relationships, but the way he defines the responsibility of husbands/parents/masters in the prevailing atmosphere of the Christian community as a whole is radically subversive. The whole section is introduced by the general exhortation to the whole church 'Submit to one another out of reverence for Christ' (Eph. 5:21).[19] The life of the whole Christian community is conditioned by reverence for the Lord Jesus Christ, which means treating everyone with humility. This means doing nothing out of selfish ambition or vain conceit, but in humility considering others better than ourselves (Phil. 2:3). It means valuing every member of the body because,

---

17. See Dunn's 'Explanation' of Rom. 12:14–21, in ibid.
18. 'The church of the New Testament self-consciously claimed the created structures of life and work in community, as we may see especially (but not only) in the so-called household codes . . .' (Oliver O'Donovan, *The Desire of the Nations: Rediscovering the Roots of Political Theology* [Cambridge: Cambridge University Press, 1996], p. 183).
19. That this is an introduction to the whole section is proved by the fact that in the following verse the verb 'submit' has to be carried over from the previous verse. What is in the text is, 'Submit to one another . . . The wives to their own husbands . . .'

however insignificant they may be in the eyes of the world, they are infinitely precious to God and have been endowed with gifts of the Spirit vital for the body's efficient operation. The submission of wives, children and servants in this context takes on a very different complexion.

However, it is what is expected of the husband, parent and master that is radically subversive. The pattern for the Christian husband's behaviour towards his wife is the behaviour of Jesus towards his church. 'Love' is the key word to describe Jesus' attitude to his church as his bride, and his love is defined by his readiness to sacrifice himself for her, to be exclusively committed to her, to forgive her, to build her up so that she is increasingly able to realize her potential; and in all this he loves her as he loves himself (Eph. 5:25–31). Gender oppression is totally impossible in the context of a marriage where the husband seeks to love his wife just as Christ loved the church. The whole relationship is taken to another plane, where a power struggle becomes impossible in an atmosphere of mutual blessing. Since gender oppression is now generally accepted as one of the key causes of poverty, the outworking of this radical perspective through the life of the church could have an immense impact.

The servant–master relationship is changed just as radically. The 'servants' in the passages dealing with the household codes were usually slaves. Looking back on the NT, as we do through the lenses of the horrors of the transatlantic slave trade and the vigorous evangelical campaign to abolish it, it is unsurprising that we are puzzled by the seeming acceptance of slavery in the NT letters and the fact that the apostles made no attempt to abolish it. First, by way of explanation, slavery was a very different institution from the slavery of the modern era. In NT times, economic production was based on household businesses. So slaves were really domestic servants who were often highly skilled workers. That does not diminish the injustice of buying and selling people like things, but there was much more scope for valuing the abilities of slaves than there was in modern slavery.

Secondly, although what is said in the NT letters indicates that no attempt was made to abolish the institution of slavery legislatively, if masters and slaves followed the prescriptions of the Christian household code in this matter, the slave 'mind' would undoubtedly be abolished. Christian slaves were encouraged to see their work as service offered to their Lord Jesus, knowing that whatever their earthly masters were like, their heavenly Master would value, appreciate and reward their efforts. Masters were likewise to treat their slaves in the way their heavenly Master treated them – as equal human beings of inestimable value. Exactly what Paul meant is probably most graphically illustrated in his letter to Philemon, which he wrote to accompany Onesimus, Philemon's runaway slave. The way Paul pleaded Onesimus' cause undermines the whole foundation of slavery. Here is a summary paraphrase of some of the things Paul said to his friend Philemon, who was a church leader and slave owner:

1. You may think he is useless because of what he did, but in fact he is quite the opposite. He is so useful to me that I have come to love him as a son. I would like to keep him with me, but I will let you take that decision (vv. 8–14).
2. You lost his services for a while so that you could receive him back, not as a slave any more but as a brother and an equal (vv. 15–16).
3. I know the tremendous respect you have for me, so if you still consider me a partner in serving our Lord Jesus Christ, I would like you to welcome Onesimus as you would welcome me (v. 17).
4. I'm happy to pay for any loss you may have incurred because of what Onesimus has done, but remember, you owe everything to me as the one who led you to Christ – that is why I'm confident that you will do more than I ask (vv. 18–21).

The striking point about the whole story is that the big issue was not just slavery: it was Onesimus' whole life and social relationships. Paul's delight and joy in his brother had a massive impact on his whole life. Church tradition has it that Onesimus ended up as the senior church leader, or bishop, in Ephesus. From runaway slave to bishop – that was the transforming result of Paul's joy.

Conclusion

The joy generated by the resurrection of Jesus unleashed the powerful centrifugal force of the Spirit into the world. The upside-down kingdom of the servant Messiah creates communities where possessions are given away rather than hoarded in a vain attempt to grasp at security. Power is given away so that the powerless can be empowered. The institutional church has all too often identified with the centripetal force of the spirit of this world, but, however ashamed we should be of this history we can rejoice that Jesus is Lord of his reconciled and reconciling community, and that this church, which has existed since Pentecost, still exists today.

15. THE CHURCH IS A COMMUNITY WHO SPEAK GOD'S WORDS

The assumption underlying this whole section on the church has been that poverty is the result of a disordered society and that Jesus has come to establish a properly ordered society. As people are gathered into the society Jesus rules as Lord, they challenge the authorities of this world and witness to the possibility of living in a renewed world order in the power of the Holy Spirit. So far the emphasis has been on the reality of living in the power of the resurrection. But not only is the church called to live the resurrection life, it is also called to speak the words of God. The two key ways in which the church speaks the words of God are *prophecy* and *prayer*.

Prophecy

Prophecy is as old as the story of God's special revelation, since Abraham was the first to be called a prophet (Gen. 20:10). As we have seen, Moses was the archetypal prophet. Fundamentally the prophet is a person called directly by God to convey his message to others. Whatever may be said about the means God has used historically to convey his message, such as dreams, visions, angelic beings, an audible or inward voice and so on, underlying everything is the reality of God's ability to communicate directly with a human being. The genius of the new covenant as described by Ezekiel is that all Israel will have the will of God written on their hearts. The implication is that those who have God's will written on their hearts are able to live it and tell it out. The Spirit of the new covenant is a Spirit of prophecy as well as a Spirit of resurrection living. On the Day of Pentecost people from many different nations heard the Spirit-filled disciples 'declaring the wonders / great deeds of God' (Acts 2:11). Peter explained the phenomenon as a fulfilment of the promise of a general outpouring of the prophetic Spirit in Joel:

> In the last days, God says,
>   I will pour out my Spirit on all people.
> Your sons and daughters will prophesy,
>   your young men will see visions,
>   your old men will dream dreams.
> Even on my servants, both men and women,
>   I will pour out my Spirit in those days,
>   and they will prophesy.
> (Acts 2:17–18)

What is so radical about this promise and its fulfilment is that the divine calling to speak God's word – to prophesy – is completely democratized. The young and old, female and male and those of low or high social standing can be filled with the Spirit and prophesy. Every believer indwelt by the Spirit has a direct line to God and can be an agent to bring God's message to the church and to the world. This is not to deny that there are those with special speaking gifts in the church and that they are even called prophets, but the ability to prophesy is universal.[1] The difference between specific gift and universal ability is a matter of scale. What believing this means for church is that we can expect to hear God speak into our situation through any member and not only to the church but also to unbelievers. This is what Paul argues in 1 Corinthians 14:24–25:

> if an unbeliever or someone who does not understand comes in while everybody is prophesying, he will be convinced by all that he is a sinner and will be judged by all, and the secrets of his heart will be laid bare. So he will fall down and worship God, exclaiming, 'God is really among you!'

---

1. O'Donovan describes prophecy as 'the archetypal charism' (*The Desire of the Nations: Rediscovering the Roots of Political Theology* [Cambridge: Cambridge University Press, 1996], p. 188).

Paul goes on to say that the expression of prophecy needs to be regulated when the followers of Jesus gather, but that does not undermine the point that the ability of many to speak the message of God can have a powerful impact on the unbeliever. What convinces unbelievers is the communal nature of the multiplicity of messages. They see a people guided by God – encouraged, rebuked, built up, judged and comforted in their relationship with God, one another and the world.[2]

The unbelievers Paul envisaged being convinced and casting themselves at God's mercy would not be doing so in response to what evangelicals have generally understood by the proclamation of the gospel. What is in view here is not the sharing of a well-honed formula but a response to witnessing the dynamic involvement of God with his people. The lordship of Jesus Christ, the reality of sin and the need for repentance and faith would probably be expressed in some of the prophecies, but conviction would be born out of *hearing* the reality of God's presence in the lives of his people through the Holy Spirit.

Neither is prophecy here in 1 Corinthians 14 equivalent to Bible exposition. As O'Donovan says:

> To prophesy is to speak a word from God to the church as it is placed here and now; to declare that the present situation is this, and not that. It is not scriptural exposition: it brings forward something new and of the moment, something not wholly predictable. Yet it is not free and exploratory innovation, but is always predicated upon careful attention to the testimony of Israel's prophets and apostles to the Christ-event. In the light of that testimony, it discovers the present.[3]

O'Donovan is using 'discover' here in its original sense of 'exposing to view' or 'revealing'. What prophets do is expose the truth of situations within the

---

2. I am conscious of the enormous amount of material that has been produced on the NT understanding of 'prophecy', and especially on Paul's understanding of it. Thiselton describes Paul's understanding of prophesying, especially in 1 Cor. 14, as 'the performing of intelligible, articulate, communicative speech-acts, the operative currency of which depends on the active agency of the Holy Spirit mediated through human minds and lives to build up, to encourage, to judge, to exhort, and to comfort others in the context of interpersonal relationships' (Anthony C. Thistleton, *The First Epistle to the Corinthians*, New International Greek Testament Commentary [Carlisle: Paternoster; Grand Rapids: Eerdmans, 2000], p. 1094).
3. *Desire of the Nations*, p. 188.

gatherings of disciples and also through the church in the world. It is in this latter context that it is right to speak about the church prophetically addressing the social evils of its generation, or, in NT terms, convicting the world of sin.

The pattern seems to be, first, prophets speaking to the church, and then the church scattered at large speaking to the wider society. It is difficult to avoid drifting into a discussion of ecclesiology at this point, but it is sufficient to say that whatever ecclesiological position we adopt, the biblical evidence at this point assumes the priesthood of all believers. Any and every member of a gathering of believers can speak prophetically into its life and through the life of the congregation into the life of the wider society. But whatever the time-specific condition of a church or the society in which it is placed, its message must be about grace and justice, because the God of the church is a God of grace and justice.

Speaking God's word in the context of empire

The people who are under the government of Jesus as they speak of their king and his grace and justice will also challenge the governments of this world. This has been true from the beginning, especially where empire is concerned. Paul was positive about some aspects of the Roman Empire. He took advantage of his privileged position as a Roman citizen on at least three occasions; it was an advantage in his missionary journeys that a section of a population anywhere he went could speak Greek; he encouraged respect for the imperial authority, because in many cases its legal framework, even if it was based on class divisions, often led to the punishment of wrongdoers and the protection of those who did well. However, he drew a clear line where ultimate authority is concerned. There was only one who had ultimate call on his life and on the life of all human beings and that was the Lord Jesus Christ. And living in obedience to this Lord, as we have already seen, cut across much of what the empire stood for.

What the Roman Empire stood for was not just in the background but an all-pervasive reality in the lives of everyone who came under its sway. In fact, that is the character of empire in any age. An imaginative autobiographical account of the conversion of the Nympha greeted by Paul in Colossians (Col. 4:15) conveys something of the ubiquity of the symbols of the empire as embodied particularly in the emperor:

> Everywhere I turned there were images of Caesar. When I walked to the market, I saw his image in the square. I saw his image in the theatre, in the gymnasium, in the temples. And the coins with which I transacted my business all bore his likeness.

> Even my household was full of his image, from the idol of the emperor in the atrium to images on my jewelry and utensils and paintings on my wall.[4]

These all-pervasive images were not in place simply for aesthetic effect, but were everywhere underlining the same message over and over again: Caesar is Lord and the peace and prosperity we enjoy come from him. The Roman poet Horace even sang that the emperor had 'wiped away our sins and revived the ancient virtues'.[5] So the emperor was even seen as Saviour as well as Lord.

It is of the essence of empire to usurp the place of God ever since the builders of Babel started work on their tower intended to reach up to heaven. Empires are founded on the belief that power must be acquired in order to ensure well-being and security. So the more power the empire can acquire, the more well-being and security there will be for its citizens. Power can only be acquired by producing wealth that can be spent on building up military capacity. As we saw in the discussion of Babel, empire is a centripetal force. Its aim is not to expand in order to do good to those who come under its sway but to increase its power and influence in order to increase the well-being and security of those able to share in its power. However, the story it tells about itself is a perfect contradiction of what it does. The stories or myths that sustain all empires speak of their benign influence. Empires are always the bringers of peace and stability, civilization and prosperity. They have discovered the best way to order human society and are out of 'altruism' imposing that order on others for their well-being. As already noted above, empires have images representing their power that can be seen everywhere and are a continual reminder of who is 'Lord' and 'Saviour'.

It is easy to see the characteristics of empire in the dominant Roman power of the NT era. But empire building did not end with the collapse of Rome. There have been many other empires since, and the dominant current 'empire' is unquestionably the US. As the heart of the capitalist economic world order it is the central hub from which that order is becoming more and more dominant in the world. Whatever may be said about the contribution the World Bank and the International Monetary Fund (IMF) could make to overcoming poverty, it is not coincidental that the headquarters of both institutions are in

---

4. Brian J. Walsh and Sylvia C. Keesmat, *Colossians Re-Mixed: Subverting the Empire* (Carlisle: Paternoster, 2004), p. 54.
5. Ibid. p. 58. Horace 65–7 BC flourished and was patronized by the emperor Octavian, who unified the empire after the chaos following the assassination of Julius Caesar, and as Augustus Caesar became the first of the deified emperors.

Washington DC. And when one looks at the policies of both institutions, it is difficult to avoid the conclusion that close geographic proximity to the US centre of power also means close ideological proximity. The way in which these institutions work is a good example of imperial patronage. Empire is built on making the less powerful dependent on the patronage of the more powerful. Both the World Bank and the IMF are agents of capitalist economics. The IMF has made loans dependent on structural adjustment programmes that are the embodiment of capitalist free-market orthodoxy, although their application to poor countries has given economic advantage to US and European commercial interests in the important agriculture sector that in the US and Europe ignores the dogmas of the free market!

A case could be made that the whole government aid effort of rich countries is also a case of 'imperial' patronage. Poor countries are made to jump through a series of hoops in order to have aid so that they can enjoy something of the benefits of the empire. Even the work of non-governmental organizations (NGOs) can take on the form of 'imperial' patronage. The NGOs represent 'developed' countries, that is, countries that claim to have achieved the goal of well-being for their populations. The poor people to be helped live in what are called developing countries, that is, countries which in many cases have hardly started the journey towards the 'wonderful' achievement of the developed countries. Those in developing countries who have a heart for the poor need to be instructed as to how to develop, and it is only to the extent that they accept the direction of the Western NGOs that they receive funding. In the process, if the agents of the Western NGO or government agency in the developing countries accept their subservient role, they are paid at a level that will enable them to live something approximating to the Western dream. This is an expression of deep scepticism about the whole development industry based on a feeling that so much of the large sums of money spent on aid benefits those who become employees in the industry, and that only a tiny amount benefits the poor. Even Christian aid agencies that claim to work on the basis of partnership need to be aware that it is very easy as the holders of the purse strings to be an imperial 'partner'.

The centralization of economic power in the US is backed by the most powerful military machine ever seen in the history of humanity. As mentioned earlier, in 2005 the US spent $420 billion on the military, which represented 43% of the total spent on the military in the whole world that year! It is true that the war in Iraq was very costly, but even if the cost of that was taken out of the total, the US military budget is still far bigger than would be required to defend US security. Such massive spending can only be for imperial ends.

Of course, the massive outlay on the military is defended as an altruistic effort to secure the cause of freedom and democracy in the world:

> If the Pax Romana summarized the Roman imperial mythology, then the Pax Americana, with its clear distinction between good and evil and its self-righteous and aggressive foreign policy, encapsulates the dominant mythology of our day. Like Rome, the United States describes itself as a nation chosen by God to bring democracy and freedom to those parts of the world 'backward' enough to endorse a different system of government and different economic priorities from those of global capitalism.[6]

What was said earlier about the meanness of the US aid budget exposes this claim to altruism as hypocrisy.

Finally the US Empire is busily capturing the imagination of the world through images becoming more and more pervasive around the world. The central brand is the American way of life, which is presented as a life of prosperity, safety, equality and happiness in countless media images around the world. But *consumption* is the central mantra of the current dominant world empire and all its talk about 'freedom' is really talk about the freedom to consume. Wherever commercial interest believes there are people with money to spend on consumption, advertising pumps out the message that a life worth living is linked to the ability to consume their products, even if, as in the case of massive corporations like Coca-Cola and McDonald's, the relatively expensive products they sell have little if any value. To get more and more people to consume goods produced by the commercial interests of the empire, advertising implies that with the good, which may actually be a bad, we buy a whole range of non-tangible qualities. Storkey lists a

> few of the inner appeals which are made, premised on buying certain goods: confidence, innocence, relaxation, love, security, power, naturalness, fun, status, comfort, peace, happy families, romantic love, friendship, excitement, freedom from stress, sex appeal, personal attraction, health, youth, happiness, serenity and many more aspects of a good life are tied to products and services.

He then comes to the obvious conclusion that seems to evade so many of us that 'the appeals of consumerism are pathetic in that they are not true.

---

6. Ibid. p. 62. For a trenchant critique of US imperial pretensions, see C. René Padilla and Lindy Scott, *Terrorism and the Iraq War: A Christian Word from Latin America* (Buenos Aires: Kairos, 2004).

Consumer goods and services cannot give the qualities they claim . . . The ability to swallow lies is one of the best indices of our ability to mess up, and we are now gulping.'[7]

So when we gather as disciples to declare that Jesus is Lord and Saviour, for our confession to be genuine, we must reject any other claim to that position. We must understand and reject the way in which the powers of this world exercise their authority in our generation in order to usurp the position that can be held only by our Lord Jesus. We need to speak much of the need to be rescued from the dominion of darkness and transferred to the kingdom of God's beloved Son 'in whom we have redemption, the forgiveness of sins' (Col. 1:13–14). We also desperately need a proliferation of prophetic speech and gift so that we can know how to live as people of the kingdom rather than people of the empire of this world. And, whatever else we say in our generation, our talk must be about the rich sharing with the poor and possessing qualities like love, joy, peace, patience, kindness, goodness, faithfulness, gentleness and self-control, which cannot be bought but come only as gifts of the Holy Spirit of God (Gal. 5:22–23).

We rejoice that many evangelical churches in the rich minority world have been awakened since the 1950s to their responsibility to use at least some of their wealth to bless the poor. We also rejoice that God has raised up many organizations to channel the money generated by the churches to where it is needed. But there is still need of the prophetic voice so that the charity of the churches does not conform to the pattern of this world and become an expression of empire rather than of the lordship of Jesus Christ.

The task is daunting, but the prophetic words of God on the lips of his people can be powerful because we serve a Lord whose words are like a double-edged sword (see Rev. 1:16; Heb. 4:12–13; Eph. 6:17). If we speak prophetically in the power of the Spirit out of the truth of Scripture, we shall not speak in vain. The word of God we have been given can change things, even if we are faced with the most powerful commercial and military empire ever seen. And we have no other weapon except the Word of God to effect change in our world, and must utterly reject the idea that the destructive power of US weaponry used to bring terror ('shock and awe') to places like Iraq can in any way establish justice on earth.

---

7. Alan Storkey, 'Post-Modernism Is Consumption', in Craig Bartholomew and Thorsten Moritz (eds.), *Christ and Consumerism: A Critical Analysis of the Spirit of the Age* (Carlisle: Paternoster, 2000), pp. 113–114. This chapter by Storkey is a fine example of prophecy.

Prayer

This makes our task seemingly impossible, but our sense of insufficiency and consciousness of the powerful forces arraigned against us brings us to the second form of speech available to us – *prayer*. In fact, our ability to speak effectively *for* God in the church and in the world is dependent on our ability to speak *to* him. The gate into life is narrow and the path difficult, but access is unrestricted. All who come humbly confessing their sin and looking to Jesus for cleansing are welcome and heard. They come by the Spirit and leave with the Spirit to live under the lordship of Jesus. So they can be told to 'pray in the Spirit on all occasions with all kinds of prayers and requests' (Eph. 6:18). Their chief concern is God's honour as manifested in his will being done on earth as it is in heaven, which is what is meant by the coming of the kingdom. The best that the Father can give to achieve this end is the presence of the Holy Spirit, and he is generous with this gift to all who ask (Matt. 6:9–10; Luke 11:13).

Peter and John, having healed a man who had been crippled from birth in the name of Jesus and proclaimed publicly to a big crowd that Jesus is the Messiah, were hauled before the Sanhedrin and commanded not to teach in the name of Jesus any more. They were also told that if they disobeyed, they would be punished. Having told the authorities that they had no intention of obeying, the apostles returned to 'their own people', the church and, having reported what had happened 'they raised their voices together in prayer to God'. What they prayed for was the ability to do even more effectively what the Sanhedrin had just commanded them not to do: 'Now, Lord, consider their threats and enable your servants to speak your word with great boldness. Stretch out your hand to heal and perform miraculous signs and wonders through the name of your holy servant Jesus' (Acts 4:29–30). God's response was to manifest his presence with such power that the place they were meeting was shaken and 'they were all filled with the Holy Spirit and spoke the word of God boldly'. But that is not all they did, because Luke goes on immediately to add, 'All the believers were one in heart and mind. No-one claimed that any of his possessions was his own, but they shared everything they had' (Acts 4:32). The prayer was for bold words, miracles and wonders; the Spirit's presence led to bold words, mighty deeds and *bold living*. Not only were they enabled to proclaim the King, but also to display the reality of his kingdom in their life as a community.

As Jesus prophesied, churches will have to face opposition from governing authorities and will need to pray for strength to continue to proclaim the truth boldly in such circumstances. But, as we have already seen, direct conflict is not the only possible relationship between church and government. The church can also pray for power to perform miracles that are really acts of goodness and mercy towards those in need. For the Jerusalem church, the miracles the apostles performed provided some temporary protection for the church, because there was popular support for a movement that helped people in need. Finally there is prayer for the churches to be the communities of the kingdom they are called to be. This is what gives churches the authority sometimes to influence the governing authorities and influence society at large, as represented by government, to order itself in a way more consistent with the kingdom of God.

This is how O'Donovan develops this point:

> By 'the power of the church', then, is meant 'the authority of the church', its effective enablement to be the political community that it is, the community of God's rule, manifesting his kingdom to the world. But such a power cannot be exercised statically: like the Kingdom itself it is wholly orientated to its own more complete manifestation. It is the power to call upon God *for power*. The prayers of the church seek one thing only, the final manifestation of God's rule on earth. Nevertheless, because it is called into existence in order to witness to that coming manifestation through its own life and word, it prays also for God's power at work within itself. Prayer is invocation of the Spirit, calling on God's power *now* to witness to God's power *then*. But since the Spirit is known through a differentiated multiplicity of gifts, prayer for the Spirit is also prayer for the various charisms, the graces given to the church's members individually for service.[8]

The focus of prayer in the NT is clearly on the churches growing and becoming what God intends them to be. When Jesus prayed for those who would come to believe in him as a result of the apostles' message, the heart of his prayer for them, as for the apostles, was that they should be one. The pattern of their unity was to be that of the Father and the Son and the cement that was to hold them together, as it held the Father and the Son together, was love (John 17:20–26). This prayer of Jesus is affirmed and expanded on in those letters of Paul that contain prayers for the churches to which he was writing (see 2 Thess. 1:11–12; Eph. 1:17–23; 3:16–19; Phil. 1:9–11; Col. 1:9–12). He did not pray that the churches would be able to influence the government to do justice so that poverty would be overcome through their efforts. What he prayed was that the churches would grow in their appreciation of the love of Christ. In Ephesians, the power he prayed they should have was the

8. O'Donovan, *Desire of the Nations*, p. 189; his italics.

power to grasp the immensity of Christ's love. He also prayed that they should have power to endure in the face of all opposition and the power to do what they wanted to do in order to fulfil their calling as disciples. He also prayed that they would grow in their knowledge of God's will and their ability to discern what was the best course of action in all the twists and turnings of life. Central to it all was that they should live worthy of their calling as the community of the kingdom and bear the fruits of righteousness/justice. Hawthorne sums up the thrust of all Paul's prayers for the churches in his explanation of the prayer in Philippians:

> And his prayer, though brief, is profound in its implications; it is a prayer for a Christian community (1) that it might overflow in an intelligent and perceptive love, (2) that it might have the ability to recognize and choose the truly essential things of life, (3) that it might be pure and never the means of hurting others, (4) that it might allow Jesus Christ to generate through it all kinds of good deeds, and (5) that thus it might be a community committed to honoring and praising God, and at the same time the cause of God being honored and praised by others.[9]

As O'Donovan rightly points out, the effective working of the Christian community is realized through the power of the Holy Spirit, who manifests himself in a variety of gifts given to individual believers. The individual is not absorbed by the community. There is unity but in diversity; there is one body but many members. This principle is also true of the Spirit himself. The presence of the Spirit in any individual means that all the gifts are potentially present in that individual; a gift is the intensification in an individual of an aspect of the Spirit's grace just as pure white light that contains all the colours of the rainbow manifests those colours as separate when passed through a prism. At Pentecost, the ability of all to prophesy was seen as evidence of the fulfilment of the promise of a new covenant. Everyone within the new covenant community has direct dealings with God and can speak the message of God into the life of the church and beyond. But it became clear very soon that some had this gift in a more intense way than others. They were recognized by the community as prophets and prophetesses.[10] In the same way, every believer was able to teach others especially in the context of congregational worship. 'Let the word of

---

9. See 'Explanation' of Phil. 1:3–11, in Gerald F. Hawthorne, *Philippians*, Word Biblical Commentary on CD-ROM, vol. 43 (Dallas, Tex.: Word, 1998).

10. In Acts 21:9, Luke refers to the four unmarried daughters of Philip the evangelist, who were prophetesses. In older commentaries, every effort is made to underline

Christ dwell in you richly', says Paul to the whole church at Colosse, 'as you teach and admonish one another with all wisdom' (Col. 3:16a; cf. Eph. 5:18b–19a).[11] But there was also a special gift of teaching that only a few members of the congregation possessed (Rom. 12:7b).

In the list of specific gifts in Romans 12 where Paul identifies 'teaching' as a gift, he also lists 'service' (*diakonia*) as a gift. Precisely what Paul has in mind in Romans 12 is difficult to ascertain, because he uses *diakonia* to describe a whole range of activities in other contexts. He uses it to describe his task as an apostle, the task of reconciliation, all the gifts, the general care that Christians should have for each other as well as the specific task of relieving poverty (Rom. 11:13; 2 Cor. 11:8; 5:18; 1 Cor. 12:5; 16:15; Eph. 2:12; 2 Cor. 9:1, 12–13). There is no need to ascertain what Paul means precisely here. It is clear that serving in a variety of ways was something all Christians were to do. To be servant-hearted is of the essence of what it means to be the disciple of one who said that he had not come to be served but to serve and give his life a ransom for many (Matt. 20:28). Yet some are called to a specific form of service focused on either spiritual or physical needs. Another example from the list in Romans 12 is 'showing mercy'. It is of the essence of what it means to be a follower of Jesus to show mercy. Jesus commands us all to be merciful, just as our Father God is merciful; he said that justice, mercy and faithfulness are 'the more important matters of the law' (Matt. 23:23; cf. 5:7; 9:13). It is incumbent for all Christians to show mercy, yet there is also a special gift/charism of showing mercy, and commentators are agreed that what Paul has in mind here is practical care for the needy.

Faced as we are with a world order essentially hostile to God and his righteousness/justice, what the church needs more than anything is the power of the Holy Spirit to continue to manifest now something of the reality of the ordered city to come. As we pray to the Father for the Holy Spirit in the name

---

the temporary or private nature of their prophesying. However, more recent evangelical commentators such as F. F. Bruce are in no doubt that the women had the gift of prophecy: see *The Acts of the Apostles: The Greek Text with Introduction and Commentary* (London: Tyndale, 1951), p. 387.

11. Commentators disagree, but it seems likely, especially in view of the passage in Ephesians, that the key way in which the whole congregation were able to participate in teaching each other was through psalms, hymns and spiritual songs. The psalms were probably the psalms of the OT, but hymns and spiritual songs would be Christian compositions, so that composing spiritual poems and music to instruct the church was inspired by the Holy Spirit.

of Jesus, we are not only asking that all who belong should have power to speak (prophesy) and serve, but also that each member should have some aspect or aspects of the Spirit's life in abundance. These gifts of the Spirit given to individuals are not only effective in building up the community of believers, which is the key testimony to the reality of the kingdom of God, but are also effective as gifted individuals live out their life of faith in the world.

The church in the world is present as a visible community, but also as individuals endowed with gifts of the Holy Spirit. The gathered and scattered presence of the church in the world are both crucial to extending the kingdom of God that results in overcoming poverty. That is an inevitable consequence of using speaking gifts to testify to the lordship of Jesus Christ, and using serving gifts to show the mercy of Jesus Christ to those in need. But speaking and acting are never mutually exclusive. Teachers who do not manifest the love of Jesus in their lives through acts of mercy are hypocrites and those who act in love towards the needy but do not speak of the love of Jesus betray their gifting. All the gifts are manifestations of the one Spirit, so it is impossible ultimately to divide words from deeds.

Wesley's reputation as an evangelist is totally unassailable. Yet he often used his outstanding 'word' gift to plead on behalf of the poor and to argue for changes in public policy for their benefit. Interestingly as a contemporary of Adam Smith he was no advocate of the free market but of market restrictions for the benefit of the poor. For example, in newspaper articles and tracts in the 1770s, he argued for a prohibition of distilling and a reduction in the number of horses kept by the wealthy for sport. He believed that the greater supply of grain that would become available as a result to make bread would force down the price and be a blessing to the poor.[12]

The Methodist movement was a movement of intense spirituality. This was the movement that really defined what evangelicalism has meant by 'conversion' for most of its history. It was also the movement that gave birth to the evangelical missionary movement that is now generally seen as one of the greatest evangelistic movements in church history. The movement also emphasized the need for a deep piety in its members, including a heavy emphasis on prayerfulness. So it is tempting at this point to write at length of the huge range of gifts and activities unleashed by the Methodist movement on behalf of the poor.

---

12. Robert F. Wearmouth, *Methodism and the Common People of the Eighteenth Century* (London: Epworth, 1945), p. 210. Smith's views on the scarcity of grain were published in 1773 in a pamphlet entitled *Thoughts on the Present Scarcity of Provisions.*

One such activity was the Strangers' Friend Societies established by Wesleyan Societies in the growing industrial cities of the late eighteenth century. Adam Clarke was the organizer of the Strangers' Friend Society in Manchester. Writing about this society in the *Methodist Magazine* in 1798, he says that those appointed to visit the 'strangers' were 'the most pious, sensible and zealous young men of the Methodist Society'. He exhorted them to 'hunt poverty, sin and disease thro' all the public haunts and private retreats' and to 'strive to lessen, if you cannot remove the immense load of human ills'. And he said of these young men that they 'were not afraid to look death in the face' as they took 'the dangerous labour on themselves of visiting . . . cellars and garrets, where poverty and distress had taken up their abode, and where the most virulent contagion had dwelt for many years with increasing, because undisturbed, malignity'. They were to offer their care unconditionally because 'Protestants, Roman Catholics, Strangers and Foreigners [had] an equal right to be relieved by it.'[13]

Some years ago I was taken by a friend to visit two towns in Africa to explore the possibility of establishing a community link for the benefit of the poor with our town in Wales. For my friend the visit was a step towards fulfilling a vision God had given him twenty years earlier when, as a newly qualified medical doctor, he spent some time working in a camp in Ethiopia during the great famine of 1984. For twenty years he had prayed and dreamt and planned and now he was convinced that the time had come for the vision to become reality. During our visit to the first town we were taken to an outlying village to see the circumstances in which village people lived and to meet a committee of Christians that had been formed in order to address some of the people's needs. We met the local committee in a building used for congregational worship by the local Anglican Church. As the committee described the challenges the village faced because of poverty, my friend broke down and wept. He describes his experience as being filled with the Spirit for the task of fulfilling the vision he believed God had given him so many years earlier. By now people from both towns have been envisioned, with the churches, schools and colleges, medical establishments, politicians and local government all involved, and a good beginning made to reducing some of the worst effects of poverty in the African town and district. And at the root of it all is persevering prayer and the exercise of the sharing, caring and showing-mercy gifts of the Spirit that have made my friend a powerful advocate on behalf of the poor in our community and beyond.

---

13. Ibid. pp. 213–214.

Conclusion

In thinking about the church and the poor, the crucial issue is not what the church does for the poor but what the church is as the governed community of Jesus. The church exists to gather people from the world into the kingdom of God in which all citizens are equally valued. As a governed society in, but not of, the world, it offers a real alternative to those under the authority of its governments. As such, even though its citizens have been predominantly insignificant people, it is often seen as a challenge to this world's governments, because those under the authority of Jesus can never give them more than a qualified allegiance. This is particularly true of empire that by definition aims for global hegemony. In this threatening context, the gathered congregations of Jesus are called to live out their lives together in the power of the Holy Spirit. As a foretaste of what it will mean to live in the new heavens and earth, the communities of disciples aspire to live a life of love. One key distinguishing mark of such a life is care for the poor, which means sharing with them, listening to them and speaking on their behalf. The only offensive weapon the church has in its effort to change the world is speech. But we believe that when we speak with the anointing of the Holy Spirit, people, including people in authority, can be convicted, change their mind and do what is good and just. It is because we believe this that we see prayer as crucial to empowering the church with the gifts of the Spirit so that the world will also be changed. The more subject to God the world becomes, the more poverty is overcome.

EPILOGUE: WHICH STORY ARE WE IN?

Throughout history our world has been characterized by a great deal of 'crying' because of oppression and injustice. Much of the volume of this crying has always been produced by the poor, and the chorus of the cries of the poor today is immensely loud. What is in view here are the cries of those who live in 'absolute poverty', as described by the United Nations. They define it as 'a condition characterised by severe deprivation of basic human needs, including food, safe drinking water, sanitation facilities, health, shelter, education and information'.[1] The people living with this type of poverty are said to be living on less than a dollar a day per person. What is more, it is estimated that there are over a billion people living with this level of economic deficit. Imagine this billion people in absolute poverty queuing up in single file for emergency supplies at your feeding station. If the line was straight and had a poor person every two feet the queue would go around the world, which is 25,000 miles, almost four times! This represents an unimaginable volume of 'crying'.

The challenge at this point is to summarize the relevance of this book to this crying of the poor.

---

1. Copenhagen Declaration on Social Development Chapter 2; Eradication of Poverty, para. 19, issued by the UN World Summit for Social Development that met in Copenhagen in 1995.

The book began by considering the root of the abuse of power that causes the crying of the oppressed. What I attempted to show was that while poverty is a social, political and economic problem, it is also fundamentally a spiritual problem. Its deepest root is in our alienation from God. Away from God our focus inevitably turns in on ourselves, and the world becomes a threatening and insecure place. Our created ability to dominate is not destroyed by our alienation from God, but the way we use this inherent power becomes self-centred and as a result we tend to use other people and the rest of creation for our own ends. This process is a reflection of a general sense of insecurity and goes hand in hand with the violence associated with securing resources by any group of people and the 'government' they endorse to achieve that end. On the small scale, we see this process at work in family, clan or tribal conflicts, and on a large scale in empire building.

Empire is the highest manifestation of the abuse of power, and empire building has been with us since Babel. Imperial propaganda has always pumped out the message that the empire's power is entirely benign and for the benefit of its subject peoples, while using its power to enrich those at its heart.[2] The church was born within the dominion of the greatest empire seen up to that time. Today the 'empire' centred in the US dwarfs Rome and any other empire since in its military and commercial might. This is the personal, local, national and international context in which I have sought to understand and expound the outworking of God's redemptive purpose especially as it relates to government and the plight of the poor.

---

2. Augustine's assessment that empire builders are like criminal gangs out for plunder is probably far nearer the truth: 'A gang is a group of men under the command of a leader, bound by a compact of association, in which the plunder is divided according to an agreed convention.

'If this villainy wins so many recruits from the ranks of the demoralized that it acquires territory, establishes a base, captures cities and subdues peoples, it then openly arrogates to itself the title of kingdom, which is conferred on it in the eyes of the world, not by the renouncing of aggression but by the attainment of impunity.

'For it was a witty and truthful rejoinder which was given by a captured pirate to Alexander the Great. The king asked the fellow, "What is your idea in infesting the sea?" And the pirate answered, with uninhibited insolence, "The same as yours in infesting the earth! But because I do it with a tiny craft, I'm called a pirate: because you have a mighty navy, you're called an emperor"' (*The City of God*, tr. Henry Bettenson [Harmondsworth: Penguin, 1972]), p. 139).

God created humankind with the ability to rule, and we have consistently abused that ability with terrible consequences as a result of our alienation from God. The more than a billion people living in abject poverty today testifies loudly to the continuing reality of our misrule. We would expect, therefore, that any attempt on God's part to redeem humankind would impact the exercise of our ability to rule. The restoration of humankind to fellowship with God and the restoration of divinely instituted government are inseparable. From its beginning with Abraham to its consummation in Jesus Messiah, this is clearly an integral element in God's redemptive purpose.

Focusing first on the divinely instituted ruler, we traced a succession from Abraham through Moses and some of the judges to the establishment of a dynasty of kings headed by David. They were rulers/leaders characterized by an acquaintance with God that grew in their understanding as they stepped out in faith in situations that seemed hopeless from the human perspective. They majored on embracing what was beyond reason in obedience to God – Abraham was prepared to sacrifice Isaac, Moses faced the might of Pharaoh with a staff, Samuel sacrificed and prayed as the Philistines amassed to attack, David walked out clothed as a shepherd armed with a sling and some stones to face the heavily armed Goliath. They were humble in the sense that they depended on God for the moral resources they needed to rule. Some, including Moses, who was arguably the greatest leader of them all, were very reluctant rulers. They were clearly rulers with an eye for the glory of God's name and the good of God's people. Seeing their role as serving God and his purposes through his people, they were not concerned about their own reputation.

They also had a passion for doing what was right and just. What Abraham had experienced of God through word and vision was absorbed into his way of life to such an extent that it gave God confidence that he would rule his large household with justice and righteousness and that he would be able to induct his family into what was right and just. When the time came for Abraham's descendants to be settled as a nation in their own land, God gave them his law as a sort of tenancy agreement conditioning their occupancy. He did this through Moses, who lived what he taught. The society envisaged by God in his law would be devout and prosperous. Putting God first, even when his demands seemed to go against reason (such as forgiving debts when observing the sabbath year of the land) would result in abundance. Obedience to God's law would eliminate poverty, but even if obedience was not total and poverty showed its ugly head, the law made provision for dealing with it. But the effectiveness of the leadership structure in administering the just laws was very dependent on both leaders and led loving and respecting the Lawgiver. The great leaders did love and respect the Lawgiver most of the time, although every one of them had feet of clay. The people they led were far less faithful and, although there were undoubtedly many faithful among them in every generation, as a body for much of their history they tended to assimilate to the idolatrous ways of neighbouring peoples and nations. When rulers and ruled turned their back on God, and Israel first and then Judah became characterized by idolatry and injustice so that God heard the crying of the oppressed coming from among those supposed to be his own people, judgment and exile became inevitable.

It was during the turbulent period of the exile of Judah that God revealed the coming of a Ruler, the Messiah, who would surpass all others. He was to be a seed of Abraham in David's line to affirm that God's redemptive purpose was to be fulfilled through Israel. But God's promise to Abraham that all nations would be blessed through his seed now comes to the fore. This Ruler's domain was to be universal. He would establish justice in all the earth. Through him the whole earth was to be filled with the knowledge of the Lord as the waters cover the sea. He would bring terrible judgment on the wicked but not at the head of invading armies. To the contrary, he was to be the prince of peace. His weapon was to be his words and his final defeat of violence would not come through inflicting but suffering it. He would be no bruiser, but the one who would be bruised for our iniquities. And his suffering would not be in vain, because by it he would bring forgiveness and a new life to many people; in theological terms, his death and resurrection would bring about a reconstituted humankind to populate a new heaven and earth.

We believe Jesus of Nazareth, son of Mary, Son of God, to be this Messiah. His resurrection proves his superiority as Ruler and exalts his example and teaching, but it was his death that released the greatest boon for humankind – the baptism of the Holy Spirit. Every reconstituted individual indwelt by God the Holy Spirit has the law, or way of life, of God written on their hearts. They all know God in this intimate inward sense. The heart, the very source of our human existence, which has been so polluted by our stubborn alienation from God, is now cleansed by the vicarious shedding of the Messiah's blood. This is why we can follow the teaching and example of the Lord Jesus. A heart cleansed and indwelt by the Holy Spirit is free to love enemies, to give alms, to be generous to the poor and to seek first the kingdom and its justice in the knowledge that, whatever happens, the ultimate judgment of our Lord on all humankind will be utterly just.

This new humanity Jesus has bought with his blood is not a disparate collection of individuals but a 'people'. Human beings as the crown of God's creation manifest what they are not only in their relation to God but also in their relation to each other and the rest of creation. Community is of the essence of our being, so it is unsurprising that community is at the heart of God's redemptive purpose. A holy nation was at the heart of the old covenant and a holy people dispersed among all the nations is at the heart of the new. This holy people is made up of gathered communities of those who worship Jesus as Lord. This means that they submit to the authority of Jesus to order their individual and corporate lives. With Jesus as their King, their head of state, their primary allegiance is to a government often at odds with the governments of this world. Historically this has often led to persecution and martyrdom. Imperial ideology has found it particularly difficult to tolerate those who refuse to accept that there could be saviours of the world other than Jesus.

What the ordered communities of Jesus do is take the risk of being alternative communities. With love and generosity they live now in their glorious future. They stumble and make mistakes, but with the renewing Spirit within they press on towards the goal of their high calling. They take up their cross daily and die to their own desires and ambitions so that they can serve their King in the blessing of others within their gathered community and beyond. When they are most filled with the Spirit, there is no needy person among them and remarkable transformation occurs in the lives of many sunk in sin and despair. Their power comes only from the Spirit. What transformation they achieve now is achieved through words of truth and deeds of love. Their words and deeds are often powerful, but they can also leave them exposed and helpless in the face of hatred and rejection. It is a risk they are prepared to take. Better to die in the service of a kingdom that will never end than live comfortably in an empire passing away. It is better to listen to the crying now and respond in prophetic speech, prayer and acts of love, because we belong to a kingdom where there will one day be no more crying, than shut our ears and say and do nothing because we belong to a kingdom in which crying will never cease.

SELECT BIBLIOGRAPHY

AUGUSTINE, *The City of God*, tr. H. Bettenson (Harmondsworth: Penguin, 1972).

BARTHOLOMEW, C., and MORITZ, T. (eds.), *Christ and Consumerism: A Critical Analysis of the Spirit of the Age* (Carlisle: Paternoster, 2000).

BAUCKHAM, R., *The Bible in Politics, How to Read the Bible Politically* (Westminster; John Knox: 2002).

—, *God and the Crisis of Freedom: Biblical and Contemporary Perspectives* (Louisville: Westminster John Knox, 2002).

BLOMBERG, C. L., *Neither Poverty nor Riches: A Biblical Theology of Possessions*, New Studies in Biblical Theology 7 (Leicester: Apollos, 1999).

CHESTER, T., *Good News to the Poor* (Leicester: IVP, 2004).

EVANS, D., with SCHERER, K., *Creating Space for Strangers: Thinking Afresh about Mission and the Church* (Leicester, IVP, 2004).

GALBRAITH, J. K., *The Anatomy of Power* (Boston: Houghton Mifflin, 1983).

GRANT, P., *Poor no More: Be Part of a Miracle* (Oxford: Monarch, 2008).

HUGHES, D., with BENNETT, M., *God of the Poor: A Biblical Vision of God's Present Rule* (Carlisle: Authentic, 2006).

MCCONVILLE, J. G., *God and Earthly Power: An Old Testament Political Theology* (London: T. & T. Clark, 2006).

O'DONOVAN, O., *The Desire of the Nations: Rediscovering the Roots of Political Theology* (Cambridge: Cambridge University Press, 1996).

—, *Resurrection and Moral Order: An Outline for Evangelical Ethics*, 2nd ed. (Leicester: Apollos, 1994).

SAMUEL, V., and SUGDEN, C. (eds.), *Mission as Transformation: A Theology of the Whole Gospel* (Oxford: Regnum, 1999).

SHENK, D. W., and STUTZMAN, E. R., *Creating Communities of the Kingdom: New Testament Models of Church Planting* (Scottdale: Herald, 1988).

SIDER, R. J., *The Scandal of the Evangelical Conscience: Why Are Christians Living Just Like the Rest of the World?* (Grand Rapids: Baker, 2005).

SIDER, R. J., OLSON, P. N., and UNRUH, H. R., *Churches that Make a Difference: Reaching Your Community with Good News and Good Works* (Grand Rapids: Baker, 2002).

STASSEN, G. H., and GUSHEE, D. P., *Kingdom Ethics: Following Jesus in Contemporary Context* (Downers Grove: IVP, 2003).

STORKEY, A., *Jesus and Politics: Confronting the Powers* (Grand Rapids: Baker Academic, 2005).

STOTT, J. R. W., *The Cross of Christ* (Leicester: IVP, 1986).

—, *The Message of the Sermon on the Mount* (Leicester: IVP, 1978).

VOLF, M., *Exclusion and Embrace: A Theological Exploration of Identity, Otherness, and Reconciliation* (Nashville, Abingdon, 1996).

WALSH, B. J., and KEESMAT, S. C., *Colossians Re-Mixed: Subverting the Empire* (Downers Grove: IVP, 2004; Carlisle: Paternoster, 2005).

WILLIAMS, S. N., *The Limits of Hope and the Logic of Love: Essays on Eschatology and Social Action* (Vancouver: Regent College Publishing, 2006).

WRIGHT, C. J. H., *The Mission of God* (Nottingham: IVP, 2006).

—, *Old Testament Ethics for the People of God* (Leicester: IVP, 2004).

YAMAMORI, T., and PADILLA, R., *The Local Church, Agent of Transformation: An Ecclesiology of Integral Mission* (Buenos Aires: Kairos, 2004).

YODER, J. H., *The Politics of Jesus*, 2nd ed. (Grand Rapids: Eerdmans; Carlisle: Paternoster, 1994).

INDEX OF SCRIPTURE REFERENCES

Old Testament

Genesis

Revelation